CHRISTIANITY AND THE WIDER ECUMENISM

CHRISTIANITY AND THE WIDER ECUMENISM

Edited by Peter C. Phan

A New ERA Book

PARAGON HOUSE
New York

Published in the United States by

International Religious Foundation
481 8th Avenue
New York, New York 10001

Distributed by Paragon House Publishers
90 Fifth Avenue
New York, New York 10011

A New Ecumenical Research Association Book

Library of Congress Cataloging-in-Publication Data

Christianity and the Wider Ecumenism / edited by Peter C. Phan.
p. 288 cm.
ISBN 0-89226-074-2 : $29.95
ISBN 0-89226-075-0 : $14.95 (paperback)
1. Christianity and the Wider Ecumenism—Congresses. I. Phan, Peter C., 1943–
BR127.C4742 1990
261.2—dc20 89–49380
CIP

Contents

Acknowledgments

THE EDITOR WISHES to thank Dr. Francis Clark, who was the chief organizer of the "Christians and the Wider Ecumenism" conference on behalf of the Council for the World's Religions, for his inspiration and outstanding example of genuine openness in interreligious dialogue.

My sincere thanks are also extended to Ronald Brown who cheerfully and expertly typed the entire manuscript.

I am deeply indebted to Dr. Thomas Halton and Ms. Stella O'Leary for their friendship and support.

My editorial labor is dedicated to Patricia Costello to whom I am profoundly grateful for the generous hospitality she offered me during my first year in Washington, D.C.

INTRODUCTION

Peter C. Phan

AN ATTENTIVE OBSERVER of theological trends in the Christian churches, especially Roman Catholic and Protestant, would not fail to notice that there has been in the last decade or so a self-conscious shift from a concern about the unity among the various Christian churches and communities (the "ecumenical movement" in the narrow sense) to the issue of unity among all world religions (the "Wider Ecumenism").[1]

Of course the Wider Ecumenism is not a total novelty.[2] The Second Vatican Council (1962–1965), a momentous religious event of our century, has already promulgated, besides a decree on Christian ecumenism, a declaration on the relation of the Church to non-Christian religions.[3] The Roman Catholic Church has established not only the Secretariat for the Promotion of the Unity of Christians but also the Secretariat for Non-Christians, as well as the Secretariat for Unbelievers. On its part the World Council of Churches has instituted its own Sub-Unit for Dialogue with People of Living Faiths and Ideologies. Lastly, the academy has maintained a long-standing interest in the doctrines and practices of non-Christian religions as the large number of courses on comparative religions offered by religious studies departments testifies.

Nevertheless, it remains true that the Wider Ecumenism understood as an official movement that engages Christians in dialogue with other believers—Jews, Muslims, Buddhists, Hindus, Zoroastrians, Taoists, Confucianists, Jains, Sikhs, Shintoists, (African) tribal religionists, and such new religious movements as the Unification Church and others—is a relatively recent phenomenon. Furthermore, in the last few years it has enjoyed a vigorous spurt of growth as the number of conferences and the spate of theological literature convincingly demonstrate.

This does not mean, however, that the Wider Ecumenism has been unanimously welcomed as a spiritual boon by all Christians or, for that matter, non-Christians. On the one hand, among Christians there are some who would insist, on the basis of scriptural texts such as Acts 4:12 ("There is no salvation in anyone else, for there is no other name in the whole world given to humans by which we are to be saved") and John 14:6 ("I am the way, and the truth, and the life; no one comes to the Father but through me"), that non-Christians religions are, if not superstition and works of the devil, at least abolished by the event of Jesus the Christ. Hence, no dialogue ought to be engaged in between Christians and non-Christians, at least on an equal footing; rather Christians should be wholeheartedly committed to the missionary task of converting pagans to Christianity. On the other hand, not a few non-Christians are suspicious of the Christians' belated invitation to interreligious dialogue and regard it as a covert attempt to manipulate them after having failed to convert them by direct methods.

Not all Christian theologians, however, entertain a negative attitude towards non-Christian religions. Some, known as inclusivists, maintain not only that non-Christians may be saved but also that their religions are ways of salvation, whether these are to be called ordinary or extraordinary means.[4] Proponents of this view, however, still insist that Christ remains normative for all non-Christian religions and include them either by being present in them anonymously or by fulfilling them. Others, labeled as pluralists, go a step further and argue that, on the basis of contemporary historical consciousness, of faith in God as Absolute Mystery, and of Christian praxis in favor of justice and freedom, the claim of Christ's/ Christianity's uniqueness, definitiveness, absoluteness, normativeness, and superiority should be abandoned. Metaphorically speaking, contemporary Christian theology must cross the Rubicon and explicitly acknowledge that other religions may be independent ways of salvation—equal or even superior—to Christianity and that there may be other saviors—equal or superior—to Jesus.

II

Whether one is an exclusivist, inclusivist, or pluralist, or some combination thereof, there is no escaping the fact that interreligious dialogue is both an urgent need of our times and—if it is to be undertaken at all—an extremely complicated enterprise. On the positive side, the means of mass communication, the expansion of technology, the ever-increasing interdependency among nations in socio-political and economic spheres, the growing feasibility of travel to foreign countries whereby one can experience first-hand cultures different from one's own, and many other factors have created a "global village" or "planetary society" in which dialogue, including dialogue with other religionists, is a matter of necessity. On the negative side, world-wide problems such as mass poverty, the destruction of ecology, religious fanaticism, and the ever-present threat of thermonuclear cataclysm cannot be left to politicians alone and cannot be resolved unless believers and unbelievers alike take a concerted action and pool their common resources, spiritual and otherwise, to promote mutual understanding and acceptance and to contribute to their solutions.

Moreover, even exclusivists, who refuse interreligious dialogue on the basis of apparently particularistic texts such as Acts 4:12 and John 14:6, or of traditional axioms such as "extra ecclesiam, nulla salus" (outside the Church there is no salvation) must come to grips with other biblical texts of more universalistic import, such as 1 Timothy 2:4 ("God wants everyone to be saved and come to know the truth"); with more inclusive impulses present in the Hebrew Scripture, the New Testament, and the Christian tradition; and with the claim of historico-critical studies that the sectarian character of certain affirmations both of Scripture and Tradition was part of the survival tactics of a minority group such as early Christianity in a prevalently hostile world.

On the other hand, inclusivists and pluralists, who are committed to interreligious dialogue, face a herculean task. Questions of methodologies and contents abound and do not admit of easy solution. Professor Francis Clark has made a helpful—by no means exhaustive—list of them:

> How do Christians regard the new movement towards interfaith understanding and religious fellowship? What should be their attitude to it? To what extent do they take part in it? What are the objectives—pragmatic, humanitarian, ethical, theological, spiritual—of those Christians who do take part in it? What are the objections of those who do not take part in it? Must the fundamental attitude of Christians to the non-Christian majority of the human race be one of missionary zeal? Does the ideal of Christian mission require rekindling, or reinterpreting, in the changed situation of our time?
>
> Or should Christian theology in this new age of world consciousness modify its seemingly intransigent claims? Should it even accept a "Copernican revolution" in thinking about the religious value of the world's religions? Does acceptance of "interfaith theology" entail abandonment of the title deeds of Christianity? Or can Christian theology find a reconciliation between the doctrine of the centrality of the person, work and grace of Christ and, on the other hand, the testimony of divine goodness and purpose manifested in other faith-communities?
>
> How indeed do interfaith ecumenists who are Christian believers combine their belief in the uniqueness of the Christian revelation, and of the place and work of

> Christ the Savior, with their belief in God's universal salvific will? In the context of a more universalist theology that embraces in God's plan the other religions of the world, how do they interpret the traditional Christian doctrines concerning the vital importance of faith in Christ, of the Church, of divine grace? Do Christian theologians who acknowledge the action of God's saving grace in other religions see it simply as a personal gift to the individual believer, or do they see a God-given function in the non-Christian religious communities themselves?
>
> What is the guidance of Holy Scripture on these matters? How has Christian tradition developed the understanding of the problem of "the salvation of non-Christians"? How are the insights of present-day biblical and systematic theologians contributing to a wider and deeper understanding?
>
> How do the Christian churches appraise the spiritual values of those other religions, whose members collectively make up the majority of mankind? What lessons can Christians learn from the values and practices of other religions? Can the theological, ritual and cultural expression of Christianity be developed and universalized by adoption of elements from those sources? If many ordinary Christians find the new interfaith outreach a difficulty, or even a threat to their faith, how should pastors and preachers respond?
>
> Is interfaith encounter and dialogue restricted to the level of mutual respect and humanitarian cooperation, or can it seek also some spiritual unity between believers, transcending the boundaries of their religions? Is mysticism the common ground? What main trends of thought can be drawn from the many important studies of world religion and interfaith relations that have been published by Christian theologians and philosophers of religion in recent decades?[5]

It was with a view to contribute to the Wider Ecumenism that the Council for the World's Religions, funded by the International Religious Foundation, an organization of the Unification Church, organized a conference with the theme "Christians and the Wider Ecumenism." The conference was scheduled to take place in Jerusalem, but because of unsafe political circumstances, it was moved to Istanbul, Turkey. It was here, in a hospitable Muslim country whose ancient cities and monuments are hallowed names for Christian history—Nicaea, Constantinople, Chalcedon, Hagia Sophia, Chora, just to mention a few—that some fifty participants, theologians, and religious leaders, from twenty nations, representing different Christian denominations and diverse theological orientations, met on May 8–14, 1988, to study and discuss how believers of different religions can promote mutual understanding, harmony, and collaboration in the service of the world. More specifically, the focus of the conference was not a dialogue between Christians and non-Christians in which comparisons of doctrines and practices of various religions and expositions on the history, values, and present condition of non-Christian religious are undertaken, (an *inter*religious dialogue). Rather, the conference was meant to serve as a forum for *intra*-Christian discussion of the varying attitudes and practices within the Christian churches towards the Wider Ecumenism as the ecumenical touchstone for Christian theology itself. It was felt that prior to an actual dialogue with other religionists, Christians must clarify to themselves certain fundamental and preliminary issues such as the possibility and necessity of interreligious dialogue for Christianity, the salvific value of non-Christian religions, the use of Scripture, the role of Christ, etc.

III

The present volume contains eighteen of the papers given at the conference. They are organized into four parts. The first part raises the question of whether the Wider Ecumenism is necessary for Christianity. M. Darrol Bryant argues that the dialogue with other world religions is necessitated not only by the emergence of the "planetary society" of our times but also by the very Christian belief in the Trinity. The three-articled faith in God as Creator, Redeemer and Sanctifier, he writes, "does not preclude dialogue with people of other faiths, but encourages such dialogue as part of Christianity's own calling to know more fully the mystery of God that has been given to the family of Christian traditions." In order to be fruitful, such dialogue, which is the new name for the perennial Christian vocation to love the neighbor as ourselves, must be, Bryant suggests, multilayered (involving every level of our being), multiform (facing inward and outward, forward and backward, along the axis of space and time), and must produce mutual transformation.

Whereas Bryant derives the necessity of interreligious dialogue from the Christian faith in the Trinity, Durwood Foster grounds the inmost wellspring of the Wider Ecumenism in the life and teaching of Jesus. In his "Christian Motives for Interfaith Dialogue," he argues that Christian dialogue with non-Christian religions must be inspired by the all-inclusive attitude of Jesus toward the people of his time, his death on the cross and resurrection, and his teaching on *agape* love. In a fresh interpretation of the episode in which the Canaanite woman implored Jesus to heal her sick daughter as recorded in Matt. 15:22–28 and parallels, he shows how Jesus was taught by the pagan woman's humility to go beyond his original commitment to the House of Israel and open himself to the Gentiles—a first encounter as it were in interreligious dialogue.

Robert P. Scharlemann, using the metaphor of Peter and Judas and a philosophical analysis of faith as a finite and free response, puts forth the thesis that "even when Jesus is understood exclusively as the revelation of God (that is, as the one and only human being who is existent deity), the non-Christian is as much a part of this revelation as is the Christian, not as the reprobate or rejected one, but as an equal participant in the salvation connected by Christians with the name of Jesus." Because faith is a free response, Peter can be Peter and does not have to be Judas, and vice versa; further because faith is a finite response, Peter cannot be both Peter and Judas at the same time, just as Judas cannot be Judas and Peter at the same time. But both Peter and Judas (Christianity and non-Christianity) are necessary to attend to Jesus as the Christ.

Geoffrey Parrinder, in his "Updating (*Aggiornamento*) Within and Without," suggests that the past exclusivistic attitude of Christians towards non-Christian religions based on a literal understanding of certain biblical texts should be reappraised in view of a more accurate reading of the Bible by means of the historico-critical method. In a sweeping survey of both the Jewish Scripture and the New Testament, he shows how certain exclusivistic texts (e.g., Mark 16:16; John 10:8, 14:6) will lose their edge if placed in their historical contexts. In closing he recommends Bishop Kenneth Cragg's method in expounding Christianity to Muslims and Islam to Christians be adopted in interreligious dialogue in general.

From his sociological standpoint Joseph E. Fichter suggests that, with the rise of secular humanism and the loss of world dominance by Western civilization, Christianity, which has been intimately bound up with European social systems, has become a minority in terms of status and prestige. In order to survive and prosper Christianity must therefore enter into the process of cultural adaption, and to carry out its task of promoting justice and peace it must dialogue and collaborate with other religions.

The second part of the book, "The Wider Ecumenism: Some Fundamental Issues," is introduced by Monika K. Hellwig's wide-ranging essay, "The Wider Ecumenism: Some Theological Questions." It first describes the Good News of Jesus Christ to the world as "the restoration of God's rule...[that is] peace among nations and among individuals, justice for all and especially for the poor and oppressed and powerless, and an end to all kinds of useless suffering." It then chronicles the process in which this Good News was related to the Good News of other religious traditions and shows how Christianity passed from the position of exclusivism to inclusivism to mutual complementarity and enrichment. In the context of interreligious dialogue Hellwig argues that evangelization is essentially a summoning forth of human hope for true human happiness, an enterprise in which the naming of what is happening (e.g., of God as Father, of Jesus as the Way, the Truth, and the Life, etc.) is secondary. Hellwig fully subscribes to the thesis that the ordinary way of salvation offered by God to all human beings is through their respective religious traditions and that conversion to Christianity is an extraordinary way desired by God for some people in order to perpetuate the witness of Jesus in the world. In such a view interreligious dialogue is a necessity since Christianity has much to learn from other religions.

In his "Rethinking Christian Doctrine in the Light of Religious Pluralism," John Hick proposes that Christian doctrines should not be regarded as divinely formulated and guaranteed propositions, but rather as "human attempts to grasp the religious event, primarily of the Christ event, and in the light of this, of our human situation as a whole." On the basis of this principle, Hick sets out to reinterpret four basic Christian beliefs. First, drawing on Donald Baillie's doctrine of "paradox of grace," and Geoffrey Lampe's "Christology of inspiration," he suggests that the Incarnation is something that happens in varying degrees whenever a man or a woman, and not only Jesus, becomes an instrument of God's love on earth. Second, for the purpose of interreligious dialogue, Hick argues that the absolutist Christology that affirms that Jesus is the "Son of God," the pre-existent Second Person of a divine Trinity, must be abandoned in favor of a non-absolutist Christology of a special "servant of God." Third, the doctrine of the Trinity must be interpreted in a way that coheres better with a non-absolutist Christology, that is, not as implying an ontologically three-personed deity but as three-fold (modalist) from our human point of view, as three ways in which the one God is humanly thought and experienced. And, finally, the exclusive soteriology that interprets Jesus' death as satisfaction, or substitution, or exemplar must also be rejected in our religiously plural world in favor of the view that Jesus is our Savior insofar as he makes real to us God's gracious presence, love, claim, and acceptance.

The problem of how to read sacred Scriptures in interreligious dialogue is addressed by Martin Forward's "How Do You Read?: The Scriptures in Interfaith Dialogue." He suggests that, besides the scholarly, historico-critical study of the Scriptures, there is a common reading of each other's Scriptures as fellow pilgrims and as friends. Friendship does not shun questions of truth for the sake of a continuing relationship, but enables matters of truth to be raised in ways in which they will be truly heard and considered. Forward proceeds to give two challenging examples of reading the Scriptures as friends, first between a Christian and a Jew (Isa. 52:13–53:12) and second between a Christian and a Muslim (Qur'an, 4:14ff.). Despite inevitable disagreements in interpretation, reading the Scriptures as friends, Forward is convinced, can help partners in dialogue cope with the pain of disagreement and hope that God will speak to them in these divergent Scriptures.

Since religious tradition is transmitted through language, interreligious dialogue must of necessity deal with the question of what religious language is and how to interpret it. Francis X. D'Sa, in his "Ecumenism and the Problem of Religious Language," suggests that in spite of the fact that Reality is continuously disclosing itself, our human understanding only grasps certain aspects of it, and this event of understanding in turn is expressed not in its entirety but only partially. D'Sa further argues that religious language, though similar in structure to ordinary language, is that which expresses the claims and appeal of Reality as Meaningfulness. It makes use of myth, metaphor, symbol, parable, and prophecy. Since religious language is essentially symbolic and analogical and therefore inadequate to the Reality it expresses, it is impossible, D'Sa points out, to make a claim of absoluteness and uniqueness for a particular religious language and system, be it Christian or otherwise. At best, each religion can claim a relative, not absolute uniqueness, and such uniqueness will be enhanced through the study of symbols of other religious traditions in interreligious dialogue and through the *communicatio in sacris mythis* of these traditions.

Another important theological issue in interreligious dialogue, especially for Christians, is how to understand the traditional maxim *extra ecclesiam nulla salus* which affirms, at least *prima facie*, that there is no salvation outside the Christian church. Joseph Osei-Bonsu traces the history and development of this axiom from patristic times to the Second Vatican Council and argues that biblical texts, both from the Jewish Scripture and the New Testament, do not lend support to the exclusivistic interpretation of this theological adage and that its use should therefore be abandoned. Finally, from the perspective of African traditional religions, Osei-Bonsu points out, such a maxim makes little sense, both because it is impossible to think that the majority of Africans, who are not Christians, are damned simply by virtue of the fact they do not belong to the Christian church, and because there exist in these African religions many elements of truth and goodness.

The third part of the volume presents the Wider Ecumenism in the context of contemporary Christian theology. Marcus Braybrooke, in his "Some Christological Implications of Recognizing the Jewishness of Jesus," points out that not a few contemporary Christian theologians have attempted to re-examine the person and mission of Jesus against the background of his Jewish milieu. It is now generally recognized that Jesus was a "faithful Son of the Covenant" and was close to the Pharisees, even though he preached the coming of the new age. Braybrooke also notes that it was the early disciples that shifted the focus of attention from the kingdom of God to the person of Jesus and that it was Gentile

(Hellenistic) Christianity that applied to him titles of divinity in the ontological sense which in Jewish context had only functional significance. Such Christological developments, however, are culturally conditioned and should not be seen as binding for all times. A Christology developed in interfaith dialogue should make clear that the focus of worship is God the Father and that the covenant between God and Israel remains valid.

In his "Are There Other 'Saviors' for Other Peoples?" Peter C. Phan expounds and evaluates the recent thesis of pluralists that the claim of the uniqueness of Christ and Christianity should be abandoned in interreligious dialogue. There may be, pluralists maintain, other saviors and other ways of salvation that are equal or even superior to Christ and Christianity. After examining the pluralists' three arguments for crossing the bridge from inclusivism to pluralism (contemporary historical consciousness, the reality of God as Absolute Mystery transcending every human conceptualization, the existence of immense sufferings apparently caused by the myth of Christian uniqueness), Phan argues, on the basis of the distinction between Christ and Christianity, that the claim of Jesus' uniqueness is a faith claim, a kerygmatic affirmation; that it has its own logic and hence cannot be validated by an examination of empirical facts. On the other hand, Phan points out, the claim of Christianity's uniqueness or superiority is a claim of fact, and therefore must be empirically proved. Such a proof may be convincing for certain aspects of Christianity and fallacious for others. Finally, for Phan it is not necessary to abandon the claim of uniqueness of Christ or Christianity as a pre-condition for a fruitful interreligious dialogue. The pluralists' thesis, in his view, is neither warranted nor necessary.

The next three chapters examine the position of contemporary influential theologians regarding the possibility and necessity of interreligious dialogue. Donald W. Dayton, while making no attempt at minimizing the exclusivistic tendencies of Karl Barth's Christocentric concentration, shows how Barth's exclusivism must be interpreted in the context of his three other theological principles, namely, his condemnation of Christianity as "religion," his universalistic soteriology, and his articulation of the relationship between "the Light and the lights."

Mary Ann Stenger, in her "The Understanding of Christ as Final Revelation," compares and contrasts the theologies of Karl Barth, Paul Tillich, Karl Rahner, and John Hick with regard to three issues, namely, whether Jesus as the Christ is the final revelation; whether the emphasis on the universality, rather than the particularity of Jesus, allows for more openness to non-Christian religions; and whether a shift should be made from Christocentrism to theocentrism for the sake of interreligious dialogue. Stenger herself has problems with any form of Christian inclusivism, and while not abandoning the Christian centering on Christ as the final revelation, she opts for a relation of that center to Ultimate Reality which is beyond finite expressions and forms.

Frederick M. Jelly carries the study of contemporary theologians a step further by including Edward Schillebeeckx. The Dutch theologian, Jelly explains, views humanity as called by God to communion with himself. This interior call, however, necessarily seeks a visible embodiment—a sacrament—in history which Christian faith professes to be Jesus of Nazareth. Jelly argues that whereas Tillich's Logos—Sarx and Spirit-Christology provide a prophetically critical principle for the continuous reform of all religions, including Christianity, Rahner's and Schillebeeckx's emphasis on the necessity of a visible embodiment of God's grace clarifies the role of the Church as an instrument of salvation in history. Both Tillich's "Protestant Principle" and Rahner's and Schillebeeckx's "Catholic Substance" are to be maintained in the Christian's dialogue with non-Christians.

The last part of the book entitled "The Wider Ecumenism in Practice" presents, very selectively, three concrete attempts by Christians at interreligious dialogue. Myrtle Sarah Langley delineates the background and offers an analysis of a report of the Board of Mission and Unity of the Church of England entitled "Towards a Theology for Inter-Faith Dialogue." The report was debated and duly received by the General Synod of the Church of England in July 1984. It marks a momentous step in "a journey of many miles" toward religious unity. Richard Quebedeaux, in his "Interreligious Dialogue: Next Step for Conservative Protestant Intellectuals?," traces the move of conservative Protestants (fundamentalists, evangelicals, Pentecostals) from an exclusivist stance toward dialogue with non-Christian religions.

From a more personal standpoint, Romesh P. Modayil, a Methodist minister, recounts his memorable experiences in interreligious dialogue, first with a militant Hindu organization, the Arya Samaj, and second with a Muslim community. From these encounters Modayil realized that ignorance was the greatest deterrent to interreligious dialogue, ignorance of the customs, habits, tradition, and culture associated with a particular religion or system of beliefs. He strongly urges that interreligious dialogue be conducted not only on the theological level but also at the practical level of sharing the whole gamut of customs and habits, language and tradition of other religions.

It is obvious that the essays collected here have only touched upon some of the issues to be dealt with in interreligious dialogue. It is hoped that they will promote a stimulus for further work toward the unity of all religions in the service of humankind.[6]

Notes

1. Hans Küng's theological career is an illustration of this shift. Whereas in his early works he was mainly concerned with intra-Christian ecumenism, in the last few years he has turned his attention towards the issue of the unity of all world religions. See, for instance, his work with Josef van Ess, Heinrich von Stietencron, and Heinz Bechert, *Christianity and the World Religions*, transl. Peter Heinegg (Garden City, New York: Doubleday & Co., 1986) and with Julia Ching, *Christianity and Chinese Religions* (New York: Doubleday, 1989).
2. The expression "The Wider Ecumenism" is taken from the title of a book by Eugene Hillmann (London: Burns & Oates Limited, 1968).
3. For an English translation of these texts, the Decree on Ecumenism (*Unitatis Redintegratio*) and the Declaration on the Relation of the Church to Non-Christian Religions (*Nostra Aetate*), see Vatican II, *The Conciliar and Post-Conciliar Documents*, ed. Austin Flannery (Collegeville, MN: Liturgical Press, 1984), 452–470 and 736–742.
4. The categories of exclusivism, inclusivism, and pluralism appear to have been given currency by Alan Race in his book, *Christian and Religious Pluralism. Patterns in the Christian Theology of Religions* (London: SMC Press, 1982).
5. Professor Clark's letter to participants of the conference "Christians and the Wider Ecumenism" explaining the conference theme.
6. For further recent literature on interreligious dialogue, see among others S. Wesley Ariarajah, *The Bible and People of Other Faiths* (Maryknoll: Orbis Books, 1989); David Lochhead, *The Dialogical Imperative. A Christian Reflection on Interfaith Encounter* (Maryknoll: Orbis Books, 1989); Eugene Hillman, *Many Paths. A Catholic Approach to Religious Pluralism* (Maryknoll: Orbis Books, 1989); Wilfred Cantwell Smith, *Towards a World Theology. Faith and the Comparative History of Religion* (Maryknoll: Orbis Books, 1989); Raimundo Panikkar, *The Silence of God. The Answer of the Buddha* (Maryknoll: Orbis Books, 1989).

PART I

IS THE WIDER ECUMENISM NECESSARY FOR CHRISTIANITY?

1

INTERFAITH ENCOUNTER AND DIALOGUE IN A TRINITARIAN PERSPECTIVE

M. Darrol Bryant

Introduction

THE WORLDWIDE ENCOUNTER and dialogue of men and women of different faiths is of profound importance for the future of Christian self-understanding and theological reflection.[1] But what that import is we will only fully know in retrospect, especially in relation to its theological significance. For many of us currently involved in the dialogue among people of different faiths, the experience has been of inestimable personal significance. For me, it has been personally transforming and enlivening both spiritually and theologically. But how that significance is to be articulated even for myself, let alone for the communities of faith of which I am a part, remains troubling and uncertain. The significance of such developments for the doctrinal and dogmatic dimensions of the Christian faith will not be known until far into the next millennium of the Christian era. And some of the most difficult and painful tasks of this interfaith dialogue will fall to the clergy, bishops, and leaders of the Christian communities of faith as they are confronted with the myriad practical and institutional questions that such a development will entail. My own hunch—and it can only be a hunch—is that future historians will look back on our time as one of epochal transition for the Christian faith and its multiform communities.[2] Our time will thus appear as yet another period in which the central dynamic and conviction of the Christian faith—that of death and resurrection—were suffered and endured as Christianity rose in faithfulness to its Triune God. For me the sign of the Christian communities' fidelity to their God is not primarily their outward successes, as important as these are to our ongoing life in time, but their inner and spiritual transformations in fidelity to the Living God.

This view should not be construed as a downplaying of the theological, doctrinal and dogmatic dimensions of the Christian faith; for me, these remain the life-giving symbols (in the classic sense of the Ecumenical Councils) of the faith. Nor should it be heard as a denial of a commitment to understanding the ontological entailments of the faith (in the sense of Anselm's faith-seeking understanding). Nor should it be understood as placing praxis before theory—a dichotomy which I regard as one of the most pernicious dichotomies to be found in contemporary intellectual life, since our lives remain one at every moment. Rather it should be heard as a word of caution at the outset of this inquiry because the task is so difficult, and the results can only be a probe seeking to illumine the twilight in which we find ourselves. We have, I believe, been led in our time into a new relationship with men and women of different faiths, but we are still a long way from understanding what this means in all of its ramifications.[3] Nonetheless, it is crucial that we begin to rethink the question of the meaning of the interfaith encounter and dialogue for the Christian communities of faith as part of our own ongoing quest for self-understanding and direction in faithfulness to the Triune God, the One made known to us as Father, Son, and Holy Spirit, as Creator, Redeemer, and Consummator.

I have invoked the name of the Triune God at the outset in order to indicate the faith in which I *approach* interfaith dialogue and the *horizon* within which I seek to understand it.[4] At this time, there are many ways in which our subject may and should be approached, but it seems necessary to indicate my particular context at the outset. As a three-articled faith, Christianity is irreducibly theocentric, yet internally differentiated in ways that allow us to see unity and diversity in a relation of *perichoresis*. Similarly, it allows us to see an analogical unity and diversity in the human order without sacrificing one (unity) to the other (diversity). But more on this later. For now, this introduction should suffice to allow me to (1) unfold some of the dimensions of dialogue itself, (2) contribute to the quest for a Christian basis and horizon for entering into and understanding the meaning of this encounter and dialogue, and (3) explore some of the questions that arise for the theological agenda of the coming millennium of the Christian era.

From Encounter to Dialogue

It is perhaps appropriate to begin with a few words about the world-historical processes that gave rise to the encounter of men and women of different faiths and the subsequent dialogue that is beginning to emerge around our common planet. It has become commonplace to observe that modern means of communication, travel, and immigration have created the historical conditions for the contemporary encounter of men and women of different faiths.[5] But this commonplace is a half-truth when it obscures the tragic events which made this possibility a reality, namely, the experience of two World Wars in our century. This worldwide experience of tragic conflict and common suffering gave rise to our dawning sense of the necessity for global community, for a truly planetary society. It was here, as the very name we have given to these wars makes clear, that we—meaning all the peoples of the world—endured the tragic and bitter consequences of failing to find ways to live together in peace across our many differences.

World War II especially brought people from all parts of the planet into collision with one another in unprecedented, and tragic, ways and numbers. The wars also accelerated the process of decolonization, which led to the emergence of new nations in Asia and Africa, a phenomenon that in many ways revitalized religious life or gave it a new focus in the process of nation-building and forging cultural identities. These processes also undermined the North Atlantic presumption that its prerogative was to bestow civilization upon the whole planet. The wars were, in tragically ironic ways, the vehicles of global revolution. Thus "whirl" has become king, but it has also created the openings wherein we might begin to meet as men and women of different cultures, societies, and traditions as well as different faiths in a new situation. The immigration of significant numbers of peoples from formerly colonized lands into former colonial homelands, the dispersion of peoples in the aftermath of war, the dislocation of huge populations in societies in transition, and the pursuit of scholarly study and religious vocations by those who have been touched by other cultures and ways of life as a result of their war experience or its consequences are among the world-historical factors that have facilitated in our time this encounter of men and women of different faiths.

What is thus emerging through the shared experience of suffering, the electronic means of mass communication, the spread of technology, and the experience of living side-by-side with people of different traditions is "a global village" (McLuhan), a "planetary society" (Rosenstock-Huessy).[6] But will that "global village" or "planetary society" be a *good* village or society? That question hangs in the balance. And one of the factors that will tip the balance is, I believe, our discovering ways that lead us to discover each other anew as members of the human family in relation to the Ultimate.

In this new situation, dialogue becomes the new name for the perennial Christian vocation to love the neighbor as ourselves. The love of the neighbor is, in Christian terms, always simultaneously the love of God. The love of God and the love of neighbor are not a disjunction, but the trinitarian conjunction of self, other, and the Ultimate.[7] Outwardly, this vocation to love God and the neighbor takes the form of the quest of justice in the global village; its inward expression is the move towards dialogue as the way to genuine community and peace among neighbors in our global village. When we enter into dialogue with our neighbor—who is everyone in the global village—then we pass from mere encounter and living side-by-side into the realm where genuine mutuality, cooperation, and friendship are possible. We move toward the good, towards genuine community. When we enter into dialogue with our neighbor, we open the possibility of reversing a history too littered with the devastating results of regarding the other as an enemy to be vanquished. When we enter into dialogue, we signal our willingness to trust the change this process will inevitably bring, the death and resurrection that await us as we live our vocations unto God.

Dialogue is, therefore, an unconditional good for Christians in this age of transition. It is not only a calling for the mystic in our traditions, as some suggest, but for believers of all sorts and conditions.[8] It is a vocation of the whole people of God. As a calling, the movement from encounter to dialogue exhibits the following aspects.

(1) Dialogue is the way toward love of neighbor, towards contemporaneity and community. As we have been thrown together by the processes of world history and the means of mass communication, the inevitable question is, how do we move from mere side-by-sideness towards community? Dialogue is the spiritual discipline and habit that can

transform our distemporaneity—that is, the fact that we come from different times and spaces and generations, different places in society and different societies, different places in our traditions and different traditions—into genuine contemporaneity, peoples living in a shared time on our shared planet and having a shared vocation towards God. Dialogue does not obliterate difference, nor does it aim to homogenize; rather, it seeks to orchestrate differences into the harmony of the whole and to acknowledge the many gifts that are required to make a genuine community. Community, as Martin Buber remarked, lies beyond individualism and collectivism.[9]

(2) Dialogue is multilayered. Everyone who has entered into dialogue has quickly discovered this fact. It involves the human, social, and ultimate dimensions of our lives simultaneously.[10] As we come into the presence and mystery of one another through the pathways of silence, word and action, we find ourselves touched and moved at every level of our being. As we break through our preconceptions, overcome our anxiety and fear, we discover that we share the ambiguities of being human even when we recognize that our humanity has been shaped by widely differing cultures and societies. We recognize that we have all been permeated by our respective social patterns and that we share similar difficulties in fulfilling our social vocations. We come to see the joy and pain, the insight and blindness, of our halting quests for the Ultimate and the presence of that Ultimate that seeks our restoration and healing. While these levels of dialogue can be distinguished and hierarchically ranked, they penetrate our lives in a relationship of—forgive me for this impossible way of putting it—"dancing around."

(3) Dialogue is multiform. Dialogue is not only multilayered along a vertical axis, but also multiform along what Rosenstock-Huessy called "the cross of reality."[11] That is, dialogue, like the human beings who enact it, simultaneously faces inward and outward, forward and backward, along the axis of space (from inner to outer and vice-versa) and the axis of time (from backward to forward and vice-versa). Thus dialogue becomes exceedingly complex. But complexity is to be expected, since dialogue is a meeting of whole human beings in their multiformity. Thus at a given moment, dialogue may be focused on the past, on our histories and their respective legacies of gifts and pains. As we together face our respective pasts, they become a shared past as they mutually interpenetrate each other and become a common past for a shared future. As we explore our histories together, we may be led to see them anew, to recover their gifts in a new configuration with our present, or to discern what from that past we need to let go as we move toward the future.

And this is just one front of the cross of reality on which we meet and where we find our way to life or death! Likewise, on the inner front, we may come to share our anxieties and fears as well as our dreams and hopes; we may learn to sing with one another and what inner dispositions and attitudes we need to give up. And so it goes in a process of give and take, of listening and speaking, of silence and sound, of seeing and being blind—not only on the front of the past and on that of the inner life behind our skins, but also at the outer front of our relation with nature and social institutions, and on the future front of the imperatives that call us. Each of these fronts of dialogue deserves more development than I can give them here, but I trust that this sample is sufficient to indicate something of the multiformity of dialogue.[12]

(4) Dialogue involves mutual transformation.[13] For those involved in dialogue, the very process itself is transforming. It is transforming not necessarily in the sense of forsaking old convictions, or even in the sense of abandoning long-standing patterns of action, but in the sense that through dialogue one can be raised to an enlivened and more vital way of being in the world.[14] Dialogue always involves risk, for it is never possible to know in advance its precise dynamics or outcome. Such prediction is impossible not only because of the factors outlined above but also because the process is existential. It involves a way of being with the neighbor as well as an exchange between two or more persons. And to the extent that there is a genuine exchange, there will be mutual transformation.

Thus far I have spoken about dialogue at a certain level of abstraction, with few considerations of the explicitly religious aspects of the dialogue, except to argue that dialogue is a way to love the neighbor. This approach has been purposeful because dialogue must be seen in something of its fullness in order to understand properly the presence of faith as the ground and form of the persons present to dialogue. Faith is the orientation of the whole self towards the whole of reality. Thus it is always present to dialogue, shaping the very perception and action of those who participate in dialogue. When we meet in dialogue, we meet as persons whose lives have been formed, to greater or lesser degrees, by faiths that have grasped our very souls and thus inform our thinking, willing, and feelings in all our being and doing. Thus faith is always present to dialogue, not only when specific issues of religious belief or practice are being considered. Furthermore, it is faith, as I have argued above, that in Christian terms should lead us to dialogue and faith that sustains us in dialogue. It is faith—our lives constituted by a living faith in God as Creator, Redeemer, and Consummator—that forms us at every moment in the dialogue with persons whose lives have been constituted by such living faiths as Hinduism, Islam, Buddhism, Judaism, Taoism,

Sikhism, etc.[15] Dialogue is thus always, by its very nature, interfaith as well as intra-religious.[16]

Having spoken in this dramatic way about dialogue, it is important to recall that dialogue has, at this point in time, been the experience of very small numbers within the family of Christian traditions and even smaller numbers from other traditions. At the same time, it is worth noting that the initiative for dialogue has largely come from the Christian communities of faith.[17] But it is my conviction that the movement to dialogue will continue and grow, and the crucial question for the Christian communities of faith is how they regard this situation. Can dialogue be entered into on the basis of the fundamental convictions of the Christian faith? Is it an unwelcome threat or a welcome challenge?

Christian Foundations for Dialogue: From Inside Out

I have already argued that dialogue is the form that the Christian vocation "to love thy neighbor" takes in relation to men and women of other faiths. Moreover, I have contended that we, as Christians, come to dialogue with others as bearers of faith in our very persons, and consequently, it is never accurate to suggest that faith can be bracketed or excluded from dialogue. At the same time, it must be acknowledged that the faith in the Triune God that we share as Christians has been articulated in an astonishing variety of ways throughout the Christian era and in our own time. This fact must be acknowledged, as must the difficulties of attempting to articulate the meaning of dialogue for those of us who as Christians feel called to the emergent dialogue. Paul Knitter's *No Other Name? A Critical Survey of Christian Attitudes toward the World Religions*, for example, documents something of the range of Christian attitudes toward dialogue.[18] A crucial question that emerges from Knitter's study is whether or not Christians can enter into dialogue with men and women of other faiths *on the basis of the Christian faith itself*. Obviously, there are those who would deny such a possibility; but here I argue that the foundations for Christian involvement in dialogue are inherent within that Triune faith itself. While such an argument cannot be fully developed here, let me offer some suggestions towards that end.

My basic conviction is that Christians must come to the dialogue with men and women of other faiths on the basis of faith itself. Otherwise, that dialogue will always be experienced as something external, a threat to be resisted or cast off. If, however, dialogue can be seen as unfolding from the inside out, from the very depths of Christian faith itself to embrace the neighbor and the mystery of the Triune God, then it can be welcomed as a further development within Christian self-understanding and its vocation to God. Thus the question of Christian involvement in dialogue—and understanding what such dialogue means—turns on the question of our understanding of Christian faith itself. What is the faith we share that, in the view outlined here, not only leads us to dialogue but becomes the horizon within which we understand or seek to understand the meaning of our dialogue with one other?[19]

(1) Faith is, in Christianity, always faith in God as Creator, Redeemer, and Sanctifier—three in one, one in three. This three-articled faith, as I understand it, thus affirms that God as God—and our humanity as from God to God—rests finally in mystery in its proper sense. That proper sense of mystery—which must be distinguished from mystification—is that while we affirm God in this threefold sense as Creator, Redeemer, and Sanctifier, we do not, nor can we, fully grasp the relations between these different "personae" of God. This recognition of mystery is not meant to deny inquiry—witness the astonishing history of reflection and meditation upon the mystery of the Trinity—but rather to remind us of the limits of the human capacity to grasp the fullness of the divine mystery and to keep us open towards the divine as the perpetual ground of our being (creation), our remaking (redemption) and our growth (sanctification). Just as the affirmation of God as Trinity both discloses our Christian experience of God as he has been made known to us and protects the inexhaustibility of Divine Transcendence, it discloses the mystery of our life as simultaneously known and hidden, even to ourselves. In this sense, then, Christian faith is radically, that is, at the root, theocentric: it is faith in God as God.[20]

Thus I must admit to being perplexed when, for example, Professor John Hick calls for a "Copernican revolution in theology," since theology is, by definition, always centered in God.[21] That there are forms of Christian thinking that are not sufficiently "three-articled" in their grasp of the object of the Christian faith is no doubt true, but more emphasis on the Trinity is not, seemingly, what Hick is calling for. Be that as it may, my point here is two-fold in relation to dialogue with persons of other faiths. First, Christianity's three-articled faith in God does not preclude dialogue with people of other faiths, but encourages such dialogue as part of Christianity's own calling to know more fully the mystery of God that has been given to the family of Christian traditions.[22] While there is no question that Christians must affirm what is given to them of God as Creator within Scripture and tradition, are we to assume that these sources exhaust the fullness of God as Creator? Or as Redeemer? Or as Sanctifier? I think not. The principle here is that the mystery always exceeds our grasp of it, and thus we must remain ever open to something more than can be given to us. And that something might be mediated to us through other traditions, even when those traditions exclude, for example, a belief in a "creator," as does Buddhism in most of its manifestations.[23]

Second, the three-articled faith provides Christians with a horizon for seeking to understand what one encounters in the dialogue with persons of other faiths. For example, Father Bede Griffiths' *The Cosmic Revelation*, written out of more than a quarter century of dialogue with persons and texts of the Hindu traditions, speaks of the Vedic revelation as part of God's revelation of Himself "in creation and the human soul."[24] In his differentiated understanding of the Christian faith, Griffiths has a way to affirm in Christian terms what he encounters in Hinduism. Some might perceive this approach as Christian "triumphalism," that is, an attempt to articulate the experience of the other in Christian terms. However, it seems to me more accurately understood as an attempt to make accessible to other Christians what he has learned in his profound dialogue with the Hindu traditions. The principle here is that our dialogue with other is mediated through our own Christian categories, even when the dialogue may lead us to enlarge or alter those categories.

(2) Faith in God as Creator is mediated to us through creation, as Redeemer through Jesus as the Christ, as Sanctifier through our growth in the Spirit. In each of these affirmations, we again encounter a fundamental mystery, one which, for lack of better terminology, I will call the mystery of the "universal and particular." That is, in addition to the mystery of the relations between the Father, Son, and the Spirit, there is the vertical mystery between creation and the Creator, between redemption and the Redeemer, between sanctification and the Sanctifier. Historically, Christian reflection has centered on the mystery of the relation of the Incarnate Word or Jesus as the Christ and the Eternal Word. But a similar principle obtains in relation to creation and the Creator, sanctification and the Spirit. While Christians affirm that Christ is, in Tillich's terms, the Bearer of the New Being, there has been from the beginning of the Christian era an awareness—often hidden or denied, but present nonetheless—that redemption is not exhausted by reference to Jesus of Nazareth. Thus there emerged a host of ways to try to articulate that profound mystery of the Eternal Word. Some found it in the doctrine of the Logos, some in the doctrine of Wisdom, and still others through that of Pantocrator or the Cosmic Christ.[25] That history is too complex to review here, but even these few observations should allow my fundamental point, namely, that Christian reflection is still open to seeking to understand more fully and profoundly the mystery of the relationship between God as Redeemer in Christ and the redemption of all people.

Thus when some interpret certain New Testament texts (Acts 4:12 or

John 14:6) to mean that there is no redemption apart from Jesus, such interpretation seems to violate Scripture as a whole. Certainly even the biblical witness affirms that before Jesus, men and women were redeemed. There is at least a profound tension between such texts and the whole of Scripture. Moreover, the very Scripture that Christians affirm as their own is, in part, shared with another tradition which does not affirm the Christian teaching concerning the Christ. Too often Christians obscure or even deny what we should most clearly affirm: namely, that the God we worship is one with the God which the Jewish people affirm. When early Christianity rejected Marcion, they rejected, in my view, every understanding of Christ that would deny the identity of the Christian God with that of the Jews. In any case, it seems to me that Christians need always humbly to acknowledge their own heterodoxical development (one I obviously affirm) of the doctrine of God. But I am straying too much from my point, namely, that in dialogue, Christians have the possibility of affirming the presence of the Eternal Word which continues to deepen and transform believers both within the Christian family of traditions and beyond. The point is not to make all into "anonymous Christians" but to transform Christians into anonymous witnesses to the Word which always exceeds their grasp.[26]

In the light of the dialogue with people of other faiths, Christians will, at least, have to come to a clearer understanding of redemption than seems to be present when we, as Christians, too quickly deny its presence outside the boundaries of the Christian church (the Catholic problem) or Christian belief (the Protestant problem).[27] I have always felt that the relevant question of Christian thinkers is whether or not there is salvation among Christians. More seriously, the question of redemption or salvation needs to be carefully re-examined. When we Christians speak of redemption, what do we mean? I would understand it in its root meaning as *salvus*, "to be made whole." More specifically, in the Christian tradition, the process of being made whole is linked to the experience of death and resurrection, of life overcoming death and restoring us to communion with God. Is that reality present only to the lives of Christian believers? To the extent that we discover, in our dialogue with men and women of other faiths, the presence of wholeness in their lives and traditions, we will be led more deeply into the mystery of redemption. How we will come to articulate that mystery, I do not yet know. As a consequence, I tend to regard some of the present attempts to articulate a "global theology of religions" or "a theology of world religions" premature, or at best, only beginnings in a process that will unfold over hundreds of years.

Again, my point is this: the affirmation that God as Redeemer is mediated in Christ as the Word does not preclude dialogue with people of other faiths. Rather I would contend that just as that affirmation should have led Christian faith to a deeper reflection on the Eternal Word in relation to Jewish faith—a failure that has had appallingly tragic consequences in the history of the West—so in relation to men and women of other faiths the Eternal Word can lead us to the most profound contemplation of the mysterious processes of redemption.[28] For Christians, such reflection and contemplation will ultimately be linked to Christ as mediator, but as mediator of "abundant life" (John 10:10) in the mystery of redemption. Thus our understanding of this mystery of the "universal and particular," or the meeting of the "human and divine" in relation to God as Redeemer, can be deepened through dialogue with men and women of other faiths. Such a deepening will have implications *both* for how Christians articulate their own understanding of Christ and for how Christians regard the faith of others. Christ is, in the perspective outlined here, the *icon* of redemption in God, and not an idol.

When dialogue is placed in a trinitarian perspective, the Christian should realize that dialogue with men and women of other faiths need not be reduced to a Christological issue. Such a reduction skews our perception of both our own faith and the faith of others. Viewed in a more vital trinitarian—or what Raimundo Panikkar calls *theandric* perspective, dialogue is the way to a deepened apprehension of the very mysteries that we as Christians affirm.[29]

(3) Faith in God as Creator, Redeemer, and Sanctifier is the Christian orientation *towards* the whole of reality, and our *way* into the Ultimate. But it is not, itself, the Ultimate. Christian faith itself is, then, the foundation on which Christians may enter dialogue with men and women of other faiths but one's understanding of that faith will be transformed by the meeting. My point seeks to move in two directions: against those who would reduce Christianity to ethics or to lightly held opinions and, simultaneously, against those who would transform faith into metaphysical rationalism such that what Christians say of the Ultimate is all that can be said. As a living faith, Christian faith is, in the first instance, a *spiritual* orientation towards the whole. It is characterized by perfect love that casts out fear and, for the Christian, it is grounded in the Creator, mediated by Christ, and consummated by the Spirit. Thus Christ as the Way, the Truth, and the Life is not, in the first instance, an abstraction but the vital mystery at the heart of faith. Believers thus bring to the encounter with other faiths their own Christian orientation to the whole as witness and testimony to the Ultimate, and, at the same time, an openness to listening and hearing others for their witness to what they have known, experienced, and articulated of the Ultimate. It is, then, on the basis of this spiritual meeting and dialogue that we can begin the

awesome task of attempting to give voice to what is there encountered.

It is at a second (not secondary) level, then, that the Christian faith is articulated in the form of beliefs, symbols, and doctrines. Such articulated beliefs, symbols, and doctrines—which then interact with the first level of vital faith—are the efforts at expression in human words, symbols, and concepts of what is given in faith as orientation. As such, the criterion is not discontinuous with Scripture, tradition, the creeds, or experience, which all have a similar goal or *telos*. When, as has often happened in the history of Christianity, the articulated expressions are reified, their spiritual power and capacity to illuminate the Ultimate may be lost in a sterile or excessive rationalism.

But, at the same time, the attempt to find ways to give voice to what is apprehended in faith is necessary and desirable. In Christian terms, the Word goes forth from silence. Hence, in relation to dialogue with others, Christians are obliged to walk a fine line, neither pretending they have nothing to say about God, nor assuming that what they say is all there is to say. It is here that we have the opening, at the level of articulated symbols and concepts, for finding forms of expression adequate both to the historically expressed and witnessed Christian faith and faith as it comes to expression in the dialogue with others. The difficulties of this task cannot be over-emphasized, but neither can the imperative to pursue the task. The desired end is not a new syncretism, or even a fusing of horizons, but ways to express our differences—and they will remain fundamental—as well as our shared insights so that we can live together in a spirit of mutual awareness, understanding, and friendship.

In summary, then, I have offered an interpretation of the three-articled Christian faith that leads us into dialogue with others on the basis of that faith itself. As a faith understood as an orientation towards the whole arising from the encounter with Jesus as the Christ, Christianity comes to articulate itself as a faith in God as Creator, Redeemer, and Consummator—one in three, three in one. This mystery of unity in multiplicity, multiplicity in unity, is both the distinguishing structure of Christian faith and the basis for Christian dialogue with men and women of other faiths. For the Christian, the very movement *into* the mystery that faith apprehends leads us *out* again in wonder to discern that presence of our Triune God in creation, history, and the lives of our fellow human beings. For Christianity, the awareness of the variety of faiths present in the human family is not simply a challenge to our understanding of Christ as Redeemer, but also an opportunity to explore more deeply God's presence to humankind as Creator, Redeemer, and Consummator whom we may meet outside the confines of the Christian communities of faith. For this God is, we believe, the God of all.

Dialogue, Community, and the Ultimate: The Way Ahead

The perspective that I have outlined here has implications for our future relations as Christians with men and women of other faiths. It seeks to move us beyond intransigence and fear to welcome the opportunity to enter into a new relationship with other faiths on the basis of the Christian faith itself. I have found that such a dialogue with others does not diminish my faith as a Christian, but deepens and enlarges it in the rhythm of the Word: listening and speaking, silence and inward meditation, dying and being reborn. It has led me to see more deeply the wonder of divine presence and absence both in my own life and in the lives of others. It has led me to a greater respect for the faith of others, including the faith I share with other Christians, and a need to discern the meaning of this type of meeting. That meaning must, I believe, be articulated for Christians in the horizon of our trinitarian faith—and in the horizons of the faith of others too.[30] And that process, as I have already asserted, will only unfold over the coming generations as faith speaks to faith both within the family of Christian traditions and across traditions.

But are we not, as Christians, obliged to give up our central claims or, as some have put it, our "title deeds" in order to enter into dialogue with other faiths? I think not. The absurdity of such a view becomes obvious if, for the moment, we look beyond Christianity and consider persons of other faiths. Would we, for example, expect the Taoist to deny the Tao as a precondition for dialogue, or expect the Caitanya Vaishnavite to deny the conviction that Krishna is the Lord, or the Muslim to forsake faith in Allah? Of course not. What we are, however, *all* obliged to give up is an *a priori* conviction that dialogue with other faiths is of no value or constitutes a denial of our own faith since we, whoever the 'we' is, already have the whole truth.

But will we not be obliged to compromise our faith in Christ? Again, I have not found such compromise necessary at all, at least not at the level of faith. But at the level of articulated doctrine, I think the answer is both yes and no. Christian faith is always in the process of finding adequate ways to articulate its faith in Christ; the whole history of Christianity testifies to this ongoing process. Thus it is misleading to assume that it is only the encounter and dialogue with men and women of other faiths that will have this consequence. (Personally, I find the emergence of a rampant historicism within Christianity itself much more troubling.)[31] Such dialogue may intensify that process, but it does not, in my view, alter it in kind. At the same time, it must be acknowledged that Christians will be challenged to find adequate ways to express what I have called the mystery of the universal and particular in relation to God as Redeemer.

What will be more deeply challenged will be the tendency among many Christians to hold faith in Christ apart from faith in God as Creator and Spirit. Seen in its three-articled context, our faith in Christ will be deepened and enlarged.

But what happens to the Christian call to "conversion"? My own sense is that we need to avoid misconstruing the issue as "dialogue versus conversion." This misconstrues the issue because dialogue is not just polite chit-chat, nor is it the scholarly study of comparative religions. Rather, dialogue is, in a Christian perspective, the means through which the Word continues to deepen and transform our lives.[32] Thus conversion is not just for the other, but a continuing process in the heart of the Christian believer. While the motivation for dialogue cannot be conversion understood as getting others to abandon their faith for mine, neither can we exclude the presence of the Spirit that will continually transform us all. The conversion we should seek as Christians is not to an extrinsic set of propositions, but to a vital interior spirituality keyed to love as the central chord in the divine symphony.

My general point here is that the movement into dialogue with men and women of other faiths does not, in advance, entail any denial of the Christian faith, but rather involves us simultaneously in the love of neighbor and God. Consequently, we may emerge from that dialogue articulating that divine-human mystery in a new way. But only time will tell. More important here is for us to recall the ends of dialogue.

The first end of dialogue is *meeting itself* in an ethos of mutual respect and mutual willingness to be together in silence and in words. Such meeting is itself the way to create mutual respect and an openness to one another because it is a shared meeting. The second end is to create the possibilities of *genuine community and peace*. Through the processes of give and take, we learn to understand one another by standing in each other's moccasins, and we learn the ways that make for community. Community on our common planet can grow only out of the life of the spirit—not out of a gun nor out of commerce. The third end is a *shared quest for the Ultimate*. Without in any way denying what has been given to each of us as persons in traditions, but rather in sharing those ways, we can come to recognize each other as fellow pilgrims. We are fellow pilgrims not because we hold the same beliefs, nor because we are really all the same underneath, but because we all know in part and yet are seeking to move more deeply into the Transcendent. Dialogue is not syncretism, nor is it a reduction of our respective differences. It is rather a way ahead. It is a way to mutual respect and friendship for the sake of global community no matter how small the community in which we now stand. Dialogue is not motivated by a desire that all be the same but by a desire to move beyond a history of mutual antagonism. It is a way to search beyond the cacophony of the present for the symphony of the community of communities that is grounded above.

Notes

1. Much literature has appeared on this subject in the last 25 years. I think that my first encounter with this question was through Paul Tillich's *Christianity and the Encounter of the World Religions* (New York: Columbia University Press, 1963). This work remains an important one, especially for reminding us that Christianity itself always stands under judgment in its encounter with other religions.
2. For a view of the history of Christianity through several epochs, see Eugen Rosenstock-Huessy, *The Christian Future Or the Modern Mind Outrun* (New York: Harper and Row, 1966) and his earlier *Das Alter der Kirche* (Berlin: Lambert Schneider, 1927–28) in three volumes and written with the Catholic Joseph Wittig. It is from Eugen Rosenstock-Huessy that I have learned much, but his views reflect a tradition that, in my view, goes back to Luther, Augustine, and Irenaeus.
3. I would even see this meeting with persons of other faiths as unfolding within the "Providence of God," but that view involves a fuller discussion than can be undertaken here.
4. I am, alas, fully aware that the Trinity is not as fully resonant a symbol of the Christian faith for others as it is for me. I am also aware, as my critics have pointed out, that my focus here on the "economical Trinity," that is, God in relation to creation, redemption, and sanctification or consummation, obscures the "inner Trinitarian" relations of Father, Son, and Spirit. This, it seems to me, is inevitable in an essay. But the criticism is, nonetheless, important and acknowledged.
5. See, for example, Heinrich Ott in *God: The Contemporary Discussion,* eds. F. Sontag and M.D. Bryant (New York: Rose of Sharon, 1982), 5–6.
6. See Marshall McLuhan's *Understanding Media: The Extensions of Man* (New York: McGraw-Hill, 1964) and his earlier *Gutenberg Galaxy* (Toronto: University of Toronto Press, 1962). It is, however, important to understand the precise sense in which McLuhan used the phrase "global village," namely, as a consequence of electronic media which obliterate space and time and put us into an immediate aural and visual relationship with one another. For McLuhan this was, in many ways, a dismaying consequence of contemporary media, since it tended to erode the more linear, rational consciousness promoted by print media. Moreover, this linking together of the entire globe in the electronic media does not overcome the incredible cultural and historical differences of the people so linked. In some ways it gives us a "false" sense of a shared world precisely to the extent that it obscures the incredibly different times and places from which we come. Thus the term "global village" is used here descriptively or metaphorically to point to an aspect of our contemporary situation and not as a glib image to suggest we are all one big happy family. Thus I have also used the idea and image of a "planetary society" which comes from Eugen Rosenstock-Huessy's *Planetary Service: A Way Into the Third Millennium* (Norwich, Vermont: Argo Books, 1978) where it is meant to indicate not a present reality but a common project and destiny to be achieved in the next millennium.

These terms are also an image of our situation that is possible only since we have moved beyond the skin of this earth to outer space from which we can look back and literally see our common planet as one. For further reading on Rosenstock-Huessy, see M.D. Bryant and Hans Huessy, eds., *Eugen Rosenstock-Huessy: Studies in His Life and Thought* (Lewiston, New York: Edwin Mellen Press, 1986).

7. See Herbert Richardson, "The Great Commandment," *New ERA Newsletter*, Vol. III, No. 2, 1983, which makes this point eloquently. I am indebted to him here—as in so many other ways.
8. Catholic literature on dialogue sometimes seems to suggest that dialogue with persons of other faiths is only for the mystic.
9. I am struck by the fact that an important source for the language of dialogue is the fruitful encounters of a small circle of Christians and Jews in post-World War I Germany who contributed to *Die Creatur*, especially persons like Eugen Rosenstock-Huessy, Franz Rosenzweig, Martin Buber, Hans Eberhardt, and Joseph Wittig. Thus in one sense the very language of dialogue—and especially a new awareness of the grammar of speaking and listening—entered the Western theological discussion out of the forge of interfaith encounter. For Martin Buber on community, see *Between Man and Man* (London: Collins, 1961).
10. While it is possible—and important—to differentiate these levels, it is also important to see how they interpenetrate each other. Thus a human act which is a social act, is also a cosmic act. The intellectual act of differentiation is also important for, as Augustine put it, "rightly ordering our loves" so that we love God as our ultimate aim and thus free society and human beings from weights they cannot bear. This point was wonderfully expressed by Huston Smith when he wrote about religion and politics as follows: "One consequence of the decline of faith and growing skepticism about 'the consolations of religion' has been that the demands placed on society and government in the name of temporal happiness have become ever more insistent and ever more unreasonable. So modernity, having spiritually expropriated the masses of its citizenry, finds their demands for religious Infinity that has been denied them. A regime which has to pacify a populace that is seeking fulfillment in the wrong place, will find its problems insuperable." See "Does Spirit Matter?," *Spirit Matters. The Worldwide Impact of Religion on Contemporary Politics*, edited by Richard L. Rubenstein (New York: Paragon House, 1987), xiv.
11. See especially Eugen Rosenstock-Huessy, *The Christian Future* and *Speech and Reality* (Norwich, Vermont: Argo Books, 1970). For an introduction to this important but neglected figure, see M.D. Bryant and Hans Huessy, eds., *Eugen Rosenstock-Huessy: Studies in His Life and Thought* (Lewiston, New York: Edwin Mellen Press, 1986), especially my essay on "The Grammar of the Spirit: Time, Speech and Society," 233–260.
12. See again E. Rosenstock-Huessy for a fuller discussion of these fronts of life.
13. See John Cobb, *Beyond Dialogue: Towards the Mutual Transformation of Christianity and Buddhism* (Philadelphia: Fortress Press, 1982), an important study, except that it mistakenly sees transformation as beyond dialogue rather than its perpetual fruit.
14. It is important to remember that in many ways the most important dialogue to result from dialogue with others is the inner dialogue wherein we speak with ourselves in silence about what we have heard, witnessed, and seen. It is often at this stage that the deepest and most lasting transformations occur.
15. I focus here only on the Christian in dialogue. It is presumptuous to speak for the

other. Moreover, it seems to me that we in the Christian community need very much to clarify for ourselves our purposes in dialogue with others, especially in North America and Europe. It was refreshing for me while on sabbatical leave there in 1986–1987 to discover that Christians in India took dialogue with others for granted. I have been moved by their example, especially that of Metropolitan Paulos Mar Gregorios, Father Bede Griffiths and Father Albert Nambiaparambil, to name but three. We Christians in the West can learn much from such figures.

16. This point is in relation to Raimundo Panikkar's *The Intra-Religious Dialogue* (New York: Paulist Press, 1978) which I basically accept. But I would point out that such dialogue remains interfaith.

17. The initiative for dialogue is, in truth, even stronger from groups like the Unification Church which, through the International Religious Foundation Inc., has made great contributions in this area despite the general hostility of many sectors of the Christian community. This point has been made by the Rev. Kenneth Cracknell who wrote the following in *Interfaith News* (Feb. 1986):

> The Unification Church (which is not an orthodox church) does more for the interfaith movement at the international level than do either the World Council of Churches Dialogue Unit or the Roman Catholic Vatican Secretariat for Non-Christians, or both of them put together.

18. Paul F. Knitter, *No Other Name? A Critical Survey of Christian Attitudes Towards the World Religions* (New York, Maryknoll: Orbis, 1986), a fine and important study. It does not, however, adequately explore the question of the spiritual foundations for Christian involvement in dialogue nor finally work with a sufficiently differentiated view of the Triune Christian faith. In this book, all questions become finally questions of Christology. Thus the issues become skewed, since many of the issues have to do with the doctrine of God as Creator and with the Spirit. This is, I might say, often an issue that has plagued Christian responses to the Unification movement. Many react as if the whole issue is Christology. But such a response barely touches the major issues. The Unification movement can much more appropriately be seen in relation to the doctrine of the spirit and eschatology.

19. What I am arguing here is not at all a theology of world religions or of pluralism, but rather an intra-Christian understanding of our own faith. Or perhaps better, I am attempting to articulate that faith, as I understand it, as leading me into dialogue and sustaining me there.

20. The Trinity has both an inner front and an outer economy. There are both the inner Trinitarian relations and their outward correlations of time and history. Both aspects remain the subject of ongoing reflection. I find myself drawn toward a Johannine perspective on this point; that is, I believe that it is illuminating to consider the third millennium as the "age of the spirit" in which our task is to discover the secret of the spirit in society and in our relations with one another.

21. See Gavin D'Costa's excellent critical study of John Hick's work, *John Hick's Theology of Religions, A Critical Evaluation* (Lanham, MD: University Press of America, 1987). For Hick's own writings, see the bibliography in D'Costa, 215–231 and especially his *God Has Many Names* (London: Macmillan, 1980). One of the most important points that D'Costa makes concerning Hick is that his pilgrimage is really through Christian theology to a certain philosophy of religion which has, I believe, become normative for his writings.

22. Dialogue is as important for intra-Christian relations as for relations with men and women of other faiths.
23. In my dialogue with Tibetan Buddhists, I have found their spiritual practice and disposition immensely attractive. And this fact of my experience stands despite, thus far, a complete inability to understand each other on the issue of God as Creator. This is instructive for me: I try to listen and I offer an account of my conviction; and I wonder why this conviction remains utterly unintelligible to those I have spoken with and, correspondingly, why I have trouble grasping their conviction on this point. But such a failure to understand one another—or perhaps better, to encounter such diverse accounts of things—does not lead either to a lessening of respect or to a desire to terminate discussion as fruitless. Rather, the underlying recognition of the spiritual depth and value of the other leads me to want to continue dialogue in the conviction that over time, some glimmers of understanding may emerge.
24. See Bede Griffiths, *The Cosmic Revelation: The Hindu Way to God* (Bangalore: Asian Trading Corporation, 1985), 109.
25. See Jaroslav Pelikan, *Jesus Through the Centuries* (New York: Harper & Row, 1987).
26. My point is that Christians do—and must—affirm that Christ is fully human and fully divine. But this affirmation clarifies only the boundaries of the mystery and not the mystery itself. Within these boundaries, Christians are free to generate all kinds of accounts of that mystery. For a comparable argument, see George Lindbeck, *The Nature of Doctrine* (Philadelphia: Westminster Press, 1984), especially 17–19, 33–41. However, I would argue that there nonetheless remains an element of "correspondence" that is crucial to faith, that is, Christ is truly God. But here a similar argument can be made in relation to Jesus and the Eternal Word, or better, the Eternal and Incarnate Word: both must be affirmed within the Christian faith, but neither is exhausted by the other.
27. See Vatican II's "Declaration on the Relationship of the Church to the Non-Christian Religions" for a crucial statement that has strengthened the movement of many Roman Catholics to dialogue with persons of other faiths. The statement is important in pointing to the way the Roman Catholic Church can gradually open itself to dialogue with other faiths, namely, through the vehicle of the Council. But what is the comparable way for the Protestant traditions?
28. For a critique of this failure within Christianity, see C. Klein, *Anti-Judaism in Christian Theology* (Philadelphia: Fortress Press, 1978).
29. See Raimundo Panikkar, *The Trinity and the Religious Experience of Man* (London: Darton, Longman, and Todd, 1973), which I consider one of the truly remarkable attempts to see the Trinity in the context of other faiths. This work is of inestimable importance. On his term *theandrism*, see especially 71–77.
30. Of course that articulation in the horizons of the faith of others must be done by members of those communities of faith.
31. This is, I believe, an important point which cannot be developed here. Let me only say that my encounter with men and women of other faiths led to a revitalization of my own faith and came as a fruitful antidote to the long debate within the Western world concerning the viability of faith at all—a debate that is present inside as well as outside the Christian churches.
32. This is of course a Christian interpretation of dialogue, but one that I believe could be shared by persons of other faiths as well.

2

CHRISTIAN MOTIVES FOR INTERFAITH DIALOGUE

Durwood Foster

INTERRELIGIOUS DIALOGUE poses for Christian faith today some momentous issues. On the one hand it is an immensely significant challenge to overcome existing parochial bigotry in response to the universalizing love, faith, and hope of Jesus Christ. There is no denying that a disheartening burden of doctrinaire exclusivism does distort Christian history and continues today not only to fulminate in the shrill triumphalism of much current evangelism but also to vegetate smugly in the indifference of mainline pastors to questions posed by other faiths. The actual good news of the Gospel, we shall argue, has always harbored a leaven of self-transcending outreach and now increasingly invites our threatened and aspiring pluralistic planet to a mutual commitment of creative openness. In concert herewith, moreover, there is a rising tide of impatience and disgust with bigotry all over the earth, and also the spreading insight that religious chauvinism is at the heart of all bigotry. But on the other hand present trends toward reciprocal respect and free exchange among religions have also called forth formidable resistance in the name of fidelity to the concrete truth each faith embodies. It is imperative that the authentic depth of traditions be preserved against a shallow syncretism that lacks all specific commitment. Accordingly, the present situation has become a decisive watershed, one slope of which leads outward to further affirmative association and common search among traditions, with the danger of superficialization and loss of substance, while the other slope inclines toward a guarding of known truth and value at the risk of exacerbating the rivalry of self-enclosed absolutisms. Those in this situation who are prepared to "cross the Rubicon" and join a radically open dialogue of truth and salvation must expect of course not just information and apologetic opportunity but rather reconception, transformation, and even conversion. It is especially the faithful willingness to plumb these possibilities that constrains further theological clarification in the current dynamic phase of the world's wider ecumenism. What is the self-understanding of the committed Christian, and *mutatis mutandis* the devotee of any faith, who consciously espouses a potential transcendence not only of her or his religion but also for the normative revelation that grounds it? No less than this, we shall hold, is required by the finality or normativity of Jesus as the Christ.

1. In the order of being as distinct from the order of knowing, the most basic Christian motive for dialogue with other faiths is that the God Christians worship is the One who creates, upholds, and lovingly wills to redeem all that is. [Cf. Gen. 1:1, 2 Tim. 4:6]. Ultimately there is no other source or ground of truth, value, or meaning in the entire universe than this One God whom to know, serve, and in communion subjoin is the paramount concern and quest of Christian existence. Accordingly, whatever manifests, registers, reflects, or illuminates the reality, purpose, and creative activity of this unique and universal God is of categorical interest and significance for Christian faith and life, so that St. Paul plausibly enjoins: "Whatever is true, whatever is just, whatever is pure, whatever is lovely, whatever is gracious, if there is any excellence, if there is anything worthy of praise, think about these things" (Phil. 4:5–6). Thinking about them, the wider ecumenist believes, means inquiring about, searching for and seeking to understand them more deeply, fully, and honestly, as only dialogue can adequately enable.

2. Not only is the God whom Christians worship the One who brings forth, undergirds, and directs to its end the whole concourse of being and becoming, but biblical-Christian faith also explicitly and emphatically affirms the universal knowability of God. "The heavens are telling the glory of God, and the firmament proclaims his handiwork" (Ps. 19:1). "He did not leave himself without witness, for he did good and gave you from heaven rains and fruitful seasons, satisfying your hearts with food and gladness" (Acts 14:17). Indeed, "Ever since the creation of

the world his invisible nature, namely his eternal power and deity, has been clearly perceived in the things that have been made" (Rom. 1:20). This ringing assertion of God's unbounded knowability is a powerful invitation to theological dialogue in all directions. For even if the actual knowledge of God has been impeded and obscured by sin, as biblical faith does perceive to be the case, it remains vastly important to trace and mine such insight as may endure, not only to establish points of contact for the Gospel newly given but also to espouse the augmentation and critique offered by "whatever has been said aright" (Clement) and is being said aright by anyone anywhere. The obscuration of sin also besets in-house Christian theology, so that its presence elsewhere is no more reason to abrogate communication outwards than within one's own circle of faith. On the other hand, the liberating but also obligating vision of Paul that "all things are yours, as you are Christ's and Christ is God's" (1 Cor. 3:21f.) has in fact continuously inspired Christian interaction with and assimilation from non-Christian sources from New Testament times till today.

3. While the whole original creation is "very good" (Gen. 1:31) and thus as such revelatory of its Author's reality and purpose, in the eyes of Christian faith a special status inheres in human beings as created in the image and filled with the Spirit of God (Gen. 1:26, 2:7). Human beings, that is to say, are uniquely potentiated as bearers of the meaning and truth of God. Note that the inestimable honor and responsibility of this capacity is imputed, in the fundamental stratum of biblical witness, not to a particular race, gender, type, class or religion, but to male and female in their shared intrinsic humanity. In principle every person is endowed with ontological truth. Prior to the plausibility of interreligious dialogue there is thus the revelatory exigency of dialogue itself, as humanity's intercommunion from the depths of its own most common identity. Or, prior to all traditions, is this not rather the binding root from which they arise, as Martin Buber so saliently saw? Indeed, "Thou hast made him little less than God" (Ps. 8:5); and when humans speak profoundly and earnestly with each other the original matter of all religion is at stake. No one who takes seriously the Christian heritage can dare spurn the dialogue of salvation with other *persons*, whatever particularizing garments they may be wearing.

4. While according to Christian understanding the universal knowability of God is severely thwarted by sin, this situation, so far from precluding, rather accentuates the value of interreligious dialogue. Sin would destroy the possibility of meaningful dialogue only were it total, but the very idea of a total sinfulness is a contradiction in terms. Sin presupposes wholesome insight as sickness does health in the body it

assails. On the other hand, were Christians themselves entirely free of sin, the latter's existence within the rest of humanity would, it is true, only enhance the value of interfaith dialogue to the extent of showing the needs of others.

But the mainstream of Christianity has always confessed that "If we say we have no sin, we deceive ourselves and the truth is not in us" (1 John 1:8). Therefore the "antithesis of sin and grace," as Schleiermacher calls it, is definitely not the same as that between non-Christian and Christian; it is rather a dynamic struggle pervading humanity as a whole. In this situation there is needed all the mutual criticism and reproof, as well as prompting and guidance, that may be forthcoming in the burgeoning encounter of traditions. Reinhold Niebuhr used to say that the goodness of human nature makes democracy possible, and the fallibility of human nature makes democracy necessary. So it is with interreligious dialogue. The unexpunged knowability of the Divine, especially as focused in the human image of God, makes dialogue possible, while the endemic corruption that spares no tradition makes dialogue necessary.

5. Although an attitude of self-centeredness and exclusive superiority does appear ever and again in the biblical literature, and even more egregiously within church history, it is remarkable how luminously biblical-Christian faith has nevertheless expressed the opposite attitude of God-centeredness and humble openness toward external sources of religious worth. In the Old Testament an extraordinary instance of this is the account of Melchizedek, king of Salem and "priest of God most high" (Gen. 14:18–20). This Canaanite holy man ministers to Abraham with bread and wine (!) and blesses him in the name of the "maker of heaven and earth." Thus the Canaanite "God most high" (*El Elyon*) is identified with Yahweh, the God of Israel, and Melchizedek is remembered in biblical tradition (Ps. 110:4, Heb. 7:7–17) as a Christ-figure.

In the later New Testament a salient example of openness and affirmative generosity toward other traditions is the eschatological vision (Rev. 22:24–26) of how into the heavenly city—the *civitas dei* or Realm of God—is brought without prejudice "the glory and honor of the nations." Thus the symbol of the final repository of all historical meaning and value is conceived, even in the sometimes exclusivistic Apocalypse of John, with a magnanimity and capaciousness befitting the God who brings sunshine and rain to all the earth (Matt. 5:45) and "who desires all to be saved and come to the knowledge of the truth" (1 Tim. 2:4). Such elements of openness pulsate throughout the biblical witness, contending with contrary impulses of ethnocentrism and religious imperialism. Here, as in many other connections, the question of a decisive norm wherewith rightly to divide and focus the scriptural and traditional witness, and at the same time monitor the vagaries of current experience, becomes as pressing and sore for faith today as it has ever been.

6. While he stands within a long and variegated tradition, which integrally participates in his manifestation by preparing, receiving, and interpreting it, Jesus as the Christ is the normative center of this whole tradition; so that Christian motivation for interreligious dialogue is and must be chiefly inspired and shaped by him. It is in and through him that the Christian envisagement of God, world, and humanity achieves climactic concretion, and it is commitment to his humble openness of inclusive love that is the inmost wellspring of Christian wider ecumenism.

a. Jesus' consciousness of God, as in the story of the prodigal son (Luke 15), joins creative power with the letting-be of personal love, wherewith the responsible autonomy of human being as God's beloved child is categorically respected, desiderated, and promoted. Salvation—the teleological wholeness of the individual, society, and indeed of all creation (Rom. 8:21)—is also essentially liberation; it turns upon a *sine qua non* of loving persuasion and thus is incompatible with coercion or deception. So Paul avers that in the ministry of Christ "we refuse to practice cunning or tamper with God's word, but by the open statement of the truth we would commend ourselves to everyone's conscience" (2 Cor. 4:2). Christ as way and life is also truth (John 14:6) which makes free (John 8:32). Christians therefore "cannot do anything against the truth but only for the truth" (2 Cor. 13:8) and for this reason are enjoined to give "rational account (*apologia*) with gentleness and reverence to anyone inquiring" about their hope (1 Pet. 3:15). On the receiving side at least, as other positions address one's own, here is surely an appealing scenario of dialogue.

b. Presupposing pervasive human sinfulness (John 8:7), the openness of Jesus to the creative spontaneity of persons is strikingly luminous in the anointment at Bethany (Matt. 26:6–13, with parallels in all the other gospels). While his disciples carp at the waste of the ointment, Jesus espouses the gratuitous act of the anointing woman as "a beautiful thing." Her ecstatic subjectivity, transcending ethical calculation, is defended even as her unpredictably free expression of love is esteemed. There is in this manifestation of the Christ, or the Christ norm, a radical endorsement of personhood in its privacy and idiosyncrasy. The Christ norm here comes to mean, not simply a self-contained plentitude of everything required, desirable, and admirable, whether in a human or a deity, but rather a standing back before the other to create free space. Though this is not all it means, it here comes to mean also and essentially a norm of self-effacing *kenosis*, or emptying, in reception and recognition of the other's act of beauty, truth, and love.

Another, equally salient, instance of receptivity and openness in the Christ norm is that of the interaction between Jesus and the Canaanite woman who begs help for her ill daughter (Matt. 15:22–28 and parallels). In this incident actual interreligious dialogue takes place. Again the unsympathetic disciples show their and our need to be taught by the Christ. They would send the woman away, but Jesus chooses to hear her. Then, astonishingly, the Christ is seen in a moment of theological dispute wherein he is gotten the better of. He says he "was sent only to the lost sheep of the house of Israel." He—the Christ himself—embodies the ethnocentric exclusion that plagues his and every tradition. "It is not fair to take the children's bread and throw it to the dogs." "Yes, Lord," the woman's humility now transcends his, "Yet even the dogs eat the crumbs that fall from their master's table." In the amazing reversals that transpire in this *religionsgeschichtlich* unique story, Jesus at first seems to have the superior position and the woman acknowledges this, sorely seeking aid for the child.

But her faith in the Christ is greater than his own, and she teaches him something inestimably crucial about his own being and mission; so that theologically, at this decisive point of his universality, she surpasses him. For a moment, as it were, the history of salvation hangs in the balance.

Then, as in the story of the woman who anoints him, the Christ recognizes and embraces the beauty, submissive humor, and truth of the Canaanite's love. The Christ norm, as hardly anywhere else in religion, becomes manifest in receptive humility, in being bested and yet assimilating and affirming the better way one did not yet know. It becomes clear that commitment to Christ means commitment to openness.

c. Given the triumphalism which the biblical witness shares with all scriptures, it was unlikely the Christ should appear as one *to whom* a beautiful original act or a decisive insight of faith is imparted. It was equally unlikely the disciples themselves should be glimpsed as unperceptive moralizers, spiritually and theologically upstaged by women, one of whom was a foreigner at that.

Yet neither of these instances is perhaps as unlikely as the Cross itself, the central reality and symbol in which the vulnerable meekness of the Christ is consummated and concluded—the supreme stumbling block and folly (1 Cor. 1:23) not only to Jews and Greeks but to every perduring form and moment of churchly pride. The Cross, in its depth of meaning, is not just Golgotha's wood and the Redeemer's suffering death at that point alone.

It is the unremitting offering by Jesus, throughout the course of his existence, of everything about him that is merely Jesus to his call and empowerment to be the Christ—to be the one, that is, in whom everything is laid open to God's future, to the disposal of universal truth and love. Especially theology and clerical authority, as modes of intended Christian faithfulness, have sustained an uneasy relationship with the Cross. For on these was and is placed the baffling duty to protect the decisive truth of that which forgoes all protection.

Only a radically dialectical mentality and praxis can hope to measure up toward this duty—a Thomas writing his summas and then, in the ashes of age, confessing their poverty, a Merton mastering the heritage of the Christian spirit as hardly any contemporary and then losing his life in quest of Eastern wisdom, a Tillich admitting the inevitable idolatry of his own passionate Christology, goading his failing body to critical exchange with Hisamatsu and a hoped-for plunge into India. If the very meaning of Jesus' existence as the Christ is to yield his entire concreteness as Jesus to his reality as the way, the truth and the life, surely the meaning of discipleship essayed in his name will also be to offer one's whole heart, strength, and mind—including of course one's creed and theology—to the ongoing transformation of the Cross.

d. No less than the Cross as a decisive motive of openness, because inseparable from its significance, is the Resurrection of the Christ. In the Resurrection the cruciform mission of the Christ continues with liberating power. Without the Cross, and the self-effacing life of love it consummates, the Resurrection loses its Christian point; it is no longer the Resurrection of the Christ. In the Resurrection, precisely Jesus' mode of life and death is ratified by God, and by those who believe in this God, as the ultimate norm of all life. "Now the Lord"—that is, here, Jesus as the Christ—"is the Spirit, and where the Spirit of the Lord is, there is freedom" (2 Cor. 3:17). Of course the God of the Old Testament was already and always the spirit. But now Yahweh God—"I Am That I Am," or "I cause to Fall What I Cause to Fall" (*eheyeh asher eheyeh*, Exod. 3:14)—is, in Christian perception, climactically disclosed in the Cross and Resurrection of Jesus as the Christ. The Spirit brooding in the begining and through all ages over the unordered and disordered deep of the world now becomes normatively manifest as the slain and risen Lamb. Thus we are to understand "that no one speaking by the Spirit of God ever says 'Jesus be cursed!' and no one can say 'Jesus is Lord'— the hallmark of Christian identity—'except by the Holy Spirit'" (1 Cor. 12:3). If commitment to Christ and him crucified is commitment to openness, the gift and fruit of his Spirit, includes the reality in us of openness, of patient outreach, of ready appreciation, and humble receptivity.

Especially for our present purposes, a most salient aspect of the Christian experience of Christ's Resurrection and continuing spiritual presence with the community of faith is the thrust of, not already having all the truth, but being led forward into it. The New Testament documents themselves, as both tradition and modern criticism agree, are obviously not based wholly on the revelation imparted during Jesus' earthly lifetime, though that does indeed remain for them a *sine qua non* of the utmost importance.

Rather it is the common self-understanding of the earliest church that the promise of Jesus that "when the Spirit comes he will guide you into all the truth" (John 16:13) is being fulfilled and will go on being fulfilled until the end of time. It goes without saying that this consciousness of not already possessing all truth which is religiously vital, but of expecting more of it as history unfolds, carries a strong implication of openness. It is one of the axial Christian premises of interfaith dialogue, even if the latter cannot be directly inferred from it. The orthodox form of Christian openness, in and for the Spirit, stops short of the spiritualistic extreme of Montanism and the *Schwärmer* of more recent times in insisting that the same Spirit, as veritably his own, "will bring to your remembrance all that I [Jesus] have said to you" (John 14:26B)—thus holding firm the link with the canonical memory of the foundational Christian event.

7. Considering the whole image of Jesus Christ, his life and death and Resurrection, but also considering the Creator God known decisively (as Christians believe) through him, and likewise further the intentional healing energy imparted to us by God in Christ through the Spirit, it is time in our deliberations to lift up as a uniting thematic principle the core Christian motive of *agape* love. Agape love, for Christian faith, is the supreme motive that underlies, informs, and consecrates all others, whether in Godself, in human beings ecclesially and individually, or in Christ as decisive revealer of God and of authentic humanity. Thus love must also be the preeminent motive of Christian interfaith dialogue, as it is the prime motive of Christian worship, evangelism, theology, social action, and fellowship. This is not contrary to, but a further determination of, what we have said above about the most basic Christian motive being the character of God. If on the other hand it is often the case that dialogue occurs more from a sense of duty, yet that is not incompatible with love, which still may be the inner root or final ground of one's sense of duty. For love ought to be the motive of all Christian motives. Certainly the best dialogue is impelled and propelled by love, though not by the "sloppy agape" that has no spine of intellectual as well as practical justice and rigor; and the wider ecumenism has happily benefited from the fact that many of its promulgators, Christians and others, truly do engender a love for one another that dissolves walls of hostility and builds valid understanding.

a. Given the fact that the Christian mission to the world is fundamentally inspired by love (primordially and normatively by God's love poured out for us in Christ), the same love motivates dialogue because it categorically respects our human brothers and sisters as responsible persons who must not be manipulated or coerced (2 Cor. 4:2ff.). This means they must be able to answer back from the depth of their rational integrity, to question and wrestle with whatever is proposed to them as truth.

Can we rightly claim to love anyone to whom we would deny this opportunity or in whom we would not cherish and encourage its development? The wrestling must proceed, as Paul says, in the light of their conscience, which is to say within the framework initially of their own existing criteria, grounded in what for them is ultimate in meaning and value. To follow emphatically what is going on within them, we also must envisage their postulates of faith and entertain their standards of value. Through mutual interlocution we must become participants in their inner struggle, as indeed they will in ours if we truly level with them as human to human. Thus at bottom every act of communicating the Gospel should be dialogical. There will doubtless always remain a relative difference between evangelism as such and dialogue, but the two can indeed never be properly separated. Evangelism should always be passing over into dialogue, and dialogue should be—not some medley of neutral abstractions—but a conversation of evangelisms, with each side's suasiveness and cogency represented as honestly as possible. Apologetics ("giving answer with gentleness and reverence," 1 Pet. 3:15) would actually appear to become ideally synonymous with dialogue. For how can we love and reverence someone to whom we do not also listen in return, not just foisting our answer upon the other but earnestly seeking to appreciate and fairly appraise her or his answers as well as questions? For there are no questions that do not imply something of answers, and no answers that do not presuppose meaningful questions.

b. To love anyone means to esteem and seek the development of their personhood, and this entails allowing space for their creativity and trying to understand and integrate into one's own continuum of worth their unique achievements. At a recent dialogue with Buddhists, a Japanese Christian shared that it had been very painful for him as a young man, and was still, to be unable to honor the spiritual and cultural treasures of his Shinto-Buddhist heritage. He could hardly stand to think, he said, not only that his forebears had no entry into the Christian heaven, but also that they might possibly be admitted if stripped of their own concrete historicity and religiousness.

A Christianity that goes to all the creation preaching would-be good news must surely be sensitive to the fact that, to a world come and coming of age, news is *not* good that demeans and ignores "whatever is gracious" (Philip. 4:8) wherever it might be found. Genuine love for our fellow human beings will eagerly look to see "if there is any excellence" and like the Keeper of the heavenly Jerusalem (Rev. 21:24) will welcome gladly the "glory and honor," such as it is, of all nations and all traditions. Interfaith dialogue is by no means the only way of doing this, but it can greatly facilitate the overall process and give access to inward and subtle treasures of spirit that may otherwise go unnoticed.

8. The central Christian conviction of God's saving love for the world in Christ (John 3:16) ramifies into many subsidiary motives for interfaith dialogue, including the urgent quest for peace, for economic justice, for racial and gender liberation, for shared insights into healing, and the protection of the natural environment. There is sore and pressing need—more than ever before—for humanity to get its heart and head together, and only the most hard-bitten secularist can deny that the earnest talking through of our planetary problems has to involve not only our ethics but also the religious roots of our ethics, not only our scientific knowledge and philosophy, but also our ultimate concerns and commitments. The various derivative and peripheral motives for interfaith dialogue are certainly valid from a Christian viewpoint, if they are consonant with, and expeditious of, the loving intentionality of the Christ norm for the whole world.

Many pages indeed could now be devoted to the elaboration of these subsidiary motives, such as peace, coping with scientism, and the struggle against sexism and racism, which often may provide the most propitious springboards today for ecumenical advance. As we have, however, now come near the reasonable limit of our present musings, we can only pronounce blessing upon such wider ecumenical enterprises and reserve our last paragraphs for a few remarks about the formidable theological tasks confronting the current inter-faith movement, which despite its powerful exigency may yet be stymied or severely hampered by a host of contrary factors.

9. While at the normative core of biblical faith there is much that inspires and indeed requires a contemporary commitment to interfaith dialogue, there are also in the Bible itself, the foundational document of Christianity, some deep-seated hazards and barriers that challenge the validity and threaten the progress of the wider ecumenism. As these are the ostensible justification to which later ecclesial and theological Christian exclusivism appeals, we shall focus our concluding brief comments upon four of them.

a. Systemically entrenched in the body of Christendom, especially in its Protestant parts, there is an inverted construal of certain key passages in the biblical witness whereby they are taken to preclude and repudiate any other saving revelation than that made available in Jesus. Probably the most notorious such passage, often thrown in the face of would-be wider ecumenists, is John 14:6: "Jesus said to him, 'I am the way, the truth, and the life; no one comes to the Father but by me.'" Bogged down by the theological illiteracy that increasingly besets the modern church—not only the laity but also much of the scholarly magisterium with its disjunctive specializations—consideration of this passage typically proceeds without any awareness that here the universal logos of God, who in the beginning "was with God" and "was God," through whom "all things were made," the "true light that enlightens everyone" (John 1:1,3,9), becomes manifest in, with, and through the concrete historicity of Jesus but not—repeat *not*!—so as to abolish or confuse the critical distinction upon which the Definition of Chalcedon and classical Christianity insist between his deity and his humanity.

The result is that the "way, truth, and life" which lead and come to ultimate fulfillment in God are not seen to be the self-transcending, outreaching, open love (the logos of God) instantiated normatively in Jesus, but are rather read as an exclusivizing absolutization of Jesus' own self-contained particularity—just the opposite of the orthodox and right Christian meaning of passage. While this exclusivist reading can in no way be made consistent with the overall sense and thrust of Scripture, and is lucidly refuted by top leaders of the church (such as very recently in Berkeley WCC General Secretary Emilio Castro) and by many individual theologians, it continues to befuddle many.

The only remedy here would seem to lie in more thorough and accurate, as well as wholistic, theological study, wherein biblical and historical, and systematic disciplines might more incisively potentiate each other, leading to more theologically relevant scholarly commentaries and to a more biblically and historically informed systematics. Unfortunately, present trends in the seminaries do not buoy very much one's hope for an increase in wholistic and responsible theological work, though the upsurge of interfaith dialogue itself does happily create incentive that could change things for the better.

b. More problematic than misconstrued passages are those elements of apparent exclusivism that really are woven into the texture of Scripture. There is no gainsaying the presence of these. For example, in Acts we read, after an account of healing "by the name of Jesus Christ of Nazareth" (4:10), that "there is salvation in no one else, for there is no other name under heaven given among men by which we must be saved" (4:12).

While the preemption of salvation for Jesus does not necessarily rule out all other revelation and possible dialogue, and while there are other considerations as well that blunt the exclusivist edge of this statement as it bears on our pluralist context today, my present intent is to acknowledge that the words and the thoughts of the Bible *are* sometimes in conflict with what I have propounded as the Christian motivation for interfaith outreach.

Another example, all the more sensitive because it is Paul speaking, is 1 Cor. 2:16: "'For who has known the mind of the Lord so as to instruct him?' But we have the mind of Christ." In this verse the Apostle applies to Christ the citation of Is. 40:13, where the "Lord" is Godself, then expressly denies the instructability of Christ, for which I have argued above (in relation to the anointing at Bethany and the Canaanite woman), and finally avers that we too have the uninstructable mind of Christ! I hold we should emulate the mind of Christ, though not that we have it, and that the closer we come to it the more instructable we will become. Though revering Paul exceedingly and drawing on him constantly as a theological source, I also regard him as fallible and deem the verse before us to be distortedly docetic or Eutychean in tenor. Scripture, though it is our canonical medium of divine revelation, has a human and fallible dimension and requires open-ended correction by the Christ norm of which it is an integral bearer. Even that norm, in whatever form it has taken in our life till now, can and does go on transcending itself, since the whole Christ is not only the historical and biblical but also the risen and living Christ. Clearly, what the Christ norm says in a particular connection will always be discussable and debatable and a matter of prayer. Objectively it cannot be completely demonstrated; it can only be finally settled, for the moment at hand, by decision that will involve risk.

c. When, following Vatican II, Paul VI proposed a "dialogue of salvation" with non-Christian religious, there were many who saw this as a radical threat to the "finality" they held essential to the Gospel. Was not the very basis of the Christian community of faith, by which it divided from Judaism, the glad certainty that Christ *had* come and the Kingdom *was* at hand? It remains a major problem, in assessing the viability of a truly open exchange with other traditions, whether a "realized" aspect, a somehow fulfilled rather than merely expectant and seeking Christian religious consciousness can be sustained. If not, it will indeed be difficult for the Christian mainstream, with any kind of fidelity to its classical past, to accommodate itself to the wider ecumenism. Does this mean that a kind of triumphalism is indissolubly part of Christianity? A solution to the demanding problems in this area may lie in the kind of distinction classically made between justification and sanctification, wherein the one theme satisfies the need for, and corresponds to, the reality of something decisive and final with respect to one's meaning and destiny, while the other theme matches the equally irrepressible truth that there is an ongoing, as-yet-unfulfilled eschatological tension. Sanctification would thus become the concept whereunder and wherein the commonwealth of faiths could enrich and assist each other as helpmates and friends, both in vision and praxis, in a mutual growth in grace, in the creative exhilaration of fashioning a Realm of Ends worthy of their brightest compossible dreams.

d. In a notable ecumenical passage (1 Cor. 1:12), St. Paul intoned: "Each one of you says, 'I belong to Paul,' or 'I belong to Apollos,' or 'I belong to Cephas,' or 'I belong to Christ.' Is Christ divided?" This was *Christian* ecumenism because, while recognizing diversity, it posited the irrefragable unity of Christ as the common norm. The ultimate problem of a *wider* ecumenism, many feel, is that there is and can be no such mutual norm, unless all faiths convert to one or a new comprehensive faith shall arise to replace existing ones. The conviction is strongly held, not only for example by a Barth but also by a Tillich, that there can be—for any single person or for any integral community of faith—only *one* ultimate norm; and that for Christianity, they would say, is Christ.

But this flies in the face of the pluralism so many of us have come to live and breathe, which is the view that the truth of another person and another faith may not already be contained in my truth, and yet have just as much linkage with the ultimate truth as my own and my community's. Can we honestly espouse this pluralism and also be committed decisively to the finality of Christ? Part of the answer, I believe, is that commitment to openness—and thus to the principle of pluralism—*is* the radical decision Jesus Christ invites and requires of us. His self-giving, kenotic love, I believe, is the secret and substance of precisely that openness, and *vice versa*. But to clarify and test this, to correct and enlarge it, to envisage it—or the better idea to which it may lead—more responsibly and adequately, that is the earnest hope of our ecumenical conversations.

3

WHY CHRISTIANITY NEEDS OTHER RELIGIONS

Robert P. Scharlemann

THE QUESTIONS of the way in which the exclusivity of Jesus, both in reference to the revelation of deity and in reference to the coming of salvation, is to be related to his universality is an old one. But there are different ways in which the answer is given. Prior to the year 70, when it was not yet clear that Christianity and Judaism would go separate ways, the universality of Christianity and that of Judaism were not distinct questions. After the break between the two religions, the universality of Christian teaching was interpreted by reference to such concepts as the *Logos*—whatever of truth had appeared anywhere was implicitly compatible with the truth manifested in Jesus as the Logos made flesh. The concept of the Logos mediated between the particularity of the Christian religion and the universality of spiritual phenomena. For what the identification of the Logos with Jesus meant was that the wisdom or the reason that was embodied in the person of Jesus was the same eternal wisdom or reason that found other expressions as well.

Hence there was, for example, no need to exclude from Christianity the moral wisdom of Stoicism or the metaphysics of pagan religions. These could be incorporated with the understanding that whatever there was of truth, no matter where it appeared, it was implicitly a part of Christianity. The same was the case with the good and the beautiful (although this latter provided more problems since it could become an enticement to idolatry). To the extent that these were positive values, they were not opposed to, but implicitly contained in, what was affirmed as the revelation at the basis of the Christian religion.

During the millennium from the seventh to the seventeenth centuries, the attitude of Christianity toward other religions was shaped by the encounter with Islam, the first encounter that Christianity had with another religion. The defensive posture into which the Christian world was pressed during that period was reflected in the exclusivism of its attitude toward extra-Christian phenomena. Even during this period, however, exclusivism did not become the sole view. The same thirteenth century that saw Innocent III proclaiming that there is no salvation outside the church also saw the astounding ecumenism (of the three monotheistic religions) at the court of Frederick II in Sicily.[1] The militarism and exclusivism of this medieval period gradually gave way—Nicholas of Cusa's *De pace fidei* was an early document of the change—under the impact of the Renaissance, the Enlightenment, and, most recently, the ecumenical movement in the Christian churches toward a more open and, at the moment, highly fluid attitude of Christianity toward non-Christian religions.[2]

This very brief sketch of the mixed and changing attitude toward other religions on the part of Christianity provides the background for any discussion today. For it is easy to forget that the anathemas expressed at the church councils were directed not at other religions but at the heretical or purportedly heretical within the Christian religion. The negative judgments passed upon the heretical within Christianity cannot be transferred to the non-Christian phenomena, whether religious or nonreligious.[3] If, for the Christian religion, Jesus is the liberator-redeemer, then, as Schleiermacher put it in his *The Christian Faith*, any statement which implies that redemptive liberation is either unnecessary or impossible is heretical; consequently, any statement which, while appearing to be true to Christian doctrine, implies that Jesus was either less than fully human or less than fully divine is heretical and needs to be rejected as such. But such a statement, when made in contexts other than that of Christian religious affirmation, cannot be heretical for the simple reason that it does not purport to represent the Christian religion.

Understanding and evaluating affirmations that do not function within the Christian religion require, therefore, a different orientation than that provided by anathematized heresies. Schleiermacher struck a new path when he aligned religions according to type and stage of development. In type religions are, he said, either ethical or esthetic; in stage, they are either immature (still oriented to "animal consciousness," that is, a consciousness that is not yet self-conscious) or mature. As was typical of nineteenth-century idealism, Schleiermacher thought Christianity represented the highest type and the highest stage of religious development.[4] If it was the final religion, irreplaceable and unsurpassable, this was only because it represented in its purest form the religious function as such. (Karl Barth later pointed out that this may not even be so. For, gauged by a Protestant criterion of the religion of pure grace, Pure Land Buddhism seems to possess the immanent possibility to become equally a religion of pure grace.)[5] Troeltsch's attack on this idealist view was based on its failure to take into account that the people who draw up typologies and stages are themselves historically conditioned in ways that they may not know. Hence, one has to take account of one's own standpoint as well as of the phenomena that are seen.[6] Barth's attack on the idealist understanding of religion came from a different direction: Christianity is not mainly concerned with itself as a religion but with that revelation, tied to the name of Jesus, which judges all religions, including Christianity, and which is equally near to and equally far from every religion.

Against this broad background, I should like to propose the following thesis: *Even when Jesus is understood exclusively as the revelation of God (that is, as the one and only human being who is existent deity), the non-Christian is as much a part of this revelation as is the Christian*, not as the reprobate or rejected one but as an equal participant in the salvation connected by Christians with the name of Jesus. The basis for the thesis is that the actuality of Jesus as the Christ involves a triadic structure constituted by the relations of Peter and Judas to each other and to Jesus. We need to forestall a possible misunderstanding by noting at the outset that the figure of Judas does not represent the reprobate, the one to be excoriated, but something else which I hope to make clear in the course of developing the proposed line of thought. From the thesis, it seems to me to follow that Christianity, even at its most exclusive, requires that there be others, not Christians, just as Jesus' living reality required that there be two, equally true responses to his appearance, those of Peter and of Judas. Understanding the Christian meaning of Jesus in this way is somewhat different not only from Troeltsch's or Schleiermacher's but also from the dialectical understanding found in the early Barth. Closer to this understanding is the one that appears in Barth of the *Church*

Dogmatics when he treats of Judas, whom he distinguishes from Paul and the other apostles by saying that in Judas the "No" to Jesus *is* the "Yes," whereas in the other disciples the "Yes" followed the "No."[7]

The intention here is to indicate that, even for an exclusively understood Christianity, the plurality of religions is not a deficiency, not something which one seeks to overcome, but a fulfillment of the meaning of Jesus' being the Christ. There are some indications in the New Testament itself of the fact that the followers of Jesus should not hope for a state of affairs in which everyone would be a follower. Such an indication is contained, for example, in the image of the followers of Jesus as the salt of the earth. Salt is the seasoning that gives flavor to the food that we eat. But no one would wish to have only salt to eat. Jesus' followers may, similarly, be the salt of the earth; but no one would want to have the salt without the food seasoned by it. Christian existence comes into its own only by its relation to worldly existence. Other indications found in the sayings ascribed to Jesus in the New Testament might include Jesus' reference to there being other folds with other sheep and the parable of the last judgment, according to which every encounter with a person in need (in person, hungry, naked) is an encounter with Jesus.

But these indications in the New Testament are not clearly or explicitly concerned with the question that is posed for us today about the relation between Christianity and the other religions. (The same would be true, of course, of the passage classically used to support the claim of Jesus' exclusiveness, Acts 4:12: "There is salvation in no one else, for there is no other name under heaven given among men by which we must be saved.") So the question must be posed carefully. It is the question whether the very structure of the affirmation of Jesus as Christ, when understood exclusivistically, does not involve the existence of at least one person who always denies what the Christian affirms. This is not to contend that the affirmation must be so understood even within the Christian community. It is, rather, to follow the methodological counsel that, in thinking through a theological matter, one takes not the easiest but the most difficult possibility. In this case the most difficult possibility is to understand how an exclusively understood Christianity can require the acknowledgment of other religions as equally participant in truth and salvation.

The Freedom of Response

The response to Jesus as the Christ is a response that is freely elicited; it is not a response that is compelled nor is it a conclusion arrived at by following the steps of an argument through the premises to the conclusion.

The affirmation of Jesus as the Christ is, therefore, different from the affirmation, for example, that all men are mortal or that the chair on which I am sitting is made of wood. It is true that in grammatical terms the assertion that "Jesus is the Christ" has the same form as the assertion "This chair is wooden" or "All men are mortal." In each of these cases a subject is combined with a predicate by means of the copula that is a form of the verb "to be." But the basis on which we make the affirmations is different. The basis for saying the chair is wooden is our sense perception and our abstract cognition. The basis on which we say that all men are mortal is our making explicit in the predicate something that is already contained in the subject. To be a human being is to be, among other things, mortal. Mortality and human being do not exactly coincide, since there are things other than human beings which are mortal; but there is no human being who is not also mortal, and for that reason mortality is a predicate already implied in the subject.

The assertion or the affirmation or the confession that Jesus is the Christ, however, has a different basis. It is somewhat similar to a judgment of perception, an empirical judgment rather than an *a priori* judgment, because it is made only in the presence of that which is designated by the subject term of the assertion; it does not simply make explicit in the predicate term a quality already contained in the subject term, and it is not an inference drawn from other judgments. Nonetheless, the predicate "the Christ" is not empirically perceptible but is a personal and free response: something in the person of Jesus elicits, from those who encounter it (or to whom it is disclosed); the acknowledgment is freely given: nothing compels it in the way that, for example, the very sight of a stone compels us to recognize it as a stone if we want to think of it as it is (a stone), rather than as what it is not (a tree), or what it could be (a statue). The acknowledgment of Jesus as the Christ does refer to a quality in him, a quality presented *to* us and not invented by us; but it is a quality that makes itself manifest in such a way as to elicit a free acknowledgment of its presence. Although it is a quality directly perceived, if perceived at all, rather than a quality inferred from other properties of Jesus, it is a quality not manifest to all those with whom Jesus came or comes into contact. The difference between its being manifest and its not being manifest is the basis for the difference between those who acknowledge and those who do not acknowledge him as the Christ. (The formula of such an acknowledgment is given briefly in this way: "He said, 'Follow me!' And immediately they followed him." It is a spontaneous response, an action made possible in this case by the enabling words of the summon.)[8]

The freedom of the response is what differentiates a judgment of "confession" from an empirical or a logical judgment. The reality (the being of the Christ) which manifests itself in this way is different from a reality that is always perceptibly or cognizably present. If there is a green leaf before me, then I can always verify its being green by looking again. (This does not, of course, rule out the possibility that the leaf, which is now green, may be brown at some other time.) But if one, like Jesus, is the Christ, then I can verify his being that only on those occasions when being-the-Christ manifests itself by eliciting a free acknowledgment.

Freedom and Finitude

The response, on which a judgment of confession is based, is freely elicited. It is never a response that anyone is compelled to make, but one that, when it is made, is made possible by the self-manifestation of that to which it is a response. But a response is always the response of a human being; and, as such, it always has the form of *finite* freedom. This implies not only that a negative response is as much elicited by the object in question as is a positive response (that much is meant by calling the responses free); it also implies that no one can make both responses. To put it more concretely: the response of Jesus on the part of Peter ("You are the Christ") is no truer to the reality than is the response on the part of Judas (if we understand Judas to be the one who says, by his actions, "You are not the Christ"). But no one can be both Peter and Judas. Paul expressed this in part by a teleology of the divine economy: the rejection of Jesus as the Messiah on the part of those from whom Paul would have expected acceptance serves the end of bringing all people, and not just the chosen people, into the economy of divine salvation. The freedom of the response means that affirmative and negative judgments of confession are equally possible (and equally true); but the finitude of the response means that every response is one or the other (the confession of Peter or the confession of Judas) but not both—one who does not say "No" says "Yes," and one who does not say "Yes" says "No." Peter's denial of Jesus, made in a moment of weakness and contradicting his earlier confession, was, therefore, of another order than Judas' *paradidonai* (handing over).

Finitude in this connection does not mean only the limitedness of our thinking and being. In one sense, of course, that is what the finite is. The finite is the limited; the infinite is the unlimited. The infinite, or unlimited, is in turn either a "bad" infinite (as Hegel called it) or a true infinite. The bad infinite is represented, for example, by the fact that we can always extend a line segment farther in either direction; we never reach an end. The good infinite is the infinite which is realized as the unity of opposites. If we think of a circle as an infinite line, it is a true infinite, or good infinite, because it unites the beginning and the end of a line. Similarly, the finitude of being means that being a subject is always a matter of being a subject over against an object; there are subjects and objects only in relation to each other. The bad infinity of being is the fact that we can "subjectify" without limit, and no matter how long we do so, the subject always remains subject and not object. The true infinite of being is the unity of subject and object, not the indefinite extension of either objectivity or subjectivity.

The infinity and finitude of freedom can be pointed out, along these same lines, by calling attention to the double awareness that we have of our own subjectivity, of ourselves in the form of "I." We become aware of the meaning of the word *I* within ourselves. I become an "I"—subject when I understand the meaning of this word, in contrast to "you," "he," "she," "it," and so on. There is an infinity in this self-consciousness because I can reflect not only upon the world and upon my own acts but also upon myself as the agent of those acts. It is a "bad" infinity in the sense that no matter how far back I step I can never step so far back as to escape from the I which indicates the origin, the zero-point, of all of my action, thought, perception, and being. I can think of things, and of my thinking of things, and of my thinking of my thinking of things, and so on indefinitely. The zero-point eludes our grasp infinitely. No matter how far back we step, we cannot include as the object of those reflections the very ego that in the here and now is doing the reflecting. The I as I, the ego as we are inwardly aware of it in self-consciousness, is a "blind spot" in the universe; I as I never appear to myself in the world. What can appear to me in the world as myself is only some past form or sequence of forms of the activity of the I of reflection. The infinity of the I is here a recessive one—expressed in the formulation that, no matter how far back I step, I cannot step away from that zero-point indicated in the meaning of the term "I."

If one side of the understanding of the self as I has to do with this infinity in the reflection of the I, the other side has to do with the absolute finitude of this very same I, the finitude which is recognized in our being absolutely bound to the temporal-spatial point indicated by our body. No matter how much we try, no matter how great our sympathy or empathy may be, none of us can exchange places with any other one. We can become aware that what sensation and feeling and thought are to each of us is analogous to what they are for the others of us. But none of us can exchange places in the sense of being somewhere other than the "here" indicated by our bodily locations. That is an absolute finitude.

Perfect Freedom

The significance of this infinite-finite freedom for the affirmation of Jesus as the Christ, when that affirmation is understood as a judgment of confession, can be made most readily clear if we look at how it appears in the triangular relationship of Peter, Judas, and Jesus in the New Testament account of Jesus and his disciples. The freedom of the response and the finitude of the freedom in that response both imply that the Messiahship of Jesus is open not only to the self of Peter, who responds affirmatively, but also to the self of Judas who responds negatively. In one sense, as the words of Peter indicate,[9] the figure of Judas is as necessary to the appearance of Jesus as the Christ as is the figure of Peter. Jesus could not have been recognized as the Christ if there had been only a Peter, or a group of Peters, nor could he have been recognized as the Christ if there had been only a Judas or a group of Judases. Being the Christ implies that there be also in relation to the Christ at least one who is Peter and at least one who is Judas. Without either a Peter or a Judas, there would be no Christ because there would be no response. With Peter or Judas alone, without the other, there would be an expression of the freedom of the response but not of its finitude. With both Peter and Judas, the infinite and finite of human freedom are brought into play. One can speak the truth about the being of the Christ either as Peter or as Judas; in both cases the speaking is free. But one cannot do so as both Peter and Judas or as someone between the two.

In that sense, Jesus' being the Christ implies the triadic relation of the three figures. Without these three members of a triadic relation, there is no true appearance of Jesus as the Christ. The three together represent the perfection of finite freedom: Peter can be Peter and does not have to be Judas; Judas can be Judas and does not have to be Peter; both of them, by being what they are on their own freely, attest to Jesus' being as the Christ. A statement about Jesus as the Christ which is abstracted from the settings of this concrete freedom could only be put in a contradictory or paradoxical fashion: in truth Jesus both is and is not the Christ. Such a statement can be formulated abstractly, but it cannot be turned into a judgment of confession concretely because, in the concrete, one is either a Peter or a Judas. But in the concrete, Peter needs a Judas and Judas needs a Peter for the perfection of freedom. Each is, as it were, the mirror that reverses the image of the other. Judas shows Peter who Peter is by showing him the image of the one he can and need never be; Peter does the same of Judas. Both of them are elements in the structure of the truth that sets free.

Christian and Non-Christian

The relation between Peter and Judas in the christological confession provides a basis for saying that Christians need for there always to be non-Christians. The "other" that Judas and Peter are for each other in the presence of Jesus is also the other that Christian and non-Christian religions are in the presence of Jesus. This is, of course, said from a point of view within the Christian religion; other religions would put it differently. The statement is meant to indicate how, from this point of view, the perfection of freedom appears in the diversity of religious traditions. The freedom of the confession that Jesus is the Christ—that this is the one and only name in which salvation is found—is perfect, or complete, in the sense that it co-exists with an opposite confession; and that the opposite confession does not annul it but establishes it. Freedom comes from recognizing that the I of which we are inwardly aware when we understand the meaning of the word *I* is present with equal absoluteness at other places besides each of ours. To recognize that it is present with equal absoluteness at other locations is to recognize that there is a dimension of absolute openness on the part of each free personal existence to another free personal existence. The universality of the I is found not by abstracting qualities from all of the individual members of the human species. It is found, rather, in that feature of self-awareness which is the radical openness to the other as other. This is different from recognizing that other persons in their own freedom are like me in my own. For what the opposition between the confessions indicates is that others may be so other than I am that they radically deny what I radically confess or radically confess what I radically deny—each of us in the freedom of our own confession.

To this extent the account of the relation of Peter and Judas to Jesus is an account that exhibits in radical form the structure of human freedom, in its infinity and its finitude. In the abstract, one would have to say that if Peter's confession is true, then the confession implicit in Judas' deed is false. Either Jesus was or he was not in truth the Son of the living God. But when we do not treat the affirmation abstractly but regard it in the context of freely elicited confession, then the essential character of Jesus as the Christ is precisely that it brings salvation by drawing with equal freedom and with equal truth both the response of Peter and the response of Judas.

But perhaps we can take another step as well, particularly with respect to the other who appears to us in the form of an adherent of another *religion*. Such an other may also serve a theological and not only a christological or existential purpose. The other from another religion serves as the one who concretely is the divine voice of judgment upon Christianity. Non-Christian religions, by their very existence as *non*-Christian, bespeak a judgment upon Christianity that is different from the judgment that Christianity might pronounce upon itself. They do so simply by virtue of the fact that it is a judgment which comes from without and not from within.

This is something different, if I see the matter rightly, from the kind of judgment of which Tillich speaks in *Christianity and the Encounter of the World Religions*.[10] Tillich too speaks of a judgment that is passed upon Christianity as it is upon all religions. But he speaks of this in the terms of the task that Christianity has to judge itself. Something has appeared within Christianity, expressed in the symbol of Jesus as the Christ; but what has appeared transcends and judges the Christian religion. Nonetheless, if this judgment is expressed in the form of the symbol of Jesus as the Christ, it is expressed in the form of a Christian religious symbol and therefore represents a self-judgment on the part of the Christian religion.

Perhaps we can go beyond this. It is not only that the Christian symbol of Jesus as the Christ is the symbol in which Christianity hears a divine judgment upon itself. It is also that the judgment upon Christianity can be expressed in a symbol that is not even Christian but a symbol of some other religion. The distinction is important. It is the distinction between saying, on the one hand, that in the symbol of Jesus as the Christ, Christianity is judging itself and saying, on the other hand, that in the symbol of Jesus as the Christ, Christianity is so radically opened to judgment upon itself that the judgment expressed upon it by another religion can be received as the judgment of God, even though it may be different from the judgment expressed upon Christianity by its own symbols. In other words, there is something in the symbol of Jesus as the Christ which exceeds even the self-judgment upon Christianity contained in it. Concretely, the other religions as religions can, therefore, do what non-religious persons cannot do. As religions, and Christian religions, they can concretely be that voice of the other who is the God of Christianity but is other than Christianity.

This would provide an additional reason for saying that Christianity needs that there be non-Christian religions. There needs to be such not only for the perfection of freedom in finitude but also for the concreteness of the divine judgment as a judgment really other than our own judgment, even our own religious judgment.

Notes

1. In 1208 Innocent III, who through great skill as well as strength of will, had used his papacy (1198–1216) to assert an unprecedented expansion of papal authority (the *plenitudo potestatis*), had those among the heretical Waldensians who wanted to return to the fold sign a statement containing his formulation that "no one can find salvation" outside "the holy, Roman, catholic, and apostolic church." The Fourth Lateran Council of 1215 adopted a similar formulation: "The universal church of the believers is one; outside it no one is saved." Boniface VIII's bull *Unam sanctam* (1302) arose during his controversy with Philip of France; it asserts that there is neither salvation nor forgiveness outside the church of Jesus Christ. On the history of the doctrine *extra ecclesiam nulla salus,* see the work of Fries cited in note 2 below, 245–251.

   That essay also contains bibliographical references. The ecumenical endeavors of Frederick II, "the first modern man on a throne" (as Jakob Burkhardt called him), hardly met with welcome on all sides. A body of scurrilous literature grew up, as he was accused, among other things, of trying to institute a better kind of faith than the three which resulted from the deception of Moses, Jesus, and Mohammed. For this side of the story, see Klaus J. Heinisch, ed., *Kaiser Friedrich II. in Briefen und Berichten seiner Zeit* (Darmstadt: Wissenschaftliche Buchgesellschaft, 1968), 207ff.
2. Some sources used both for this historical sketch and for representative contemporary evaluations of Christianity in relation to other religions: Heinrich Fries "Das Heil in Christus," in Heinrich Fries, *et al.* "Kirche und Religionen—Begegnung und Dialog," vol. 2: *Heil in den Religionen* (Sankt Ottilien: EOS Verlag, 1982), 212–270; John Knox, *The Humanity and Divinity of Christ* (London, New York: Cambridge University Press, 1967); Gerard S. Sloyan, *Jesus in Focus: A Life in its Setting* (Mystic, Conn.: Twenty-Third Publications, 1983); Paul Tillich, *Christianity and the Encounter of the World Religions* (New York: Columbia University Press, 1963).
3. This is something that Schleiermacher expressly formulated in his dogmatics, *The Christian Faith*. He set forth the position that the heretical within a religion is analogous to a diseased element within an organism. The danger of the heretical lies in the fact that in appearance the heretical is difficult to distinguish from the nonheretical; it gives every appearance of being a sign of health, not the sign of an attack on the living organism. Hence, the anathema that is pronounced upon the heretical is as important as is the diagnosis of a diseased element in a living organism. But the rejection of a disease in an organism does not define the relation of one organism to another organism.

   Similarly, the rejection of heresy within Christianity is not definitive of the relation of Christianity to the non-Christian. Thus, there is no possibility, for example,that the doctrine of Islam could ever be considered "heretical" to Christianity. Even if it is the case that an affirmation rejected within Christianity as heretical is identical in meaning to an affirmation appearing in another religion (one could think of the Qur'an's denial of divinity to Christ), the rejection is not transferable from Christianity to the other religion.
4. The position more recently taken by Carl Braaten—to the effect that, whereas many religions offer salvation, the salvation connected with the name of Jesus is different in being a salvation from the power of death—seems to me to be "idealist" in this

same sense. See Carl Braaten, "The Uniqueness and Universality of Jesus Christ," in *Christian Dogmatics*, ed. Carl E. Braaten and Robert W. Jenson (Philadelphia: Fortress Press, 1984), 565ff. The position is taken in a more open, dialogical, and hypothetical way than one normally associates with idealist typologies. But one wonders whether the result is not foreclosed by the following: "If we really believe that the uniqueness of Jesus lies in his universality, that his identity is always being mediated through the concrete events of history, then we should be open to exploring what the non-Christian religions can contribute to our understanding of the universal identity of Jesus Christ....Every culture has to ask of Jesus in its own way, 'Are you the One who is to come...?' Every people will have to answer, 'Who do you say that I am?'..." (567).

5. Karl Barth, *Kirchliche Dogmatik* I/1 (Zöllikon-Zürich: Evangelischer Verlag, 1960, 5th impr.), 372–377. One could add that the points on which this form of Buddhism seems to fall short of Protestantism by being too easy a way of salvation might in fact make it even more a religion of pure grace. A recent exploration of Barth on this question is that of Charles T. Waldrop, "Karl Barth and Pure Land Buddhism," *Journal of Ecumenical Studies* 24, 4 (1987): 574–597. Waldrop's emphasis seems to me to be slightly wrong, when he asserts that Barth was mainly concerned to show that Christianity was the true religion; for Barth's main concern seems to me to have been to show that the truth in religion did not lie in its form of religion at all, but in the revelation of God contained in it. Apart from that reservation, it seems to me that Waldrop's article corrects some of the prevailing misunderstandings of Barth's position concerning other religions.
6. This argument was developed in his book *The Absoluteness of Christianity* (1901). Later, in the 1920s, Troeltsch proposed that the concept of "individuality" could best explain the relation among the world religions: it is not the task of Christianity to try to convert adherents of other religions (although in particular cases there may be such conversions, either to or from Christianity) or to understand other religions as being on the way toward Christianity as the absolute religion; rather, it is the task of the religions to assist one another in achieving the stage of their own maturity. Cf. Ernst Troeltsch's *Die Absolutheit des Christentums und die Religionsgeschichte* (Tübingen and Leipzig: Verlag J.C.B. Mohr, 1902) and his later *Christian Thought: Its History and Application*, ed. Baron von Hügel (New York: Meridian Books, Living Age Books, 1957).
7. See Karl Barth, *Kirchliche Dogmatik* II/2, 559.
8. Even in the New Testament, there are, of course, suggestions of occasions on which a kind of inference is involved. For example, in John 9—that remarkably long account of the healing of a blind man—there seems to be an inference involved in the man's saying that Jesus could not be "a sinner" because no such person could have cured a man born blind. But even if this were taken as a serious argument, it is not the basis of the blind man's response to what had happened to him in the meeting with Jesus.
9. Acts 1:16; similarly, Jesus in John 13:21ff., although in this latter case it is not a matter of what "must" be but of what "will" be so.
10. Paul Tillich, *Christianity and the Encounter of the World Religions*, 77.

4

UPDATING (*AGGIORNAMENTO*) WITHIN AND WITHOUT

Geoffrey Parrinder

THE MEETING OF Christians and non-Christians today, greater than at many times in the past, and increased by the ease of modern communications, has occurred at the same time as other radical changes.

1. The *aggiornamento*, of which Pope John XXIII spoke in the Second Vatican Council, applies to many areas of Christian thought and practice. Especially important for our present concern are some of the effects of modern critical study of the Bible and early church history, upon views of the mission of the church and its relations with other religions. The exclusive, or condemnatory, attitudes held by many Christians in the past towards members of other faiths, need reappraisal in the light not only of better knowledge of those religions but also in view of critical interpretations of Scripture and tradition. By 'critical' is meant, of course, not the destructive but the scientific study of the texts and the uses to which they may be put.

Two simple illustrations may be given. Until this century in some churches it was prescribed (and is now optional) that the Athanasian Creed or *Quicumque Vult* should be recited in public worship at great church festivals: Christmas, Easter, Whitsun, etc. This creed stated baldly that "except every one do keep whole and undefiled" the Catholic Faith, "without doubt he shall perish everlastingly." This declaration damned the great majority of the human race, not only unfaithful Christians but members of all other religions, since Christians are in a minority in the world and always have been. But in recent times, at least, the value and authority of this creed have been questioned: Did it come from Athanasius? What other authority has it? Should it be used in liturgy? Is it consistent with a Gospel of love?[1]

It might be claimed that such a dogmatic statement is based on the Bible. For example, Mark 16:16: "He that believeth not shall be damned." This quotation is taken from the Authorized or King James's Version, but although its style is splendid this translation is uncritical, sometimes using dubious sources, and to accept its authority without reserve may land one in strange company. For most of us know and accept that this verse comes from one of the false endings of Mark, which is not found in the most ancient manuscripts and early commentaries, and it is regarded as a later addition by Protestant and Roman Catholic scholars alike.

The critical study of the Bible, then, may be taken as necessary in the exposition of the Christian faith today, and this has a clear bearing on attitudes towards other religions.

2. Christianity is unique among religions in adopting, treasuring, and using, the scriptures of its parent religion and including them within its canon of Holy Writ. Buddhism grew out of Hinduism, but rejected the Hindu Vedas and other sacred texts and compiled its own scriptures. Muslims believe that Jesus and Moses brought the Word of God, but this was corrupted by their followers, so that wherever Jewish and Christian Scriptures differ from the Qur'an it is the latter that Muslims hold to be always correct.

In Christian usage the Hebrew canon of Scripture has been accepted as an Old Testament, a designation to which strict Jews object, though some liberals use it because it is current and understandable. For Christians, on the one hand there is the statement that "one jot or one tittle shall in no wise pass from the law, till all be fulfilled" (Matt. 5:18). But on the other hand the same evangelist records sayings that indicate a fulfillment already come: "You have heard that it has been said, An eye for an eye, and a tooth for a tooth. But I say unto you...." (Matt. 5:38).[2] The tradition was that God had spoken those words to Moses; but there is a new, or greater, or revised divine authority.

It has been a general Christian principle that the Old Testament is fulfilled in the New, that with the coming of the Christ there is a new order, in which the old Law is not abolished but it is to be interpreted according to the law of love. It must be said, however, that Christians have not always accepted this principle, and even today there are strong voices which assert for the whole Bible a literal interpretation and an inerrancy that defeat the understanding of the Bible as a development, a record of the growth in human understanding of life and of the divine.

It is too easily declared that "the Bible says," without considering that the Bible is a complex collection of documents from many hands and different dates. If there is divine inspiration it is of *humans*, limited and fallible, not of an unalterable text. For example, in recent debates on homosexuality in various churches there has been the cry, "the Bible says." This usually referred to Lev. 20:13 which decreed that "if a man lie with mankind...they shall surely be put to death." Debaters who quote this verse as divine condemnation of homosexuality do not normally continue to the second clause and demand the death penalty, though it is hard to see why not, on a literal acceptance of these verses as the word of God. On the other hand, it must be said that it is not known whether or how often the death penalty was applied. That this issue was later debated in rabbinic circles for similar cases is evident from John 8:5: "Moses in the law commanded us, that such should be stoned: but what sayest thou?"

Those who demand a literal interpretation and application of the whole Bible often turn to 2 Tim. 3:16: "All scripture is given by inspiration of God." Professor James Barr has remarked recently that "this famous text, the most overworked in the entire Bible in fundamentalist religion, says none of the things that fundamentalists think it says."[3] The verse says nothing about the historical accuracy of the Bible, or which Scripture is central to faith, or which are the inspired books of the Old or New Testaments. In fact, when this epistle was written, whether by Paul or another, most of the New Testament was probably not yet written down, no canon of Old or New Testaments had yet been fixed, and therefore it cannot refer to the Bible as we know it, but only in a general sense to the Law and some of the Prophets. The rabbis were still debating the value of Ecclesiastes and the Song of Songs, and it would be long before the church accepted the validity of Jude or Revelation.

3. Not only may developments in the Bible be traced, say from Joshua to Hosea, or from Jephthan to Isaiah, but critical study has made us aware of different hands or schools and dates in the composition of the Old Testament (in the New Testament also, as will be stated shortly). There are different authors traceable in the early books of the Bible, and this is widely accepted, though not by fundamentalists or by strictly Orthodox

Jews. That Moses wrote the Torah or Pentateuch is still almost an article of faith in these quarters. How Moses could have written of his own death (Deut. 34:5–7) is an old objection, though no less valid for all that.

Liberal Jews generally accept the non-Mosaic authorship of some of the Pentateuch. For example, a recent Jewish book says: "Tradition would have it that Moses wrote all of the laws in the Pentateuch. Clearly this is not so, the ceremony of the first fruits, for example (Deut. 26:1–10), or the proclamation of the Jubilee, are backward projections, from a later time when the land had long been settled."[4]

Yet the same writers declare that "there can be little argument that the religion which Moses impressed upon his people was monotheism. Furthermore, it was ethical monotheism." But there has been much argument on these matters among Christian scholars, and some would not see true monotheism emerging before the time of Isaiah or even later. Did Moses exist? Was he literate? What was his faith? But in discussions with Jews we must be careful not to tread on corns.

The example of the non-Mosaic authorship of some of the Pentateuch must suffice at present, since we want to go beyond this to the relation of the Bible as a whole to Christian faith and especially to its mission and attitudes to other religions. But some of the prophets, in particular, have important views on the relation of their God to other nations.

At one time Isaiah envisaged all nations coming to worship the Lord of Jerusalem (Isa. 2:3), but later apparently the same prophet saw other peoples as children of God along with the Israelites: "Blessed be Egypt my people, and Assyria the work of my hands, and Israel mine inheritance" (Isa. 19:25). Later still, Malachi said that God was worshipped better among other nations than in Israel: "From the rising of the sun even unto the going down of the same my name is great among the Gentiles; and in every place incense is offered unto my name" (Malachi 1:11). There is room here for the development of a theology of inter-religious understanding, and a recognition of the divine presence in different religions, rituals, and Scriptures.

4. The critical study of the New Testament is liable to raise more acute objections, and yet it has brought light and understanding to many problems. The status and relationships of the four Gospels are of central importance, and that they were accepted as canonical at least by the end of the second century is a tribute to their worth.

The first three, Synoptic, Gospels contain material from various sources. It is commonly agreed that Mark is primary, and nearly all of his material is found again in Matthew and Luke. These last two Gospels also share another important collection of sayings of Jesus (called Q, *Quelle*, source), and further Matthew and Luke have other material from oral or written sources. These give the 'synoptic' or overall picture of the principal events and sayings in the life of Jesus.

When we come to the Fourth Gospel, John, however, there are serious problems and some of these relate to other religions or teachers. The differences, in style and content, between the recorded sayings of Jesus in the Synoptics, and the long discourses in John are noteworthy. Some of the narratives of John seem straightforward, even where they differ from the Synoptic parallels, though statements about the Baptist may reflect later controversies. But the long discourses may appear to be reflections and developments by the evangelist himself.

The foregoing is a brief summary of the consensus of biblical scholars, but its application to our particular subject can now be illustrated. In John 14:6 are the words: "I am the Way, the Truth, and the Life: no man cometh unto the Father, but by me." Every speaker on relations with other religions knows that this verse is quoted endlessly against suggestions that there may be ways to God, or people of devout life, in other religions than Christianity. There is no other way, it is held, and even that "all that ever came before me are thieves and robbers" (John 10:8). Should this exclusiveness rule out Moses and the prophets, not to mention Buddha and Krishna?

On the face of it this verse suggests a very restricted, if not arrogant, claim by the Christ. But are these words the *ipsissima verba* of Jesus, recorded (how?) at the Last Supper? Or are they reflections of the writer and other Christians several decades later? Viewed as the faith of the evangelist, this confession may be more comprehensible.

First, the abstract nouns, Way, Truth, Life, are similar to other titles used in this Gospel. Scholars have noted that in the Synoptics Jesus is shown as using homely illustrations, with detail taken from daily life: sowing the seed, wandering sheep, a Prodigal Son, a Good Samaritan. These depict the kingdom of God, or the love of God and humanity, in simple but profound fashion. In the Fourth Gospel there are generalities: Living Bread, True Vine, the Door, the Good Shepherd, the Way, etc. These may be taken as the attributes of the risen Christ as seen by the evangelist, and they are understandable in the light of faith. Similar exclusive claims are found in other religions, stressing the supremacy of their Way and their Lord.

Some interpreters have suggested that John 14:6 refers specifically to coming to God as Father. But God is often called Father in the Old Testament, and also in Hinduism, though not in Islam. The Psalmists, Isaiah and Malachi all call God Father, and it would hardly be claimed that they did not come to him in this relationship.

But if John 14:6 is taken to indicate the universal Logos, "the light that lighteth every man" which had been mentioned in John 1:9, then a wider viewpoint is obtained. Such a verse, and others like it, may be seen in the context of the Gospel as a whole, not in isolation, and the apparent exclusiveness may be tempered by inclusiveness found elsewhere.

The late Archbishop William Temple commented on John 1:9 as follows: "By the word of God—that is to say by Jesus Christ—Isaiah and Plato, Zoroaster, Buddha, and Confucius, uttered and wrote such truths as they declared. There is only one Divine Light, and every man in his own measure is enlightened by it."[5]

Isaiah was not a Christian, in a narrow sense, but he has always been regarded by Christians as a forerunner of Christ and the book that bears his name is treasured in the Christian as well as in the Jewish Bible. Plato used to be called a 'pagan' (a derogatory word), but he is the father of western philosophy and he has long been baptized, so to speak, into Christianity. Zoroaster was a prophet, though outside the Semitic tradition, but he was a monotheist and some of his ideas influenced both inter-testamental Judaism and early Christianity. The Buddha and Confucius were very different, and some of their teachings are strange to the Semitic world view; but they have been among the most influential teachers of Asia, and they are now widely studied in the West. Both of them believed profoundly in a spiritual world, and their truths must come from God, said Temple, if all truth comes from the one Divine Light.

Briefly, our interpretations of John should be inclusive, not exclusive, one verse tempered by another.

5. The Synoptic Gospels, however, are also documents of faith, written from various standpoints of the evangelists and their sources and the circles in which they moved. No doubt they are earlier than John, and they purport to record "all that Jesus began both to do and to teach," even if they are not detailed biographies in the modern fashion. Sometimes they seem clearly to express the faith of the later church, rather than that of the historical Jesus, as in the Trinitarian formula at the end of Matt. 28:19.

When we consider the picture of Jesus and his teaching obtainable from the Synoptics, various matters appear. Jesus was a Jew. His mission was restricted to the Jewish people. He preached the kingdom of God, yet the church emerged, chiefly among Gentiles. These things are important, in the light of relations with Jews today, and with Muslims and members of other religions.

It is now widely held that the religion of Jesus was that of a faithful Jew, though of Galilee rather than Judea. Much of his teaching was akin to that of the Pharisees, with whom he had much in common; but the later church, in conflict with some Pharisee leaders, tended to exaggerate the differences between them and Jesus. The death of Jesus was the decision of the Roman ruler ("he suffered under Pontius Pilate"), in league with Sadducee priests, their stooges. The old accusation that 'the Jews' killed Christ, all of them at that time, and perhaps with guilt upon all of them down through history in the crime of 'deicide,' was a gross and wicked libel which led to vicious persecutions of Jews down through the ages and gave a background to the terrible Holocaust of our own time. Yet it must be admitted that seeds of such anti-Semitism may be traced to some of the Gospels: "the Jews sought the more to kill him" (John 5:16 and 18); "then answered all the people, and said, 'His blood be on us, and on our children'" (Matt. 27:25).

Jesus was a Jew, and he only preached to Jews. He ate with Jewish "publicans and sinners"; but he never, as far as we know, sat at table with a Gentile. He sought "the lost sheep of the house of Israel," ate with Zaccheus as "a son of Abraham," and told the Syro-Phoenician woman that "the children must first be filled" (Mark 7:27). If he healed the centurion's servant, he did not go into his house (Matt. 8:8). It is remarkable that these incidents were recorded in Greek Gospels intended mainly for Gentile churches.

On the other hand, the narrowness or exclusiveness of Judaism should not be exaggerated, and Galilee was probably more open to outside influences than Judea. Reference has been made to the universalist spirit of some of the prophets who recognized the worship of God among the Gentiles. And then there was Zoroaster and the great Persian influence on later Jewish thought. Matthew tells of Wise Men following a star to Bethlehem, like the Gentile kings that are foreseen in Isa. 60:6 bringing gold and incense. These "wise men" are called Magi, a title of Zoroastrian priests in Persia, and whatever may be thought of the nativity story it is known that Zoroastrian beliefs had spread far and wide and influenced popular Judaism. The difference between Pharisees and Sadducees, that "the Sadducees say that there is no resurrection, neither angel, nor spirit: but the Pharisees confess both" (Acts 23:8), suggests the effect of such Zoroastrian beliefs. There is no doubt, from the Gospel evidence, that Jesus shared such ideas.

Professor Mary Boyce, a leading authority on Zoroastrianism, has recently emphasized that in the Middle East at that time educated men, including Jews and Persians, "both spoke and wrote in Greek." Therefore "Zoroastrian doctrines were familiar then, through written works, to learned Jews."[6]

6. Jesus preached the kingdom, what followed was the church. Such a statement may have a superficial appeal, but it is important to try to discover how and why the church came into existence, and to flourish chiefly among Gentiles. Was the resultant church a natural development

of the teaching and work of Jesus? If not, why they did the evangelists seek to record his *life*, faithfully and at length?

It is a further remarkable feature of the Christian Scriptures that, not only do they include the Hebrew texts of the Jews, but they do not, apart from a few phrases, include the Aramaic words that Jesus spoke. All the New Testament is in Greek, though probably all its writers were Jews, apart from Luke-Acts. The evangelists were not philosophers, or merchants, but ordinary Jews, yet no doubt they were selected by their communities for their fluency in writing Greek. Each of them has an energy of his own, through which faith shines, as anyone knows who has heard Alec McCowan recite the whole of St. Mark's Gospel by heart.

The Jewish scholar Geza Vermes is critical of those Christian writers who claim that we can know nothing of the life of Jesus, that the Scriptures are utterances of Christian prophets at liturgical gatherings. On the contrary, says Dr. Vermes, "if the evangelists were primarily preoccupied with teaching Christian doctrine, how are we to explain their choice of *biography* as their medium? They cannot have been influenced by tradition; no Jewish convention exists that the sayings of the sages should be transmitted in this way. Anecdotes conveying them abound in rabbinic literature, but nothing by way of similar biography has been handed down and there is no reason to imagine that one ever existed."[7]

The strong link between Jesus and the Gentile churches is shown by the Greek Gospels, and they are free from some of the major Pauline themes. All down the ages the Gospels have held the church to the life of Jesus, and in significant ways the history has been more central than in some other religions.

7. It is Paul who is often regarded as the man who made the break from Judaism. And if there have been sympathetic studies of Jesus by Jews in modern times, it is hard to find one of Paul, and some Gentile writers have also been very critical of Paul. Paul has been called variously "the Apostle of the Gentiles," or "the First Christian," or "the Second Founder of Christianity," or "the Myth-Maker."

Two recent studies may be mentioned. The ex-nun Karen Armstrong in *The First Christian*[8] says that she has long admired Paul but she accuses him of morbidity, masochism, and intolerance. Yet her casual errors do not inspire confidence in her scholarship. She writes of Jesus as "a Jew of Judea," and says that Mary Magdalene was a prostitute who "probably also slept with the Roman soldiers." But there is no evidence at all in the Gospels that this Mary had an immoral life, and the legend comes from later speculation.

More devastating and detailed is Hyam Maccoby's *The Myth-Maker, Paul and the Invention of Christianity*.[9] This Jewish scholar proceeds, by a series of rhetorical questions, to declare that "Saul was not a Pharisee, and not even a Jew by birth. His parents were Gentiles, and Saul was a convert." That Paul asserted explicitly that he was a Pharisee and of the tribe of Benjamin, is regarded as protesting too much. That Luke also affirmed that Paul was a Pharisee, twice in Acts, is ignored.

There are many questions, which cannot be discussed in this short space. Clearly Paul was not "the first Christian," for even Maccoby declares (on what evidence?) that James, the brother of Jesus, became leader of the church in Jerusalem "immediately" after the Crucifixion.[10] But doubtless Paul became the Apostle of the Gentiles, and a crucial difference from James and other Jews was over commensalism.

Jesus had eaten with "publicans and sinners," to the scandal of the virtuous. It was only logical that this commensalism should be extended to Gentile converts, and this is what Paul did. Galatians 2 gives the setting. Paul ate with Gentile Christians at Antioch, and when Peter arrived from Jerusalem he joined in at first. But when some Judaizing Christians came down from James to see what was going on, Peter withdrew from the common table, so that Paul "withstood him to the face."

Maccoby asserts that the rabbis acted similarly to Jesus; but he does not show anywhere that they ate with publicans and sinners, and never that they shared tables with Gentiles. Jews had their special dietary laws, and if they respected those of others they were not allowed to eat with foreigners, though apparently Abraham had done so with Melchizedek.[11] This was an issue on which the new religion passed from being a national faith, or a reform sect within Judaism, to becoming a world community. Here there would be "neither Jew nor Greek, neither slave nor free, neither male nor female."[12]

With all Paul's faults, and they need not be denied, such as some loose statements about the Law, some views on women and marriage, his opposition of flesh and spirit, yet Paul had the genius to see that the Gospel of Christ had a universal application. There are still Christians, and not only in South Africa, who will not eat with Christians of different color; the church's attitude to slavery was long one of tolerance; persecutions of heretics and Jews were a disgrace; and Paul himself gave women an inferior place. But the principles of universalism had been enunciated, and there is a real continuity between the openness of the Galilean Gospel and that of the Pauline epistles.

8. It is sometimes said that Christians are Jews who believe that the Messiah has come, and although there is more to Christianity than that, Christians started from here. It began with Peter's confession, "Thou art the Christ" (Mark 8:29); and Jewish Christians, in Jerusalem and elsewhere, held to this basic faith along with Gentile converts. Even the

Ebionites ("poor men," some Jewish Christians), of whom Maccoby makes much, held that Jesus was "the Son of God from the Christ that came into him." They seem to have rejected belief in the Virgin Birth, but Paul also does not mention it despite his highly developed Christology.

Once Jesus was accepted as the Christ, crucified yet risen and reigning in glory, the way was open for both faith and liturgy to express the centrality of Christ. Prayers through Christ, and invocations of him (Acts 7:59) led, perhaps inevitably, to the doctrine of the Trinity.

That there were differences of interpretation was, again perhaps, inevitable. Jewish Christians might take the title Son of God to refer to the King or Messiah, as it was used in the royal Psalms, while to Gentiles it might suggest one of the pantheon of Greek or Roman deities. The early centuries witnessed acrimonious wrangling, out of which the creeds emerged and were imposed. After its separation from Judaism, and the disappearance of the Jewish Christians, the church developed Greek and Latin terminology, though the Bible remained with its Hebrew thought. With the coming of Islam in the seventh century, there was a closing of the ranks.

In modern times there has been an opening up, and efforts have been made to interpret the faith to people of other religions in language which is mutually comprehensible. There are dangers, however, of further closing of ranks, with fundamentalist Christians opposing fundamentalist Muslims. Each is convinced of its absolute rightness, which implies the other's absolute wrongness; and there is a willingness to use any means, force, or economic pressures, to impose the particular faith. There is blind trust in an infallible book, a rejection of any critical study, and 'liberal' becomes a dirty word.

9. To suggest a more excellent way, in charity and mutual understanding, I close with an example of Christian doctrinal statement and exposition, addressed to members of another religion.

Bishop Kenneth Cragg has devoted most of his life to understanding Islam and expounding Christianity to Muslims. Two of his recent books on Jesus and Muhammad are models of the "wider ecumenism."[13] But I refer to an earlier work, *The Call of the Minaret*, with its "call to interpretation."[14] Here Dr. Cragg expounds orthodox Christian doctrine, in a careful manner which avoids or denies past exaggerations and which outlines the faith in a way that a Muslim may understand. Indeed, a Muslim imam told me that if Bishop Cragg's exposition of the Trinity was true then there was little in it to which a thoughtful Muslim could take exception.

Kenneth Cragg wrote primarily for Muslims, but what he said could apply equally to Jews. We all start, and "cannot proceed except on the understanding that we are both firmly and equally believers that God is One." This is because "we both stand squarely in the Hebrew tradition: 'The Lord our Lord is ONE Lord.'"[15] Christians are not tritheists, and must not give the impression that they are; they are monotheists as firmly as are Jews and Muslims.

The Christian doctrine of the Trinity is distinctive, but it is Trinity in Unity, God the Father, Son and Holy Spirit. "It does not consist, as there has been a tendency among Muslims to suppose, of God, Jesus, and the Virgin Mary."[16]

Muslims have objected to the notion that God has a son, in the manner of pagan chiefs and deities who begat many sons and daughters. This is far too human or anthropomorphic an idea of the eternal and transcendent God. So Cragg insists that "the terms 'Father' and 'Son' have no physical significance and are used analogically." Christian teachers said that Christ was "begotten, not made." He was not a creature. But "begotten" also must not be understood in a physical sense. It is evidence of the divine care for his mankind, which "begets" or "generates the activity of redeeming love in the historic Christ."

Other Christian terms and phrases also should be used carefully. "That 'God was in Christ' rather than that 'Jesus was God' is the classic exposition of this truth." Not that "God became man," but that the Son of God or the Word "became flesh," is the Biblical phraseology. So "the phrase 'God the Son' means God in self-revelation in the Person of Jesus."[17]

The doctrine of the Trinity, Bishop Cragg continues, is necessary in order to gain some conception of the divine nature and activity: "A bare unity, philosophically understood, is a barren one....Entire transcendence is in the end a blank agnosticism."[18]

There are some analogies with other religions, which can only be hinted at here. In Islam the Qur'an is the speech of God, and it has been spoken of as "the Word made Book." Further, the Prophet Muhammad, the mention of whose name is always followed in Muslim circles by the reverent ascription "peace and blessings of God be upon him," is given countless titles of adoration in devotion.[19] And for orthodox Judaism the Torah is regarded as almost divine, and Moses is the greatest of all prophets.

10. "Time would fail me" to explore these matters farther. The direct encounter with men and women of different religions, the "wider ecumenism," needs to be undertaken with all the help of scholarship and experience that is available. It is my contention that modern critical studies of the Bible and of tradition are essential tools for the understanding of Christianity and its interpretation to the world. There needs to be updating within, so that there can be updating without. A searching

examination of our own sources will help make clear whether and what kind of a mission the church has for different areas of the modern world.

The Christian message is not served by setting out a series of propositions, of questionable validity and outdated expression, or by imposing a collection of proof texts from a supposedly infallible Bible. In the past our fathers, and mothers, were ignorant of neighboring religions, even of the Jews in our midst, and persecution arose from misrepresentation. Today, as never before, there is the possibility of mutual understanding, unless the forces of blind dogmatism, Christian, Islamic or Marxist, close us again within narrow limits, with all the dangers of explosion inherent in such limitations.

Notes

1. See Hans Küng: "The other religions were regarded formerly as lies, works of the devil and—at best—vestigial truth;.... Now they are recognized as ways of salvation." *On Being a Christian*, English translation, paperback edition (Glasgow: Collins, 1978), 91.
2. Exod. 21:24; Lev. 24:19; Deut. 19:21.
3. James Barr, "Fundamentalism and Biblical Authority," in *Heaven and Earth*, ed. A. Linzey and P.J. Wexler (Worthing, Sussex: Churchman Publishers, 1986), 29.
4. D.J. Goldberg and J.D. Rayner, *The Jewish People*, (Harmondsworth: Viking, Penguin Books, 1987), 16, 197.
5. W. Temple, *Readings in St. John's Gospel* (MacMillan, 1945), vol. 1, 10.
6. Mary Boyce, *Zoroastrianism: A Shadowy but Powerful Presence in the Judaeo-Christian World* (London: Dr. William's Trust, 1987), 11.
7. Geza Vermes, *The Gospel of Jesus the Jew* (University of Newcastle, England, 1981), 4.
8. Karen Armstrong, *The First Christian* (London: Pan Books, 1983), 16, 34.
9. Hyam Maccoby, *The Myth-Maker. Paul and the Invention of Christianity* (London: Weidenfeld and Nicolson, 1986), 59ff.
10. *Ibid.*, 5.
11. Genesis 14:18.
12. Galatians 3:28.
13. Kenneth Cragg, *Muhammad and the Christian* (London: Darton, Longman and Todd, 1984); *Jesus and the Muslim* (London: Darton, Longman and Todd, 1986).
14. Kenneth Cragg, *The Call of the Minaret* (New York: Oxford University Press, 1956), 271ff.
15. *Ibid.*, 308.
16. *Ibid.*, 316.
17. *Ibid.*, 315.
18. *Ibid.*, 317.
19. See C. Padwick, *Muslim Devotions* (London: S.P.C.K., 1961), 137ff, 152ff.

5

CHRISTIANITY AS A WORLD MINORITY

Joseph H. Fichter

WE ARE MEETING for this conference in an area that is now dominated by the faith of Islam. Asia Minor was first Christianized by the early disciples of Jesus, and their successors established large dioceses and flourishing churches. Ancient Byzantium became Christian Constantinople which in turn became Islamic Istanbul. The previous church steeples in every town and village have been replaced by mosques and minarets. There is now hardly a Christian to be seen in the country that hosted the councils of Nicea and Ephesus. Christianity has become a minority religion among the people who have turned to Allah.

About fifteen years ago I discussed this same topic under the same title in my book *Organization Man in the Church*. I said that "the relative disappearance of Christianity from the Holy Land and the Middle East generally may be attributed to many factors—military invasions, political turmoil, large migrations of people, as well as religious conversions. There are other parts of the world where Christianity never penetrated, or where it barely set down its roots and then failed to grow."[1] There are now well over one billion Christians in the world, but this still leaves about two-thirds of the world's population who are non-Christians.

It seems most appropriate then that the Council for the World's Religions should select Istanbul as the site for a Christian discussion of the "wider ecumenism," that reaches beyond the boundaries of Christianity. Hans Küng has suggested that we ought to have a greater openness toward all non-Christians. After endless conferences of intra-Protestant ecumenism and intra-Christian ecumenism "we have irrevocably reached the third ecumenical dimension, ecumenism of the world religions."[2] The Second Vatican Council called itself a "sacred ecumenical synod" because one of its chief concerns was the *Unitatis Redintegratio* among all Christians. It also produced a separate Declaration, *Nostra Aetate*, which discussed the Relationship of the Church to Non-Christian Religions.

In an effort to foster unity and love, the Council focused on Buddhists, Hindus, Jews, and Muslims, and recognized "what human beings have in common and what promotes fellowship among them." It is therefore the official teaching of my Church that "all peoples comprise a single community, and have a single origin, since God made the whole race of men dwell over the entire face of the earth. One also is their final goal: God. His providence, His manifestations of goodness, and His saving designs extend to all men against the day when the elect will be united in that Holy City, ablaze with the splendor of God, where the nations will walk in His light."[3]

Most of the mainline Christian churches, and an increasing number of world religions, are now discussing inter-faith relations. I have had the good fortune of participating in another kind of ecumenical council, the Assembly of the World's Religions, at which its founder, Sun Myung Moon, said "we urgently need to purify the religious atmosphere into one in which believers can have living faith, and every soul can communicate with God. In God's paternal heart and His great love, there is no discrimination based on color or nationality. There are no barriers between countries or cultural traditions, between East and West, North and South. Today, God is trying to embrace the whole of humankind as His children. Through interreligious dialogue and harmony we should realize one ideal world of peace, which is God's purpose of creation and the common ideal of humankind."[4]

Religious Minorities

It is not my intention to speak of the decline and downfall of the Christian religion. The world of religion is changing rapidly, but we must try to maintain a balanced perspective. The "scientific" predictions of Marxists and atheists about the disappearance of religion have been proven false. Christianity is moving unevenly—slowly in its formal hierarchic structures, but flourishing in its Pentecostal and fundamentalist manifestations. There appears also to be a revitalization of Islam after the revolution in Iran.

The social scientist who talks about minorities is usually not talking about numbers, or quantity, but about a social category of people of low status and prestige. In this sense Catholicism was a social minority in New England a century ago, as well as now in North Ireland and other heavily Protestant regions. Differential social status is relative to the power and prestige of other social collectivities in the population.[5] Episcopalians are a numerical American minority but are generally people of high social status and prestige. The social status of Baptists may be high in rural Georgia and low in urban Massachusetts.

In what sense then can we currently speak of Christianity as a minority religion? According to available statistics, there are well over 1.5 billion Christians in the entire world, experiencing low status in places like China and Russia. Muslims are said to number about 840 million (although the Islamic Center in Washington claims there are more than one billion). Hindus number approximately 650 million, and Buddhists 607 million. It is an interesting fact that Judaism, a vigorous world religion, counts almost 18 million, and is outnumbered by 32 million Shintos, and 20 million Taoists.

It must be understood that the social status of a religion does not emerge from its inherent qualities, or from the validity of its beliefs and practices. Religion must be seen as one of several major institutions in the culture. The true believer, whether Muslim or Christian or Jew, would like to think that multitudes are won over because their religion is the revealed truth of God. The historical fact is that European Christianity spread all over the world in company with the military and commercial might of the colonial nations. The European explorers and conquerors everywhere ascribed minority status to the native peoples and their religion. The status of a religion rises or falls with the status of its adherents.

One may then hypothesize that the status of Christianity declines with the declining status of the Western nations, while simultaneously the non-Christian nations of the world are growing in prestige. The religious superiority of Christianity was closely allied with the secular superiority of Western civilization. The end of the colonial era in India, Africa and Asia has accompanied the decline of Western missionary activities. The significance of both the culture and the religion of the West has been lowered at the same time that a resurgence of native religion has brought competition to Christian missionaries who are no longer welcomed. The importance of Christianity has declined with the decreasing power and influence of the Christian nations.

In their discussion of "Christian Presence," Warren and Taylor say that "for more than four centuries the expansion of the Christian Church has coincided with the economic, political, and cultural expansion of Western Europe. Viewed from the standpoint of the people of Asia, and to a growing extent from that of the peoples of Africa, this expansion has been an aggressive attack on their own way of life. Quite inevitably the Christian faith has for many in these lands been inextricably bound up with the Western aggression. But it has also to be admitted quite frankly that during these centuries the missionaries of the Christian Church have commonly assumed that Western civilization and Christianity were two aspects of the same gift which they were commissioned to offer to the rest of mankind."[6]

Secular Ecumenism

Western civilization has offered gifts other than Christianity to the rest of the world, sensate gifts that have become universally desirable. Owen Thomas remarks that "Modern science and technology have created for the first time in recorded history a pattern of civilization which is effectively universal, a unitary global society based on industrial production and rapid communication."[7] This is a way of saying that the main factor of global unity need not be Christianity, or any other so-called "world" religion at all. What the rest of the world wants from the West may have nothing to do with religion.

The common assumption among social scientists is that unity, or solidarity, needs the continuing support of a core of shared values. It is Durkheim's thesis that the common adherence to a religious value system is the main factor of social solidarity. In some historical instances it appears that nationalism, as in Nazi Germany and Fascist Italy, served the purpose of reflecting social solidarity. This is precisely the thrust of world communism that promotes universal brotherhood without a religious system of behavior and belief. All the needs of humanity can now be provided through the application of Western technology under the direction of the Party. It is probably true to say that "in terms of belief, ritual and organization, communism is the major religion of the Soviet Union and China."[8]

What we are suggesting here is that secular alternatives are being developed—have probably always existed—that would replace Christianity, or any other world religion. From a functional perspective, one may say that non-theistic belief systems often provide the solidaristic motivation to displace religion. "A contemporary American may develop such a faith in the power of science, may make it so much an object of devotion, that it can fairly be said that science is his religion."[9]

Secular humanism, or some other non-theistic belief system, is probably growing faster than any strictly religious system in the Western world. Tillich, in his study of comparative religions, said that "the main characteristic of the present encounter of the world religions is their encounter with the quasi-religions of our times."[10] These modes of thought are based on secularism as portrayed in liberal humanism, scientism, nationalism, where the all-embracing "ultimate concern" focuses on a non-religious system of values. The discussion about secularism indicates a great shift from the dominance of organized religion to the dominance of non-religious systems. The acceptable Western "mission" to the Third World comes in the form of technological skills in the production and distribution of material goods and services.

World Dominance

The uneven distribution of Christians in the world population today, as well as the large cleavages within Christianity, may be largely attributed to non-doctrinal and non-theological factors. The so-called Great Schism between East and West, which became permanent in 1204, was surrounded by cultural competition and power struggles. The rejection of papal authority by Henry VIII and the subsequent autonomy of the English Church from the Mother Church cannot be fully explained unless we recognize the contemporary political, military, and economic rivalry between the English and the Spaniards. One need not belabor this point in discussing all the "national" churches that sprang up in the wake of the Reformation and the subsequent sectarianism that still constitutes what H. R. Niebuhr called the "scandal" of Christian disunity.[11]

Aside from these internal dislocations, there is the broad historical fact that Christianity has been predominantly Europeanized. This was the case with the Roman Empire, especially at and after the time of Constantine's Edict of Milan (A.D. 313). From then on it appears that, wherever European civilization penetrated, it brought Christianity along with it. The ecclesiastically inspired Crusade of the eleventh century attempted to "restore" the true religion to the Holy Land by making use of the military, economic, and political resources of Christian Europe. Centuries later, the explorers and colonizers out of Europe brought their culture-bound religion to the new world of North and South America.

It was a European religion they disseminated, and this seems to be a large reason why Christianity was never really Africanized, nor took root in China and India. Can we fault the organized *Ecclesia* for not penetrating the East, for not reaching the untold millions, for historically binding itself almost exclusively to Western civilization? Obviously, religion is institutionalized in every culture, but this does not mean that religion has to be organizationally tied in with particular forms of political, economic, and other social structures.

It is seen now as a mistake that the Christian religion was identified with a national system, or for that matter with an imperial system of government and society. The blunder of Christianity was not that it became an organized *ecclesia*, but that this organization tied itself in with exclusively Western forms. It was natural then, and an historical accident, that the tremendous power and influence of the Western world carried along with it the influence of Christianity. One does not discredit the message and intent of Christ if one says that Christianity was spread less on its own merits than on the momentum of Western civilization.

The Cross and the flag went with empire and conquest and colonization, whether the empire was Spanish or Portuguese, French, or British and even though there were often bitter disagreements between bearers of the Cross and bearers of the flag. As Kenneth Cragg remarks, "their relation has been more complex and ambiguous than Western assumption or non-Western accusation has generally recognized. Yet, that they were broadly parallel is not in doubt. European commercial expansion provided the occasion of Christian mobility, and imperial authority, in its turn, utilized, or shielded, or answered missionary imagination. 'Their gain,' Drake had said of the penetrated lands, even in the sixteenth century, 'shall be the knowledge of our faith and ours such riches as their country hath.' The priest and the preacher could not long exclude the merchant, even when they had preceded him."[12]

Bishop Cragg's remarks may well be applied to the missionary experiment among the Paraguay Indians in the seventeenth century. An adaptive culture and society were there established under Christian auspices, with the direct intention of protecting the Indians from exploitation. The Paraguay Reductions ultimately succumbed to economic greed, governmental neglect, and military power. It was another in the list of failures to demonstrate the socio-cultural flexibility of Christianity, which could have flourished outside of Western and European dominance.

Bringing the good news of Christianity to all the "new" lands implied a kind of Christian optimism that Westerners could bring enlightenment to the heathen darkness, everywhere, and thus "raise" even ancient civilizations to our own bright level. This was an illusion, as Albrecht says, "the product of both political and theological errors. The political miscalculation was to assume that these countries would remain for years under the control of Western 'Christian' governments which would provide the umbrella for the Christianizing process. The theological mistake was to identify Christianity and a particular civilization. Today the umbrella of Christian culture has unexpectedly folded."[13]

Must the theological error persist, even after we have recognized the political error? The collapse of empire, the birth of new nations in Africa, and the rebirth of independence in India and China, as well as the establishment of the United Nations—all of these have meant a realignment of power relations throughout the world. In a sense, out of the reshuffling of the last half-century the United States has emerged at a position of enormous power, wealth, and influence. In spite of the "bad image" as the new economic imperialist and exploiter, and as the military blunderer in Southeast Asia, the United States by its sheer technological success plays a predominant role in the modern world. This technology is what the rest of the world wants; we like to think that they should want also our concepts of personal freedom and civil rights.

Even this kind of remark indicates a certain prideful optimism that we of the Christian West are accustomed to display. We have so much that the rest of the world wants. This pride extends sometimes to the conviction that we, and only we, possess the true religion. Arnold Toynbee had suggested that contemporary Christianity ought to show some repentance for its presumed monopoly of God's grace. In commenting on this point, Hocking declared that "what chiefly stood in the way of the message of the Nazarene in the Orient has been less the political and economic tempers of imperialism, than a certain lack of contrition on the part of many of its messengers."[14]

Repentance and contrition imply a willingness to make reparation, but basic to all this is the repudiation of ethnocentrism, especially the kind that has set up an idolatrous self-image of Western Christianity. "We are always relapsing from the worship of God into the worship of our tribe or of ourselves; and therefore we Christians, whether we are Western Christians or Eastern Christians, tend to treat Christianity as if it were the tribal religion of our particular civilization. In the West we tend to treat it as something that is inseparable from the West, and even as something that derives its virtue not so much from being Christian as from being Western."[15]

Religion Is Culture-bound

One of the unavoidable verities about religion is that it becomes institutionalized in the culture where it exists. This is not peculiar to religion; it is true also of familial, educational, political, and economic institutions. In sociological terms, a cultural system is the sum of its institutions, which in turn are made up of the shared repetitive behavioral patterns of the people. Institutionalized religion cannot escape culture; it is a constituent of the cultural system. This means that Christianity, like any other world religion, is always culture-bound, but it does not mean it has to be bound to only one culture form or system.

If Christianity then is to be universal, it must also be flexible enough to be institutionalized differently in a variety of cultures. This is similar to the concept of the organized church, as explained by the Fathers of the Second Vatican Council. The Church, which is "sent to all people of every time and place is not bound exclusively and indissolubly to any race or nation, nor to any particular way of life or any customary pattern of living, ancient or recent. Faithful to her own tradition, and at the same time conscious of her universal mission, she can enter into communion with various cultural moods, to her enrichment and theirs too."[16]

The fact that Christianity presents itself in a variety of cultural forms is abundantly apparent when we look at the cultural pluralism of Catholicism itself. Even within the United States, how else can one explain the differences in religious attitudes and behavior among Catholics of Italian, Polish, German, and Irish background? Unless one makes unscientific racial or biological assumptions about human behavior, how else can one understand the diversity (and even conflicts) in the last century between American Catholics of German and Irish descent?

It is generally agreed that American Catholicism has been fashioned more by Irish influence than by any of the many other religio-cultural influences that came with European immigration. By sheer weight of numbers of Irish people in the Catholic population, and of Irish clergy and bishops, religious Sisters and Brothers, this cultural predominance was to be expected. One need make no value judgment, of either boast or blame, concerning this historical development. These remarks simply underline the sociological fact that Catholicism, like any other organized religion, is significantly affected by the sociocultural system in which it exists.

The typical Catholic tourist from the United States visits Mexico and finds religious customs "strange." He is assured by the tour guide that these people really are "Roman" Catholic, but he still feels that they do not act like Catholics. He will probably agree with the remark of Raimundo Panikkar: "It is obvious that the same religion that has undergone different cultural, historical, temporal, and spatial experience takes on completely different forms, which from the point of view of an outsider may be interpreted as completely different religions."[17]

It is this cultural coloration that people see, when they know that the religious behavior of British Catholics differs so greatly from that of

Italian Catholics. Both England and Italy, however, are within the larger framework of European Christian civilization. Can one say that all cultures are receptive to Christianity, or are some cultures clearly hostile, or at least alien to the Christian religion? It is suggested, for example, that the religion and culture of India are so inseparably interwoven that "assimilation of the Indian culture means at the same time assimilation of Hindu religion,"[18] yet one-third of the population of the State of Kerala in India is Christian.

To use another example, one may suggest that the Christian religion cannot adapt to the communist culture, but this conclusion probably emerges from a misunderstanding of the definition of culture. Certainly, Christian religious practices have existed alongside totalitarian political institutions, rigid educational institutions, and non-capitalistic economic institutions. The fuzziness in the analysis of the relation between communism and Christianity comes from a failure to distinguish between a cultural system and a social structure.

It is the flexibility of cultural forms which is important in this context, rather than the cooperation, indifference, or antagonism of the organized political structure against either the organized religious structure or the cultural religious institution. The failure of Christianity to adapt itself to the cultures of India, China, and Japan exemplifies this point, rather than any antagonism against Christianity on the part of the social authorities of India, China, and Japan.

Religion Is Culture-adaptive

To clarify this distinction we must look again at modern Israel, where religion is both culturally and structurally tied into the total system. Here we see a repetition of the "Church-State" problem that has plagued so many Western countries. "Obviously, the present relation is unsatisfactory," says Mordecai Kaplan: "Religion cannot be free to develop, as long as the leaders of an entrenched Orthodox minority exercise exclusive authority over a large area of civil law and religious practice for the entire population."[19] Objections to the current arrangement in Israel are raised also from an extremely Orthodox group called the "Neturei Karta," who label Zionism nothing more than "Gentile nationalism." They argue that the Jews, having been exiled by Divine Providence, must lovingly accept their sentence and "should not seek to enter *Eretz Yisroel* in a body before the predestined time."[20]

Both the non-Orthodox Jew who wants the separation of Church and State, and the deeply Orthodox Jew who opposes Zionism, seem to be making the same argument from different points of view. Judaism as a religion should not be identified with a place and a government. The eternal spiritual message of Judaism is universally adaptive and transcends any particular cultural system and social organization. What bolsters their argument is the historical fact that without a homeland for almost two millennia, the Jews continue to exist religiously in a variety of cultures. One can appreciate both the nostalgic "homesickness" of the Jew in the diaspora, and the tremendous pride of the Jew who is now building the State of Israel. At the same time, one can appreciate the practical desire to keep the Jewish religion from becoming nationalized.

From the point of view of cultural assimilation, what is happening in Israel, in bringing together religious Jews from different ethnic backgrounds, is analogous to the American Catholic experience in bringing together immigrant Catholics from various national backgrounds. The intention in Israel is to develop a distinctive national culture within which religion is a supportive and integrative institution. If this is the case, then to be a Jew means to be an Israeli and vice versa; whereas, in the United States one cannot say that to be a Catholic means to be an American. Furthermore, there is still a large Jewish diaspora in which a religious Jew can be culturally French, American, British, or whatever. Alfred Lilienthal makes this point when he says that "Jews are individuals who profess Judaism," some of whom may be Israelis and some Zionists, but to be a Jew does not necessarily mean to be also an Israeli and a Zionist.[21]

It appears that the more historical a religion is—like Judaism, Christianity and Islam—the more likely it is to be culturally adaptive. These three are called the "Western religions" by Christopher Dawson, but there is no reason to believe that the "Eastern religions," Hinduism and Buddhism, are not also essentially and potentially culturally adaptive. There is indeed a growing interest among Westerners in these Eastern religions and an increasing willingness on the part of their representatives to make contact—as well as converts—among Europeans and Americans.

The historical—and frustrating—evidence that Christianity need not be imbedded in European civilization, and that this religion is adaptive to other cultures, was in the work of the Jesuit missionaries to China and India in the sixteenth and seventeenth centuries. What they did was to "purge our Christianity of its Western accessories," and this is what Toynbee says is the first thing we must do in our approach to the non-Christian religions.

The Jesuits realized they were in the presence of high and ancient Chinese civilization for which they developed great respect. They not only adapted the Christian liturgy, celebrating Mass in Chinese instead of Latin, but also interpreted architecture, music, philosophy, and theology in accord with the Chinese culture. Malcom May judges that China, "with an ethical tradition 4,000 years old, with the unity of spirit, both national and continental, was ready at the end of the sixteenth century to absorb Christianity."[22] Although these innovations were officially approved by Pope Paul V in 1615, they were rescinded by Pope Benedict XIV in 1742, and all missionaries were ordered to take an oath against Chinese rites.

This brilliant anthropological approach, and the controversy that accompanied it, are now only historical monuments to an ethnocentric European Christianity. We need not recount the complicated story of its suppression, but we may well ask whether even at this late and enlightened date the principle of cultural adaptation of religion has been accepted. To be sure, Africans and Asians have been raised to the episcopacy, and emphasis placed on the training of native seminarians and statements made about entering into "communion with various cultural modes."

In spite of all this, the decree of Vatican II on the *Missionary Activity of the Church* is very cautious about creative adaptation and initiative and still stresses the importance of jurisdiction and organization and supervision. In commenting on this decree, Eugene Smith remarks that "the missionary call of every Christian—inescapable in his faith and baptism—is rightly stressed. The participation of the laity in mission, however, is to be channeled by the hierarchy. Fulfillment of the missionary obligation which the Christian discovers in Christ demands opportunity for individual creative initiative and experimentation which the hierarchial controls assumed in this document would seem severely to restrict."[23]

The World and the West

There is no question that perceptive thinkers have changed this ethnocentric attitude, or have had change forced upon them by the realities of the modern world. With the growth of instant communication we have come to learn more about the global situation than ever before. With the knowledge that more than one nation now possesses an accumulation of destructive power that can devastate the whole world, we begin now to question even our capacity to survive. There are indeed hopeful people like Robert Slater, who "see new pros- pects of world community which offer hope of something more than survival. In this situation what are significantly called the forces of religion—forces manifestly resurgent today—cannot be ignored."[24]

The "One World" of the United Nations was not to be a new form of imperialism; neither is Hocking's "World Civilization," nor Slater's "World Community." The new People of God is meant to be universal, and whatever is meant by the "Coming of the Kingdom" is yet to be realized. Vatican II said that "earthly progress must be carefully distinguished from the growth of Christ's Kingdom. Nevertheless, to the extent that the former can contribute to the bettering of human society, it is of vital concern to the Kingdom of God."[25] Before lapsing into optimism about either worldly or religious unity, we had better look at the contemporary facts of disruption and disunity.

Pope Paul VI's encyclical *Progressio Populorum* sees the dilemmas that have resulted from the maldistribution of the world's resources. "Social conflicts have taken on world dimensions. The acute disquiet, which has taken hold of the poor classes in countries that are becoming industrialized, is now embracing those whose economy is almost exclusively agrarian; farming people too are becoming aware of their 'undeserved hardship.' There is also the scandal of glaring inequalities, not merely in the enjoyment of possessions but even more in the exercise of power. While in certain regions a small restricted group enjoys a refined civilization, the remainder of the population, poor and scattered, is deprived of nearly all possibilities of personal initiative, and oftentimes even its living and working conditions are unworthy of the human person."[26]

The Pope does not employ revolutionary rhetoric, but he is pointing out the same harsh facts discussed in stronger language by revolutionary writers and orators. The fact is that 80 percent of the world's resources are in the hands of only 20 percent of the world's population. These are the citizens of the First World, formed in the European Christian civilization, namely Caucasian and well-educated, technologically advanced and holding the power of large-scale organizations. In broadest terms, this First World is made up of the nations that are sometimes called the North Atlantic Community.

The Second World, typified by Russia and Japan, gets along well without Christianity, escapes the domination of the First World, has appropriated much of the technological expertise, and is now in the process of developing its own resources. It is the so-called Third World, largely Asian, African, and Latin American, that contains the suffering masses of humanity. Its people are poor, multi-racial, with little training in technological skills, victims of exploitation and oppression. But these geographical lines are drawn a little too neatly to express reality. Pockets of the Third World are represented by many blacks in the United States. Pockets of the First World are represented by the ruling classes of Latin America.

What is going on in much of the Third World today is the gigantic shift from colonial to national status. At the very time when transportation and communication are drawing us together, when the possibility of economic and political cooperation seems within our grasp, when representatives of the world religions are moving in an ecumenical direction—at this same time the former colonial peoples are setting up independent nations. Nevertheless, it seems that the process of so-called "Westernization" is taking place more rapidly than it did under colonization.

When cross-cultural borrowing becomes voluntary it becomes selective. It is now quite clear that westernization, or Europeanization, does not necessarily mean Christianization. If it is true that the Third World, and to some extent the Second World, are avid for westernization but indifferent to Christianization, we must acknowledge the probability that Christianity will never be the universal world religion.

Notes

1. The essay draws freely on chapter 8, "Christians as a World Minority," 123–142, in *Organization Man in the Church* (Cambridge: Schenkman, 1974).
2. Hans Küng, "Preface," 10, in Willard G. Oxtoby, *The Meaning of Other Faiths* (Philadelphia: Westminster, 1983).
3. *Declaration on the Relationship of the Church to Non-Christian Religions*, art. 1.
4. Sun Myung Moon, "Dialogue and Alliance," 96–101, in Darrol Bryant, John Maniatis, Tyler Hendricks, eds., *Assembly of the World's Religions* (New York: Paragon House, 1986).
5. H. Paul Chalfant, Robert Beckley, C. Eddie Palmer, *Religion in Contemporary Society* (Sherman Oaks: Alfred Publishing, 1981), chapter 12, "Religion and Social Stratification."
6. M. A. C. Warren and John Taylor, "Presence," 219–236, in Owen C. Thomas, ed., *Attitudes Toward Other Religions* (New York: Harper & Row, 1969).
7. *Ibid.*, Owen C. Thomas, "Introduction," 1–28.
8. J. Milton Yinger, *The Scientific Study of Religion* (New York: Macmillan, 1957), 198.
9. *Ibid.*, 190.
10. Paul Tillich, *Christianity and the Encounter of the World Religions* (New York: Columbia University Press, 1963), 5.
11. See *passim*, H. Richard Niebuhr, *The Social Sources of Denominationalism* (Hamden: Shoestring Press, 1954).
12. Kenneth Cragg, *Christianity in World Perspective* (New York: Oxford University Press, 1968), 19.
13. Paul Albrech, *The Church and Rapid Social Change* (London: SCM, 1961), 199.
14. William E. Hocking, *The Coming of World Civilization* (New York: Harper, 1958), 186.
15. Arnold Toynbee, *Christianity Among the Religions of the World* (New York: Scribner, 1957), 94.
16. *The Church in the Modern World*, art. 58.
17. Raimundo Panikkar, *Religionen und die Religion* (Munich: Heuber Verlag, 1965), 83.
18. *Ibid.*, 85.
19. Mordecai Kaplan, *Questions Jews Ask* (New York: Reconstruction Press, 1956), 414.
20. Yerachmiel Domb, "Neturei Karta," in *Zionism Reconsidered*, Michael Selzer, ed. (New York: Macmillan, 1970), 44.
21. Alfred Lilienthal, *What Price Israel?* (Chicago: Regnery, 1953), 243.
22. Malcom Hay, *Failure in the Far East* (London: Spearman, 1953), 169.
23. Eugene L. Smith, "A Response," in Walter Abbott, ed., *Documents of Vatican II* (New York: America, 1956), 631–633.
24. Robert L. Slater, *World Religions and World Community* (New York: Columbia University Press, 1963), 1.
25. The Church in the Modern World, *Gaudium et Spes*, art. 39.
26. *Populorum Progressio*, art. 9.

PART II

THE WIDER ECUMENISM

SOME FUNDAMENTAL ISSUES

6

THE WIDER ECUMENISM

SOME THEOLOGICAL QUESTIONS

Monika K. Hellwig

THE CLOSE INTERACTION of peoples and nations in our times makes the call to a wider ecumenism both important and urgent in an entirely new way. Yet the possibilities and limitations of Christian participation in this wider ecumenism are deeply rooted in our Christian history. This paper, written from a Roman Catholic perspective, is a reflection on the present and future implications of that history. It is not meant to provide any new research into the past, nor to provide an historical study of any period or movement in detail. It is intended to offer some perspectives and suggestions for discussion, drawn from the history that we all know, at least in its broad outlines.

It seems to me that the questions we must consider in relation to the wider ecumenism from a theological point of view come to focus around the following:

1. What is the Good News of Jesus Christ for the world?
2. How does it relate to anyone else's good news?
3. How are we as Christians called upon to share and bring the Good News of Jesus Christ?
4. Does God speak to us in other ways, as well as through Jesus of Nazareth?

5. Does our faith require us to listen to other voices or to exclude them? What can we expect to learn from others, and in what ways?

In any situation of religious faith, national loyalty, or particular cultural traditions, human beings shape their own identity by patterns that lead through a phase of differentiation by exclusion to a phase of complementarity comfortably accepted through a dialogic inclusiveness. This is easy to observe in sex role development in children who, when they first become aware of sex role expectations in their society, tend to stress separateness and difference in extreme forms until a certain measure of maturity allows rejection of otherness to turn into acknowledgment of complementarity. Something similar seems to happen in most aspects of our human culture and socialization. In order to establish a position we withdraw, stress differences, and maintain separation perhaps even to the point of isolation. It may seem in this phase a matter of the greatest importance not to allow oneself to be "tempted" by exposure to the "others" and their views and behavior. Yet truly mature people like to travel abroad and learn about the ways and ideas of other peoples—enjoy trying their food, attending their entertainments, attempting their language, and trying to understand their politics.

Common sense observation suggests that Christianity falls into this pattern, both in the broad sweep of its history through the centuries and in the development of particular communities of believers. In the context of the Catholic tradition this is not theologically troublesome because it is a well-established principle that there is a certain continuity between faith and reason, manifested in several ways: in establishing the grounds of credibility for making the "leap" of faith, in seeking a thorough and coherent understanding of the content of faith, and in drawing conclusions for action from the tenets of the faith. Common sense observations are, therefore, theologically significant, and we may expect that patterns of human development and adjustment will turn out to be relevant in matters of faith as elsewhere.

The Good News of Jesus Christ for the World

The Hebrew context in which the gospel was first proclaimed was not rejected by that gospel but acknowledged and brought into sharper relief. Chapters 1 and 2 of Luke's Gospel have Zachary, Mary, Simeon, and Anna all acknowledging that this moment and this person, Jesus, initiate the fulfillment of Israel's hope. Chapter 4 has Jesus himself stressing his continuity with Isaiah. In the early chapters of the Acts of the Apostles, the disciples of Jesus continue after his resurrection to worship in the Temple and to frequent synagogues outside Jerusalem. But from this beginning there developed a long—indeed a very long—period of differentiation, hostility, rejection, and condemnation between Christians and Jews. This lasted until a certain maturity was reached. In medieval times, in spite of prejudices prevailing in the population at large, great Jewish and Christian scholars found the maturity that enabled them to exchange learning and understanding in the philosophy that grounded their theology. The churches at large have come to the point of dialogue with Judaism only really in our own times, to learn at last that the New Testament (and therefore the whole Christian faith) cannot be fully known except in the context of the continuing hope and fidelity of the Jewish people.

To those who followed Jesus in his lifetime, the Good News which he preached conveyed a meaning that they recognized. The post-resurrection faith in Jesus as savior must, of course, refer to what Jesus preached in the first place, adding the risen presence of Jesus and the new life of the community as new pledges of the trustworthiness of the message. The message itself had not changed; it was the imminent realization of God's reign in the world of human affairs. That is what "Kingdom of the Heavens" meant in inter-testamental rabbinic discourse, and Jesus, according to the Gospels, did not redefine this term which he so frequently used. As the traditions of Israel had described it for centuries, the restoration of God's rule would mean peace among nations and among individuals, justice for all and especially for the poor and oppressed and powerless, intimacy with God and trust in God's providence, and an end to all kinds of useless suffering. That was Israel's expectation and Jesus in the Gospels nowhere takes issue with that expectation, but rather claims that its fulfillment is at hand.

This hope is not really particular to one people, nor is it difficult or obscure for others to understand. It goes to the heart of human experience and captures a sense of alienation that all can recognize as their own, as well as expressing a longing that finds a ready resonance in the aspirations of all human beings. It is surely because the traditions of Israel had long acknowledged the Noachic covenant as one in which God embraced all the Gentiles that the followers of Jesus reached out, after an intense struggle of discernment, to Gentiles as well as Jews. And doubtless it was because this Hebrew insight was true that the gospel of Jesus spread rapidly across the known world of Mediterranean civilization and was embraced by successive waves of barbarian invaders of the ancient empire.

As Christianity gained ground in the first centuries, the question of inclusion or exclusion from the promised reign of God arose again in relation to the so-called pagans. In answer to the question we find those who are anxiously exclusive, claiming the radical discontinuity with everything else that human traditions of hope and promise have to offer. But we also find those who, like Justin the Martyr of the second century of Christian history, have a more inclusive vision in which the gospel of Jesus Christ is seen as expressing a hope and promise to which both the prophets of Israel and the philosophers of the Greeks have tended.[1]

It may seem puzzling at first glance that this kind of tolerant inclusiveness was not extended to the positions which the Christian writers of the second and subsequent centuries defined as heretical. However, there is an important difference. Those positions claimed to be within the Christian tradition and therefore called for a discernment as to what really constituted that tradition. For any community to maintain its coherence and specific character and to work towards its purpose, it is of course necessary that certain alternatives be excluded. Thus it is easy to understand the harsh rejection of Marcionite and Montanist positions and to realize why Gnosticism could not be tolerated when it presented itself as a mode (perhaps *the* mode) of Christian spirituality. Yet it is clear that such rejections do not in themselves cut off the possibility of dialogue with these traditions once they are seen as other. It simply takes time in history to establish the distance that allows them to be seen as other and therefore mitigates the threat that they present.

A particularly interesting historical example of this has occurred in the case of Islam. Islam offers the same kind of challenge to Christians which Christianity offers to Jews. When Islam proclaims that Moses and Jesus were great prophets but that Muhammad was the last and greatest prophet who received the final and definitive revelation, there is a direct conflict with the Christian claim of definitive revelation and salvation in Jesus Christ. It is not just a question of another tradition and another approach, but a claim of supercession which negates or diminishes the claims made by Christians. Jews have, of course, long had to wrestle with such claims against their own tradition, as successive generations of Christians identified the Old Testament or ancient covenant with an antiquated or outmoded one.

But from among the Jews who wrestled with this in the course of a long history of persecution and discrimination comes the remarkable insight of Yehuda Ha-Levi, medieval scholar and mystic, who wrote that Israel was like a seed buried in the ground and trampled under foot, from which grew a tree with two great branches, Christianity and Islam. For centuries Israel would be despised, but when the tree and its branches came to maturity and bore fruit, it would be apparent that the seed in that fruit was the seed of Israel that was planted in the beginning.[2]

The remarkable parable is like a commentary on the nature of the good news of salvation. What is really the meaning of the gospel and really the nature of salvation is in some sense only to be known retrospectively. But, unless the reality in which we live, the reality which we call creation, is absurd, then all the authentic hopes and strivings of human hearts and human traditions must converge in the ultimate realization of salvation, and even in partial and intermediate realizations. The Christian gospel always falls short of concrete, positive descriptions of salvation. It gives us poetic imagery, and it gives us negations of all kinds of suffering and injustice, but it does not give us a positive description. The reason, surely, is that even by faith we are incapable of such a description, and yet we are capable of moving towards a goal seen dimly and partially. But precisely because we can only see it dimly, partially, by analogy and by negation, we have cause to enter into dialogue with others on the good news of salvation, not only because we have something to tell them but also because we have something to hear from them.

The Christian Gospel and the Good News of Other Traditions

It is a matter of intimate concern to the Christian believer and particularly to the theologian to ask in what way the Christian gospel is related to the good news of other traditions. This is true not only of the explicitly religious traditions, but also of such as Marxism that claim to carry a message of hope for the human race. If our own understanding of salvation and the means to it are true, does it mean that the expectation of other traditions is illusory, or is it possible that both are true, and if so, how?

One can read the words of Jesus to the woman at the well in Samaria (John 4:21–24) in two ways. When Jesus says that the dispute between Jews and Samaritans over the proper place of worship is irrelevant, it might be lightly assumed that he meant that both Jews and Samaritans were wrong because Christians would have the monopoly on true worship. But in a quite different level of discourse it appears that the answer transcends all particular traditions and is concerned with the human authenticity of the approach to God in any tradition.

Medieval theology gave some thought to this under the rubric of asking what happened to the unbaptized. After considerable discussion a standard answer emerged, suggesting three kinds of baptism: the baptism of water which explicitly initiates people into the church and thereby into the grace of Christ; a baptism of blood in the case of those who are believers and seek admission to the Church but are martyred before their initiation; and the baptism of desire which is not the explicit desire of baptism but simply a quest after the truth and a desire to do what is right on the part of those who have not had the opportunity to learn of Christ as their savior.[3]

It is noteworthy, however, that this answer validates the quest of the individuals concerned because of their "invincible ignorance of the truth." It falls short of a validation of their own religious or other traditions as availing unto salvation.

A modern form of this argument was proposed by the great Catholic theologian, Karl Rahner, when he spoke of persons outside the Christian faith as "anonymous Christians" (Christians in their basic orientation, but without claiming the name of Christians) as long as these persons were in good faith. Moreover, he also spoke of those in good faith outside the Christian community as acting upon "an enquiring Christology," which put them in communion with Christ who was in search of them by a kind of magnetic attraction.[4]

Yet all such positions are based on the assumption that the other traditions are in error because there is really only one true faith, albeit God will not punish anyone for invincible ignorance. This persistent understanding caused, and subsequently was reinforced by, such utterances as that of Tertullian in the early third century, that outside the Church there is no salvation, or that of the Athanasian creed originating some centuries later, that if anyone wishes to be saved before all things it is necessary that he hold the Catholic (i.e. the Nicene) faith.

Yet a thorough study of such texts in their original context suggests a careful and nuanced interpretation. Both the texts just mentioned were originally warnings to those tempted to go into schism from the body of the church. These people were already members of the church, setting themselves in opposition to the community. Warning the members of one's own community not to stray from the way of the salvation offered by that community is clearly very different from declaring that members of other faith communities have no hope of salvation. It is true that many Christians throughout the ages endorsed the latter kind of declaration, but those authoritative texts mentioned above cannot be quoted in support of the position because they were not addressed to members of other traditions.

With this background, modern Christian theology has not been able to avoid the question whether there is salvation in other traditions. It is axiomatic for Christians that salvation is by charity. Therefore it is not outside the realm of experience and observation whether a teaching or way of life contributes to salvation. When we know, for instance, that Mahayana Buddhism teaches selflessness, peace, detachment from material possessions, and compassion, we know that it moves its adherents to charity, and we know that charity is the behavioral expression of that habitual grace that is incipient salvation. Similarly, when we see in the modern world people such as Mohandas Gandhi, for whom all barriers between peoples are eliminated, for whom the forgiveness of injuries is a daily way of life, for whom the love of God and the love of fellow human beings are inseparably united, and for whom the restoration of dignity and freedom to the oppressed is a lifelong preoccupation, then we are looking at people who have learned from other traditions how to enter into the restored Reign of God (as we might put it in our Christian vocabulary).

It might still be objected by some that salvation has to do with the outcome of life beyond death and that this is beyond our observation. There are several answers to this objection. In the first place, the biblical notion of the restored reign of God in creation, which Jesus took over without redefinition, does not place salvation beyond death or outside history and our world. It places salvation in this world among the living. The doctrine of resurrection arose in the inter-testamental period as a declaration of hope against the apparent scandal of the deaths of the faithful before the advent of God's redemption. It is true that in the light of the resurrection of Jesus, the early Christian communities gradually learned to focus more on that aspect of salvation that transcended death. But this did not shift their hope away from this world of our experience until considerably later.

It is noteworthy that there was a shift in the fourth century of Christian history. The first three centuries, during which Christians were mostly poor, powerless, and liable to persecution, testify to a hope focused on the return of Christ in glory to bring our history to consummation by turning over the kingship to the Father.

With the Constantinian establishment, the pattern of expectation changes. There is less focus on general eschatology; life and liturgy present the emperor as ruling in the name of Christ, as though the kingdom of God were already realized in history. Hope is therefore focused more and more in the course of time on the outcome for the individual after death.

With the move northwards of Christianity among the barbarian peoples there were mass conversions of the scantily instructed. The promises of the gospel were less understood than accepted on hearsay authority. We know that symbolism was taken literally in ways not originally intended. The connection between transformed life and salvation is less a matter of shared experience than of ritual guarantees. Salvation becomes more arbitrary—a reward given to individuals beyond death for ritual and moral conformity to rules laid down by the Church—rather than the restoration of God's reign of peace and justice among human beings in all their affairs. It is easy to see that in such a context phrases such as "no other name given to us under heaven by which we might be saved" take on a quality that places them beyond examination by human intelligence. Yet all such expressions arose originally from the experience of the followers of Jesus and their reflections on that experience.

Evangelization: The Sharing of the Good News

There has been a certain anxiety among Christians that the wider ecumenism necessarily entails infidelity to the commandment of Christ to go forth and teach all nations. The topic of evangelization has appeared prominently and explicitly in modern Christian discourse but has been seen as antithetical to ecumenism both by those who wanted to promote missionary outreach and by those who wanted to promote ecumenism, each feeling threatened by the other.

The issue goes back to the question of what is meant by evangelization—what it really means to give good news. It seems sometimes to be taken for granted by Christians that evangelization consists mainly of words—telling people that Jesus is savior and that they should therefore be baptized. A simple exercise in empathy is enough to realize that from the receiving end this is not good news because it is devoid of content. The words assume an experience which the outsider does not have, and they make no sense whatever without that experience. Even to proclaim that Jesus died to save us from our sins is devoid of meaning outside the experience of a community living in the grace of the resurrection, living a transformed and transforming life. There have been others, even in our own time, who have died that fellow human beings might have a better life—Gandhi, Martin Luther King, Che Guevara, Stephen Biko, soldiers in battle, rescue teams, and so forth. The proclamation that Jesus died to save all human beings is quite irrelevant unless and until those to whom it is proclaimed really experience a connection that makes the death of Jesus a championing of their own cause.

But perhaps we should understand evangelization in a very different way. If the Good News is essentially the rebirth of hope for the human race because the reign of God is being restored, then evangelization is essentially the summoning forth of human hope—true human hope for true human happiness. The *naming* of what is happening is then secondary. Furthermore, if the restoration of God's reign in the world is a matter of peacemaking, justice, community, compassion, and deep trust in the transcendent source of our being which we call God, then the primary mode of evangelization is the mode which Jesus employed first:

healing, overcoming of evil spirits of hatred and fear, summoning forth of community and courage, and so forth. The naming of God as Father, of Jesus as the Way, the Truth, and the Life, and all that goes with it, is then a secondary process in service to the primary concern of the actual living of lives and relationships.

The consequences of this for interfaith conversation are enormous. It implies that there should be no real conflict between evangelization and ecumenism. To rouse human hope by peacemaking, healing, community-building, and works of justice and compassion, is to appeal to others at the level of total experience—their own experience which they will interpret and name according to the tradition which they have learned in their own upbringing among their own people. It is only when there is a common experience of a present process of salvation that a conversation about the naming and interpretation of the experience can meaningfully take place. If the conversation is about a shared experience, there can be no doubt that the language and interpretation of the other tradition contains truth, even though we may think it is not the most apt or complete or helpful way of expressing what is happening. When our discourse turns to the transcendent dimension of salvation—that dimension which eludes direct observation and scrutiny because it is understood to transcend even death—we have no basis other than our present experience on which to interpret and evaluate what are of necessity very broad analogies in our ways of representing ultimate salvation.

Are There Other Channels of Revelation?

Another approach to that same very important question about our relations as Christians to other traditions of hope and worship is the question of where we might look for the divine self-revelation. The Psalms, which we as Christians take into the heart of our worship from the traditions of Israel, direct us to look for the self-revelation of God in nature all about us. The Psalms proclaim that nature tells of the power and splendor and greatness of God, but also of the divine fidelity and maternal tenderness and compassion. But the Psalms direct us also to look for the self-revelation of the divine in our own lives, consciences, experiences, and yearnings, and in the history of our people and of their relationships with other peoples. Jesus took up these indications in many ways. He seldom used abstract or strictly religious vocabulary and modes of expression in calling people to be alert to God's self-revelation. Instead he referred to the weather of his native land, to the affairs of craftsmen, shepherds, and farmers, to the concerns of parents and housewives, to the events of Israel's most recent history, and so forth. In these kinds of observations, Jesus encouraged people to reflect upon what they themselves could learn in the course of their common experience about the ways and attributes of God.

It was for this reason that Justin the Martyr, already mentioned above, could write without hesitation that God spoke to the Hebrews through the prophets and to the Greeks through their philosophers. It is for this reason also, that great Christian thinkers like Origen, Augustine, Anselm, and Aquinas, could seek for a fuller understanding of the divine revelation by drawing on the philosophers of the great pagan traditions. It was for the same reason that the medieval Christian scholars could seek for God's truth in the writings of Arab Muslims and of Jews. And more particularly, Aquinas did not hesitate to write of the Law of Nature (implanted by the Creator both in all creation and in the minds of human beings) as a law accessible by consultation with all persons of good will, no matter what their religious persuasion might be. In other words, the whole project of scholastic theology and philosophy was based on the understanding that God is revealed in many ways to all peoples and in all cultures and places and times. History is likewise resonant with great missionary figures who made the same discovery about the particular religious and cultural expressions of the peoples to whom they had been sent—Matteo Ricci in China, Roberto de Nobile in India, Isaac Jogues and his companions in North America.

In our own times there is an increasing awareness, expressed by the Third World Liberation Theologians and others, that it is not only in the philosophical heritage of other traditions that we must seek for truth to round out our understanding of God's self-revelation, but also in the disciplined self-reflection of contemporary peoples represented in the social sciences. If it is true that God speaks to us in events and relationships, then we listen best when we do all that is possible to see and evaluate these events accurately and fully. The social sciences are a continuing attempt to help towards this on the technical, quantitative, measurable, observable side. But it is noteworthy that in the social sciences all can participate equally whether Christian or Marxist, whether Buddhist or Muslim, Hindu, or Jew. The relationship between accurate observation and evaluation, between data collection and the interpretation of the meaning with regard to human redemption, is one that is subtle and may be seen very differently by different traditions, but the factual basis offers common ground for conversation. That people are starving when there is food in the world, that there are huge refugee populations when land for settlement is available, that many are afflicted by blinding and crippling diseases in a world where the remedies for these conditions exist—all this is matter for common concern. All this calls for conversation about our ultimate expectations and hopes and the convictions on which these expectations and hopes rest.

Likewise, on the positive side, the fact that Gandhi's *swaraj* movement and Martin Luther King's civil rights movement were successful, the fact that major diplomatic initiatives of our time have achieved conflict resolution, the fact that nuclear-disarmament talks are being held at all between the most powerful and dangerous nations of the world—all these things also are a common basis, not only for gratitude and celebration, but also for serious conversation about the convictions and hopes on which they rest.

Certain authors of our times, such as Eugene Hillman[5] and Heinz Schlette,[6] have raised the question in a more sharply focused way: is there true revelation and salvation in the other religions? It has long been customary in Catholic circles to speak of *vestigia*, or traces of God's special revelation through time. This term implies that the truth which Christians can recognize in the other religions is to be attributed to casual dissemination of the true (Judeo-Christian) revelation from time to time, assimilated into and surviving in the other religions, possibly in "distorted" form. According to this view, the people in these other religious traditions may indeed be saved, but that will be, so to speak, in spite of their own religion which has distorted the truth of revelation. This was a patronizing and rather presumptuous attitude. The authors cited above, Hillman and Schlette, present the insistent question whether peoples of other religious traditions must not be understood according to Christian faith to be saved precisely because of their own religious traditions.

Moreover, this question has become more urgent as we have come to realize that the proportion of Christians to the total world population is not growing but shrinking. Even in the West, people are being converted in substantial numbers to Islam and the eastern religions. In response to the question, there is a growing consensus with the position that Heinz Schlette takes: that the ordinary way of salvation offered by God to all human beings is through the respective traditions of their own people, and that conversion to Christianity is an extraordinary way desired by God for some people in order to keep alive the impact of Jesus Christ in the world. This does not answer all the problems, but it offers a viable basis for true dialogue.

Christian Faith and Other Voices: What Can We Learn?

From the above it certainly follows that there is honest reason and purpose for dialogue with the other religious traditions, and indeed with all other traditions offering hope for the human situation and the human race. But there remains the question of what it is that we hope to accomplish by such dialogue, what we expect to learn.

All religious language is necessarily analogical. We speak of matters that can be observed, so to speak, from one end while they are inscrutable at the other end. No human language or expression, therefore, can contain the whole truth simply and absolutely. There are many ways of approaching the truth, many analogies that might be used in trying to express it. Moreover, because we as Christians believe in the universal salvific will of God, we must assume that God is self-revealing to all that search in good faith, and is self-revealing to them in a linguistic, cultural and historical mode that they can understand.

But if this is true then each of the other religions represents such a mode of the divine self-revelation. These traditions must then be seen not only as the truth of searching human reason but also quite appropriately as the truth of a gracious God coming to meet, and even anticipating, that searching human reason in those other traditions as in our own. Moreover, if the self-revelation of God is first and foremost in our very being and in the totality of our experience, then the verbal formulation is a human undertaking for us Christians as well as for all others. This means that to some extent we are all fumbling and struggling to give utterance to something that is greater than our speech and our intellectual concepts, to which our imagination leaps expectantly by analogies.

If all this is true, then what we expect in conversation with those of the other religious traditions is growth in our own understanding and growth in our own faith wherever that may lead us. We expect new insights, knowing that these are not a threat but rather a promise of ultimate convergence beyond anything we can predict or anticipate. We expect to find complementarity of approach, of vision, of expectation, and of redemptive action. Jesus himself spoke of strangers coming from the east and from the west to sit down with Abraham in the Kingdom. He reacted with a kind of startled delight to the approach and deeper awareness of the Samaritan woman at the well, the Canaanite woman seeking healing for her daughter, and the centurion in quest of compassion for his servant. Jesus said about strangers that if they were not against us they were with us in their efforts towards driving out the evil spirits of hatred and fear and enslavement.

The wider ecumenism would appear, then, to be authentically in the footsteps of Jesus. It is he who draws our attention to the realization that in God's eyes the Sabbath and all religious observances are for the benefit of human persons. Religious traditions do not exist in their own right, to subordinate human persons to ritual formality and correctness.

Notes

1. I am indebted to Professor Agourides of the University of Athens for the reminder that, while modern Christians of the West tend to cite Justin in order to persuade Christians to take the other traditions seriously, Justin's own purpose was to persuade those of the other, dominant, traditions to tolerate Christians.
2. Yeudah Ha-Levi, *The Kuzari*, transl. Hartwig Hirschfeld (New York: Schocken, 1964), 227.
3. Cf. Gregory Baum, "Baptism of Desire," in *Sacramentum Mundi*, ed. Karl Rahner *et al.* (New York: Herder, 1968), Vol. I, 144–146.
4. The discussion, which took place in 1965–1966, largely in the journals, *Stimmen der Zeit* and *Theologie und Glaube*, is summarized with complete references in Louis Roberts, *The Achievements of Karl Rahner* (New York: Herder, 1967), ch. 8.
5. Eugene Hillman, *The Wider Ecumenism* (New York: Herder, 1963), and *Many Paths: A Catholic Approach to Religious Pluralism* (Maryknoll, N.Y.: Orbis, 1988).
6. Heinz Schlette, *Toward a Theology of Religions* (New York: Herder, 1963).

7

RETHINKING CHRISTIAN DOCTRINE IN THE LIGHT OF RELIGIOUS PLURALISM

John Hick

I PROPOSE TO START from our modern historical awareness that Christian doctrines should not be regarded as divinely formulated and guaranteed propositions, but rather as human attempts to grasp the religious meaning, primarily of the Christ event, and in the light of this, of our human situation as a whole. The history of Christian theology is thus part of the history of human thought, each phase of which is linked to some particular epoch and cultural environment, with its distinctive assumptions and modes of thought. As an aspect of the historical character of Christian thinking, broadly political and social factors, related to the needs, problems, and opportunities of the church at different times, have also affected its development.

The central event whose meaning, and the further implications of whose meaning, Christian theologians have sought to understand, is of course the life, death, and rising again of Jesus the Christ. The significance of this event as it was experienced by the first disciples was, naturally, initially expressed by them in the religious categories available to them. They applied to Jesus both the distinctively Jewish concepts of the 'messiah' (*Christos*) and the Danielic 'son of man,' and the wider 'son of God' metaphor which was common in the ancient world as a title for kings, emperors, and holy men who were believed to stand in a special relationship to God. These concepts provided ways of recognizing Jesus as a chosen servant of God, fulfilling (in the case of the 'messiah' and 'son of man' titles) a unique salvific role within the divine providence. But it was the 'son of God' metaphor that spoke to the larger Gentile world and that accordingly came to play a central role as the gospel was carried, by Paul and others, out into the Roman Empire.

In its original Hebraic meaning this offered a way of affirming the religious significance of Jesus as the charismatic preacher and healer in whose presence God seemed utterly real and the Kingdom imminent. But in due course the pressures of persecution provoked an escalation in the Christians' understanding of the lord for loyalty to whom they were being persecuted, and there began the transformation of the metaphorical 'son of God' into the metaphysical 'God the Son,' the Second Person of a divine Trinity. This transformation congealed into official dogma at the great theological Councils that were required by Constantine's adoption of Christianity as the official religion of the Roman Empire. Thereafter Christianity was burdened with the idea, which has never been satisfactorily explained and has accordingly acquired the status of a holy mystery, that Jesus had two distinct natures, one human and the other divine.

In the doctrinal system into which Christian thought began to be marshalled, three central elements cohere together—the doctrines of Atonement, Incarnation and Trinity. The inner logic connecting them is not difficult to discern. If salvation is made possible by the infinite sacrifice of Christ's death, Christ himself must have had infinite value; he must indeed have been divine—God incarnate. (The argument was to be classically expressed by St. Anselm in his *Cur Deus Homo*?) And, as we shall see later, to accommodate Jesus' deity the idea of God had to be expanded in a way which resulted in the doctrine of the Trinity.

All this was intelligible and appropriate within the historical circumstances in which it occurred. If the new Christian movement was to withstand the persecutions of the first two centuries, and then to provide moral and spiritual leadership to the Roman Empire and Western civilization, it needed the prestige of a divine founder who was the sole source of salvation. However, all this lost moral credibility when it became the ideological instrument for the savage persecution of the Jews, and for the military Crusades against Islam, in the medieval period. This exploitation of Christian theology to serve the purposes of human greed, by categorizing its targets as religious enemies—murderers of Christ, Mohammedan infidels—continued in the modern period with the religious validation of the imperial expansion of the West during the seventeenth to nineteenth centuries. This was seen as a great civilizing and redeeming mission in which the Christian world was saving Africa, South America, Asia, and Oceania from spiritual darkness and cultural depravity.

In our own century the continuing persecution of the Jews—expressing the violent reaction of Christian absolutism against those whose existence most directly contradicts that absolutism—has continued on an unparalleled scale in the Nazi attempt to exterminate the Jewish people. And today, in yet another wave of new consciousness, we are becoming aware of the ways in which Christian absolutism, embodied in a patriarchial hierarchy, has been in every century a powerful instrument for the oppression of women.

Thus what began in the early Church as a natural, and in that sense innocent and appropriate, affirmation of the full salvific authenticity and adequacy of the Christian Way, has become a basis for persecution, aggression, and exploitation on a gigantic scale. It is accordingly now necessary to ask whether such a dangerous ideology is really essential to the Christian stream of salvation, or whether in the continuous development of Christian thought the time has come—or is indeed already overdue—for a rethinking of the central complex of soteriological, christological, and trinitarian doctrines.

A second historical circumstance calling for such a reappraisal is our greatly increased awareness today of the spiritual values and salvific efficacy of the other great world faiths. If by salvation we mean a radical turning from self to the ultimate Reality that we Christians know as God, and thus a transformation of human existence from self-centeredness to Reality-centeredness, then so far as we can tell this takes place to about an equal extent within each of the great world faiths. This is intended as a negative rather than a positive conclusion. For it is extremely difficult to make responsible comparative judgments in this area. Indeed all that we seem entitled to say, on the basis of contemporary observation and the records of history, is that there is no good reason to think that our own tradition has been salvifically more effective than any of the others.

II

But in that case there is a lack of congruence between traditional Christian theology and the religious facts. For if Jesus was God the Son incarnate, and if (as Christianity has always either assumed or asserted) this is the only occasion on which God has become incarnate on earth, then Christians can have a uniquely full and direct knowledge of, and relationship to, God. Others have seen nature as pointing to God, or have received divine messages and laws through their prophets and Scriptures. But Jesus' disciples met God face to face; and his church is the continuing body of those who share in that memory, made contemporary every day in the sacraments. For Christianity is the only religion that was founded directly by God in person, and that, as the continuing Body of Christ, is the direct vehicle of God's work on earth. Given these premises it was entirely natural for Christians to conclude that God wants all human beings to be drawn into the Christian fold.

Inheriting this traditional conception, and relating it to our contemporary concern with the problems of religious pluralism, we must ask to what extent the traditional theology entails that Christians are in a religiously privileged position. Was God's self-revelation and personal presence in Christ so momentous, so decisive for human salvation, that those who have responded to it in faith are significantly better off than those who have not? Does the difference even amount to that between finding and missing salvation?

In previous centuries the usual Christian answer was positive, to the extent of accepting the implication that non-Christians forfeit salvation. The Roman church affirmed that *extra ecclesiam nulla salus*; while the Protestant missionary movement was largely predicated on the belief that outside evangelical Christianity there is no salvation. And there are still many Christians today, particularly within the evangelical wing of Protestantism, who believe this. But mainline Christian thinking has, roughly since the end of World War II, moved—however tentatively—from the older exclusivism to an inclusivism which acknowledges the spiritual values of the other world religions, and the fact that salvation is taking place within them, while still insisting that all salvation is dependent upon the atoning death of Christ. Salvation remains, by definition, Christian salvation; but it is available in principle to all human beings, whether Christian or not.

At this point the question recurs as to the religious advantage of Christian, in distinction from Muslim, Buddhist, etc., commitment. Is it easier for a Christian to be saved—so that a larger proportion of a Christian than of a non-Christian population may be expected to find salvation? Or is it that salvation can be realized in this life by Christians but only after an encounter with Christ beyond death by non-Christians? Neither of these answers is compatible with the observation that, so far as we can tell, the salvific transformation is taking place now, in this world; and is taking place, so far as we can tell, to about an equal extent within each of the great historic ways.

It is thus not easy, and indeed perhaps not possible, having once entered into our contemporary awareness of the other world religions as authentic contexts of salvation, to find a viable way of maintaining the religious superiority of Christianity.

But if we let go the assumption of religious superiority, do not the doctrines which both grounded and safeguarded that notion, giving Christianity a central role in universal salvation-history, lose their point? I think that they do. On the other hand however, a proper concern for continuity prompts us to ask whether there may not be non-absolutist forms of these traditional doctrines which should continue into the future. For Christian doctrines have in the past survived the influx of challenging new information by evolving into new forms. I believe that this is in fact possible in the case of each of these central themes. Religiously viable and attractive interpretations of them are already emerging which express important and authentically Christian insights, but which do not entail the objectionable Christian absolutism of the past.

III

Conceptions of divine Incarnation are available today which not only do not require the absolutism entailed by the traditional Chalcedonian Christology, but which are also much closer than it to the earliest Christian understandings of Jesus. Some of the leading Roman Catholic thinkers of recent decades—Karl Rahner, Edward Schillebeeckx, Hans Küng—have been pointing, though sometimes with cautious obscurity, in this direction. I shall, however, use as my examples two Protestant theologians, one a Presbyterian and the other an Anglican.

The Presbyterian is Donald Baillie, who was a Professor of Theology at St. Andrew's University, Scotland, and whose *God Was in Christ* (1948) was described by Rudolf Bultmann as "the most significant book of our time in the field of Christology."[1] Baillie focused attention upon what he called the paradox of grace, the fact that when human beings do God's will their deeds are both free and responsible human acts and yet also the work of divine grace within them. The paradox was classically expressed by St. Paul when he wrote, "I worked harder than any of them, though it was not I, but the grace of God which is in me" (1 Cor. 15:10)—he worked vigorously, and God was working in and through his labors. This paradox, Baillie suggested, provides the clue to the union of the divine and the human in the life of Christ:

> What I wish to suggest is that this paradox of grace points the way more clearly and makes a better approach than anything else in our experience to the mystery of the Incarnation itself; that this paradox in its fragmentary form in our own Christian lives is a reflection of that perfect union of God and man in the Incarnation on which our whole Christian life depends, and may therefore be our best clue to the understanding of it. In the New Testament we see the man in whom God was incarnate surpassing all other men in refusing to claim anything for Himself independently and ascribing all the goodness to God. We see Him also desiring to take up other men into His own close union with God, that they might be as He was. And if these men, entering in some small measure through Him into that union, experience the paradox of grace for themselves in fragmentary ways, and are constrained to say, "It was not I but God," may not this be a clue to the understanding of that perfect life in which the paradox is complete and absolute, that life of Jesus which, being the perfection of humanity, is also, and even in a deeper and prior sense, the very life of God Himself? If the paradox is a reality in our poor imperfect lives at all, so far as there is any good in them, does not the same or a similar paradox, taken at the perfect and absolute pitch, appear as the mystery of the Incarnation? (pp. 117–118).

Now on the face of it, and indeed I think in Baillie's own intention, this is still an absolutist Christology in that it claims that the paradox of grace was exemplified in Christ in an uniquely absolute way which is normative for the whole world. However, the deeper logic of Baillie's proposal changes the shape of the issue in such a way that a non-absolutist Christology becomes possible. But before showing this let me refer to a second author, Geoffrey Lampe, who was Regius Professor of Divinity at Cambridge University at the time of his death in 1980. In his Bampton Lectures, God as Spirit (1977), he offered a "Christology of Inspiration." He suggested that for God to become incarnate in human life is for God to inspire men and women to act as God's servants. Thus "God has always been incarnate in his human creatures, forming their spirits from within and revealing himself in and through them" (p. 23). We may indeed "speak of this continuum as a single creative and saving activity of God the Spirit towards, and within, the spirit of man, and of his presence in the person of Jesus as a particular moment within that continuous creativity" (p. 100). And within this continuum "God indwelt and motivated the spirit of Jesus in such a way that, uniquely, the relationship for which man is intended by his Creator was fully realized" (p. 11).

Thus Lampe agrees with Baillie in holding that divine incarnation consists in human beings, through free responses to divine grace or inspiration, becoming to the Eternal Goodness what his own hand is to a man—to use the words of the *Theologica Germanica*. This is something that is taking place in varying degrees throughout the ages and throughout the world but that both Baillie and Lampe believed took place to an uniquely total and absolute extent in the case of Jesus.

These two theologians did their work prior to the recent intrusion of the problems of religious pluralism into Western theological consciousness, and they do not seem to have noticed that their approach radically changes the logical character of the belief in Christ's uniqueness. For the traditional Chalcedonian theology, it was true by definition that divine incarnation was confined to this one instance; for among human beings only Jesus of Nazareth was also, ontologically, God the Son. But on the principle proposed by Baillie and Lampe *all* moments of free human response to divine grace or inspiration are, in their varying degrees, instances of divine incarnation. In so far as any man or woman responds freely to God's promptings, enacting the divine love within some earthly situation, to that extent God's love has become incarnate. And if we now want to add that this occurred to an absolute extent in and only in the life of Jesus, we are no longer uttering a definitional truth but making a momentous factual claim. The support for such a claim has to come from historical evidence concerning the lives of Jesus and of other great religious figures. Thus what for Chalcedon was an *a priori* truth, the logical implicate of a presupposed system of doctrine, is for a paradox-of-grace or an inspiration Christology an empirical claim having its basis in the known facts of history.

This changes radically the status of the traditional claim to Christ's and therefore Christianity's unique superiority. The older Christology required only the *permission* of history. The evidence did not have positively to establish Jesus' sinlessness and unique spiritual superiority, but merely had not to contradict it. (For evidence that Jesus was morally evil would have been incompatible with Chalcedon.) But a paradox-of-grace or an inspiration Christology is only entitled to assert a unique superiority for Jesus in so far as positive historical evidence authorizes this. But in order to substantiate historically Baillie's assumption that in the life of Jesus the paradox of grace was exemplified to "the perfect and absolute pitch," or Lampe's that Jesus was inspired by God to an uniquely full extent, we should need to know far more than we can in fact responsibly claim to know. Baillie's and Lampe's traditional assumption parallels that of J.A.T. Robinson's "It is in Jesus, and Jesus alone, that there is nothing of self to be seen, but solely the ultimate, unconditional love of God," concerning which the New Testament scholar Dennis Nineham asked:

> Is it, however, possible to validate claims of the kind in question on the basis of historical evidence? To prove an historical negative, such as the sinlessness of Jesus, is notoriously difficult to the point of impossibility...The sort of claims for Jesus we are discussing could not be justified up to the hilt by *any* historical records, however full or intimate or contemporary they might be, and even if their primary concern was the quality and development of Jesus' inner life and character.[2]

This impossibility of establishing as a fact of visible history that the presence of divine grace or inspiration in Jesus was absolute leaves open the possibility that there may have been other lives in which God was at work in different ways but to an equal extent. But of course the same lack of historical evidence that prevents us from making absolute claims about Christ likewise prevents us from making them about Moses, Gautama, Muhammad, or any other figure of the ancient world. Within each tradition the soteriological efficacy and adequacy of the stream of religious life that has flowed from the founder can properly be affirmed. As Christians we can, and must, say of Jesus that he is the one who has made God real to us and who has opened our hearts to the absolute claim of God upon our lives. It is his intimate awareness of God as heavenly Father, his profound and secure trust in God and consequent dedication of his life to God's work, his ability to channel the creative divine power in healing, and his unforgettably demanding and inspiring teachings, that have drawn us into or confirmed us in the Christian way.

But in order for this to be the case we do not need to attribute to Jesus an absoluteness that precludes all human moral and spiritual limitations; nor do we need to believe that he was the pre-existent Second Person of a divine Trinity. We can be content to think of our lord as it seems that his earliest disciples thought of him after his resurrection—as, in Peter's words at Pentecost, "a man attested to you by God with mighty works and wonders and signs which God did through him in your midst" (Acts 2:22).

IV

That the doctrine of the Trinity was not part of the original gospel, but emerged as an explanatory theological theory, was decisively acknowledged by Emil Brunner:

> When we turn to the problem of the doctrine of the Trinity we are confronted by a peculiarly contradictory situation. On the one hand, the history of Christian theology and of dogmas teaches us to regard the dogma of the Trinity as the distinctive element of the Christian Idea of God, that which distinguishes it from the Idea of God in Judaism and Islam, and indeed, in all forms of rational theism. Judaism, Islam, and rational theism are Unitarian. On the other hand, we must honestly admit that the doctrine of the Trinity did not form part of the early Christian—New Testament—message, nor has it ever been a central article of faith in the religious history of the Christian Church as a whole, at any period of its history.[3]

He concludes that "The ecclesiastical doctrine of the Trinity, established by the dogma of the ancient Church, is not a biblical *kerygma*, therefore it is not the *kerygma* of the Church, but it is a theological doctrine which defends the central faith of the Bible and of the Church" (p. 206). For while God was incarnate on earth as Jesus the messiah, God was also in heaven, upholding the universe and hearing prayer. And so a distinction was required between God the Father, in heaven, and God the Son, on earth. It might have been possible for Christian thought to rest content with a binitarian doctrine of Father and Son without going on to hypostatize the Spirit as a third co-equal Person, thus constituting a Trinity. Indeed in the New Testament period the Spirit was often regarded simply as the spirit of Jesus (e.g., 2 Cor. 2:17, Gal. 4:6), rather than as a third independent divine reality. However, three-fold distinctions are very wide-spread in religious thinking and may possibly express some deep-seated tendency of the human mind. At any rate, from whatever cause, Christianity came firmly to adopt a trinitarian model.

In the long history of Christian thought the understanding of this trinitarian idea has moved in two significantly different directions. These are, on the one hand, ontological or social, and, on the other hand, economic or modal. Interpreted in the former way, the Father, Son, and Holy Spirit are three persons in something like, or analogous to, the modern sense of a 'person' as a unique center of consciousness, will, valuation, and purpose. The Trinity constitutes a community of persons so intimately inter-related in mutual love and moral unity as to be "three in one and one in three." Among its merits, this conception makes it possible to speak of God as Love prior to and independently of creation; for we can think of the three divine Persons who together constitute the Godhead as eternally loving one another.

Such an understanding of the Trinity requires, as its second Person, a pre-existent Son or Logos who became incarnate in Jesus of Nazareth. This in turn has required, as the Council of Chalcedon insisted, that Jesus Christ had two complete natures, one human and the other divine—with all the perplexing questions that this notion has provoked. It has likewise led with seeming inevitability to the Christian absolutism which many of us today are intent upon avoiding.

The other kind of trinitarianism, and the one that coheres better with a non-absolutist Christology, sees the 'persons' of the Trinity, not as ontologically three but as three-fold from our human point of view—as three ways in which the one God is humanly thought and experienced. On this view the names of Father, Son, and Spirit do not refer to distinguishable divine persons, any more than do the various names of God in Jewish tradition, or the ninety-nine Beautiful Names of Allah in the Qur'an. It is indeed interesting to note that the Qur'anic Names can be marshalled, if one wishes so to arrange them, under the three broad heads of God as omnipotent creator and ruler of the universe (e.g., *Al-Khalig*, the Creator; *Al-Malik*, the Sovereign Lord; *Al-Bari*, the Evolver; *Al Mutakabbir*, the Majestic...), and God as gracious and forgiving (e.g., *Ar-Rahman*, the Gracious; *Ar-Rahim*, the Merciful; *Al-Ghaffar*, the Forgiver; *Al-Wadud*, the Loving...), and God as intimately present to us (*Ar-Rashid*, the Guide to the Right Path; *Al-Barr*, the Source of All Goodness; *Ash-Shadid*, the Witness; *Al-Mughni*, the Enricher...).

The New Testament says that "God is light and in him is no darkness at all" (I John 1:5) and the Qur'an says that "God is the light of the heavens and the earth" (24:35). The infinite divine Light is refracted in the varieties of human thought in many different ways. The Islamic tradition has preferred variety and profusion in its naming of the Infinite, while the Christian tradition has preferred a more restricted and intellectually controlled schema. But basically the idea of the Trinity, understood modalistically rather than ontologically, is a way of speaking of the divine complexity and versatility. The limitless richness of the Godhead is fragmented in our finite thought and experience; and the number of distinguishable concepts in terms of which we chose to think of it is optional. The three-ness or the ninety-nine-ness of the divine nature, as humanly described, are matters for human preference and decision.

Clearly, such an interpretation of the trinitarian symbol is compatible with a full acceptance of religious pluralism.

V

Christians have generally thought of salvation as being, by definition, Christian salvation. It has meant being forgiven and accepted by God because of Jesus' atoning death, and so becoming a member of the redeemed community, the Church. But seen in the broader context of the history of religions this is one version of the radical human change from sinful or blind self-concern to a new orientation within or towards the ultimate divine Reality. In Christianity the unsatisfactory state is diagnosed as a sinfulness stemming originally from pride or self-centeredness, and the new orientation is described as a filial relationship to God as the heavenly Father. In Judaism the contrasting states are ones of willful disobedience to God and the joy of living in accordance with God's law. In Islam: forgetfulness of God and a total self-surrender (*islam*) to and peace with God. In the Hindu traditions a self-concern expressing ignorance (*avidya*) of our true nature, and the realization of our true nature in or as the eternal reality of Brahman. In Buddhism: the suffering and anxiety of ego-centeredness and the serene selflessness of nirvana. I suggest as a generic formula that salvation/liberation is the transformation of human existence from self-centeredness to Reality-centeredness.

In the Christian version of this the human problem is seen as guilt in relation to God, and the solution divine forgiveness, with its transforming effect on the believer. This is one way, appropriate to the religio-cultural mentality developed in the Semitic faiths, of thinking and experientially grasping and being grasped by the profound reorientation in which salvation/liberation consists. And for those of us to whom God has been made real and present by the spiritual impact of Christ, and who have begun to participate as his disciples in the salvific transformation, it is clear that Christ has been in some way the instrument of our salvation—our savior.

But in the history of Christian thought the theological explication of this instrumentality has taken strange forms. For approximately its first thousand years the Church was content with a medley of metaphors of Christ defeating or cheating the devil. It was Anselm in the eleventh century who provided the first coherent theory, that of Christ's death as constituting the infinite satisfaction for the infinite wrong done to God's honor and majesty by human sin—a theory based on the medieval European conception of the honor of a feudal lord and the satisfaction that has to be made when this is impugned. This has remained central to Catholic atonement theology.

The churches of the Reformation have added the penal-substitutionary theories according to which Christ bore on our behalf the punishment that was justly due for human sin. He thereby met the inexorable requirements of divine justice, enabling God to forgive all who take Christ as their lord and savior. And within the Reformed traditions there also developed, in reaction to these somewhat harshly juridical conceptions, exemplarist theories to the effect that Christ's death saves us by making visible on Calvary the dreadful character of human sin, in that it causes even God to suffer, so bringing us to repentance.

These theories all presuppose an absolutist Christology. It is because Jesus was God incarnate that his death had infinite value and so could atone for the infinite wrong of human disobedience to God, or could show God bearing the effects of human sin. None of these theories is, then, appropriate as a Christian account of salvation/liberation in a religiously plural world.

But if we go back to the recorded teachings of Jesus we find that we do not need any such theories. He seems to have taught that God, our loving heavenly Father, is ready and willing to forgive us and receive us into the Kingdom as soon as we truly repent, embodying this repentance in forgiveness to one another. Thus in the Lord's Prayer we are taught to speak directly to God and to ask for forgiveness. There is no suggestion of the need for a mediator, or of the idea that the heavenly Father's forgiveness was conditional upon Jesus' death on the cross—a death which had of course not taken place at the time when Jesus was teaching his disciples how to pray. And, in the parable of the prodigal son, the father, who clearly represents God, did not require a blood sacrifice before forgiving his penitent son. As soon as he saw his son returning he "had compassion, and ran, and fell on his neck, and kissed him...saying 'For this my son was dead and is alive again; he was lost and is found'" (Luke 15:20, 24). In the light of such teaching we can say that the basic flaw in the Church's atonement theories (other than the exemplarist) is that they assume that something that in the nature of the case cannot be bought, namely authentic forgiveness, was bought by the death of Christ.

But why, then, the emphasis from the beginning on Jesus' death as somehow instrumental in our salvation? The answer, I think, lies in the idea, accepted in the Jewish society of Jesus' time and presupposed by Jesus and his disciples, that the death of a righteous martyr somehow works for the good of Israel. As John Downing concludes in a study of this aspect of first-century Judaism, "people thought in terms of human beings making atonement for others by means of their sufferings and death."[4] To quote John Bowker, "the understanding of suffering as a potential means of grace, not only for the individual, but for the whole community of the faithful, became the key to the Jewish response to suffering and persecution. 'He who gladly bears the sufferings that befall him brings salvation to the world' (B. Taan. Ba)."[5] The idea is also illustrated by this quotation from the second-century Rabbi Shim'on:

> When the righteous are seized by disease or affliction, it is in order to atone for the world. Thus all the sins of the generations are atoned for. When the Blessed Holy One wants to bring healing to the world, He strikes one righteous human among them with disease and affliction; through him He brings healing to all.[6]

And so it was that Jesus, aware of the imminence of his own martyrdom, could speak of giving his life as a ransom for many (Mark 10:45).

Thus the efficacy of Jesus' death was not in any way magical or juridical. He was not engaged in a plot to cheat the devil, nor was he bearing God's just punishment on our behalf, or showing God's suffering at human sin—except (and here we come back to something like the exemplarist theories) in the sense that all 'sons of God,' in voluntarily bearing the bitter resentment and hatred of so many in the presence of transcendent goodness, show forth something of the love/compassion that lies at the heart of Reality.

VI

And so within the existing variety of modes of Christian thinking there are ample resources for the development of doctrine in ways that are compatible with the pluralistic perception that Christianity is one among a variety of independently authentic ways of salvation/liberation. In order to continue to be Christians in a religiously plural world, we do not have to reject any of the great traditional themes of Christian thought; but we do need to use them in ways that are appropriate to our own situation in a world which has become consciously one. We do not need to reject the 'son of God' language in its application to Jesus, but rather need to understand it in its original Hebraic sense as designating a special servant of God. We do not need to reject the idea of the Trinity, but to understand it in its modalistic rather than in its ontological sense. We do not need to reject the identification of Jesus as our savior, but need to see him as saving us by making real to us God's gracious presence and love and claim and acceptance.

Since all of these ideas are already widespread within modern Christian consciousness, we can safely say that they constitute today a viable form of Christian faith. But we are at the same time aware that absolutist interpretations of all these themes are likewise widespread. They continue among most of the official and semi-official theologians of the churches. In addition to this there has been a considerable swing towards a fundamentalist Christianity, linked to right-wing political attitudes which are inimical to salvific human liberation. A struggle is going on for the soul of Christendom, and as theologians today we are privileged to be involved in that struggle.

Notes

1. Quoted in D.M. Baillie, *The Theology of the Sacraments, with a Biographical Essay by John Baillie* (New York: Scribners, 1957), 35 n.
2. *The Myth of God Incarnate*, ed. John Hick (London: SCM Press and Philadelphia: Westminster Press, 1977), 188.
3. *Dogmatics*, Vol. I (London: Lutterworth Press, 1949), 205.
4. John Downing, "Jesus and Martyrdom," *Journal of Theological Studies*, Vol. XIX, (1963), 284.
5. John Bowker, *Problems of Suffering in Religions of the World* (Cambridge University Press, 1970), 37.
6. *Zohar* 3:218A. Cited by Daniel Chanan Matt, Introduction to *Zohar: The Book of Enlightenment* (London: SPCK and New York: Paulist Press, 1983), 19. See also Matt's list of similar passages in his note 50, 196.

8

HOW DO YOU READ?

THE SCRIPTURES IN INTERFAITH DIALOGUE

Martin Forward

A LAWYER ASKS Jesus the very important question, "Teacher, what shall I do to inherit eternal life?" And Jesus replies, "What is written in the law? How do you read?" (Luke 10:25f.).

How we read Scripture is crucially important. All Scriptures need to be interpreted, and a variety of interpretations is often possible. For example, let us examine the lawyer's question in Luke. Both he and Jesus know that the love of God and then of neighbor lies at the heart of obedient faith. But how do they know? It is an interpretation of Scripture, which both men share, that it is so: the command to love God and neighbor is put together from different parts of the Pentateuch (Deut. 6:5 and Lev. 19:18). Within this shared interpretation of the meaning of Scripture, there is disagreement. The lawyer is interested in *who* is his neighbor, but Jesus' parable of the good Samaritan shows that our Lord reads from his Scripture *how* to be a neighbor to others.

How radical Jesus' parable was and is! By focusing on the quality of loving and not on who may or may not be loved, Jesus, at least implicitly, called into question notions which limited God's love, and ours, to a part of the human family.

The author of Luke-Acts resonated to this striking theme of neighborliness. The parable of the good Samaritan illustrates his characteristic portrayal of God's universal love and compassion, especially for the poor, the needy, and the outsider. If God is the kind of God Jesus showed him to be, nobody is outside his love, nor should be outside ours. Yet Mark (12:28–34) records the command to love God and neighbor in quite another way. Mark's concerns, his characteristic interpretations of the meaning of Jesus, are other than Luke's. This does not mean that one or other of the evangelists must be mistaken in his reading of the importance of Jesus. They were different people, with different temperaments, writing in varied circumstances to separate audiences. We are dealing here with a matter of *insights*, not with who is right and who is wrong.

Nor should we think of the lawyer as wrong. Rather, he needed the wisdom and compassion to hear the Scriptures afresh, so that they could lead him to deeper truth and understanding. One of Luke's characteristic themes is journeying or pilgrimage: faith is the way which encourages believers to deepen and broaden their vision of God.[1]

The Scriptures are constantly interpreted. They yield up different insights, depending upon who reads them, where, and in what circumstances. Indeed, the Hebrew and Christian Scriptures are themselves interpretations of God's activity in his world. When a Christian studies a passage of Scripture, he or she interprets what is already an interpretation.

The story of Philip's meeting with the Ethiopian official (Acts 8:26–40) shows that the Scriptures need an interpreter. What it does not make clear is that a variety of interpretations is possible. We shall see that not everybody would agree that the prophecy of Isa. 53 is about Jesus!

The fact that Scriptures need an interpreter in order to make sense has important consequences. For example, the use of proof-texts, whether John 1:19 or 14:6, Acts 4:12 or 10:34f., surely requires much more careful handling than has often been the case. Why were these verses and the contexts in which they appear written? For whom were they first written? What have they to say to Christians today, and will they say the same things in New York, Toronto, Leicester, Ibadan and Bombay? Certainly, the relationship between *eisegesis* and *exegesis* needs to be reexamined. There is always a tension, when we read the Bible, between reading it for what *it* says, and out of it what *we* need to find. *Eisegesis* is not altogether naughty; rather, scholars of Scripture have to advise us how we may accommodate it with integrity in our Bible study.

Moreover, Luke's account of the lawyer's conversation with Jesus raises the issue of what can be agreed on as central to faith (in their case, a common reading of their Scripture that love of God and then neighbor is crucial for the believer to ponder and live out) and what remains for insight and encounter and disciplined imagination to discover.

Such issues are for detailed discussion elsewhere. This paper proposes that people of faith can read each other's Scriptures with integrity and profit and illumination. For once we grant that a reading of our own Scriptures contains a measure of choice, *eisegesis*, and creative insight, it becomes hard to maintain a conviction that all other Scriptures are opaque to us, because we read them in the light of our own concerns and presuppositions. So, in part, we read our own!

If we are to read each other's Scriptures together, there are some preliminary necessities. We need a certain confidence in handling our Scriptures, and another's. Pilgrims will not necessarily be scholars. Some of us will read the Scriptures in translation. We shall rely on the writings of linguists, or on those participants in dialogue who have acquired a language or two. Our aim is that God may speak to us through the Scriptures. We must therefore read the Scriptures as competently as we are able. Scholarship is a tool to that end; we must neither scorn it, nor be terrorized by it.

I have written that our aim is that God may speak to us through our reading of each other's Scriptures. This means that another preliminary necessity to such a reading is the admission that we can encounter God, or rather, he can reveal himself to us, within an alien Scripture. There is not the space here to spell out the implications of the Johannine *logos* passage[2] (and other passages, especially in Hebrews and Pauline or Deutero-Pauline writings in the New Testament). But the insight there that God is for everyone everywhere as he was revealed in Christ, suggests that he is at work in the faith of others, and therefore in their Scriptures, a construct of that faith.

Wilfred Cantwell Smith has shown how it might be possible to perceive truth in the holy book of Islam. In his lecture, *Is the Qur'an the Word of God?*[3] he argues that the Qur'an has become true for Muslims when they have assumed it to be so and lived out its demands. Western scholars have had other aims in studying it. They have analyzed and studied it as a seventh century A.D. Arabian document. If they asked, "What would these sentences convey to me if I believed them to be God's word?," rather than, "What is here that has led Muslims to suppose that this is from God?," they would more effectively understand what has been happening for centuries in Muslim lands. This is a profound insight.

Maybe we should take this insight a little further. If we are open to see what another's Scripture means not only to him or her but also to us, we might suggest what that Scripture could come to mean. The dialogue described below between Christian and Jew, and Christian and Muslim will illustrate something of what I mean. Put simply, we may see in each other's Scriptures new and important insights, to be pondered and lived out.

Some people will be worried about this possibility, and will raise the specter of heresy. But that which is different from what we are used to is not always wrong. Indeed, many differences are not issues of truth, but matters of cultural and linguistic diversity and the like. Too many religious people confuse the ephemeral things of tribal identity with the everlasting truth! Conserving institutions like religions should and do examine novel insights carefully, but at best their members acknowledge new truth when they see and experience it.[4]

God is well able to take care of himself, though to listen to many religious people one would not think so. We do not need to worry overmuch about misinterpreting him, so long as we sincerely and expectantly wait upon him. Rather, we need to believe that God forgives and abides and communicates, despite both our untoward enthusiasms and our faint-hearted conservatism. After all, in such dialogue we do not aim to reshape doctrine but to encounter God. We may put it another way: we do not expect such encounters to change the substance of what we believe, but to confirm it and build upon it.

A very important preliminary necessity to such readings together is friendship. Not large groups, but two or three people who love and trust each other, should read the Scriptures together. They can be angry with each other, yet cope with that anger. They can explore holy things with a sense of humor that will not be misunderstood. Those who are not friends often lack the sensitivity such a reading requires. They may wish to score points, or to humiliate, or to condescend. His/her religion makes a person of faith deeply vulnerable. To talk of it to another is to risk a great deal: "I have spread my dreams under your feet; Tread softly because you tread on my dreams."[5] Hence the need for friendship that scorns the crusading mentality, that seeks to understand and learn, as well as to share and to offer.

Friendship does not shun questions of truth for the sake of a continuing relationship. Rather it enables matters of truth to be raised in ways in which they will be truly heard and considered. To scorn and sneer and score points: such a way does not incline the victim to ponder the jibes of the aggressor. But when we hear or speak the truth, as friend to friend, in love, that is a different matter. Then we are willing to hear, and the other will hear us too. For the Christian, this is not a simple tactical ploy. The Lord Jesus listened to people, valued people, loved people. No doubt some sneered at him for being the friend of sinners (Matt. 11:19; Luke 7:34). The point is surely that only by being the friend of someone, or at least friendly and open towards them, can you hope to change them, or be changed by them. Jesus' openness to others meant that he, too, was able to learn. For example, he, a Jew whose land was occupied by a foreign power, was amazed to discover the deep faith of a Roman soldier (Matt. 8:5–13; Luke 7:1–10). Surely, Christians must follow their Lord's example of openness and friendliness.

I shall now examine two passages from different Scriptures. The first raises issues for a Christian and a Jew, the second for a Christian and a Muslim. It is an exercise of the imagination discovering what *could* be the agenda and course of the discussion. Of course, dialogue about the Scriptures does not move along preordained paths! Obviously, more or other things can be said about the selected passages than the reflections offered here. However, people who have engaged in such readings together have a fair idea of the journey's itinerary! But perhaps the ride will be less rough than I describe it, or possibly more difficult.

The first passage is from the Hebrew Bible, Isa. 52:13–53:12. This is the last of the so-called 'Servant of the Lord' passages found scattered in the utterances of the unknown prophet of the Babylonian exile, recorded in chapters 40–55 of the book of Isaiah.

Although, if he or she is wise, the Christian will not mention the words 'Old Testament' at an early stage of the conversation, it is quite likely that his/her Jewish partner will raise the issue. If so, dialogue could be stifled almost at birth! For the Christian, the New Testament (or covenant) fulfills the old. The definition of the chosen people is widened to include the Gentiles, and the church is the means by which God brings all people into his covenant love. The Jew believes differently. The so-called 'Old' Testament is in fact the Hebrew Bible, a complete Scripture in its own right, whose boundaries were fixed *after* the life of Jesus, and whose teaching was developed in *mishnah* and *talmud* by the rabbis in the centuries following the destruction of Jerusalem by the Romans.

Either the Christian or Jew must be right, and the other wrong: or both could be wrong; surely, both cannot be right! So, at least, it would seem. What, then, is the point of a Jew and a Christian sitting down before a common possession which yields up radically different meanings to them? If dialogue is merely a matter of seeing as others see, then there may be some purpose, measured by deeper understanding. But if it is primarily about truth, then it is difficult to envisage how the presence and will of God can be discerned in such contrariness.

However, there is a way through this apparent *impasse*. It arises from a careful examination of the nature of Jewish religion at the time of Jesus, and its historical development. At that time, Judaism was hardly a unified phenomenon. Of the very different interpretations of Jewish religion represented by (among others) the Pharisees, Sadducees, Zealots, and followers of Jesus of Nazareth, only the first and last survived the war of 66–73 against Rome. Modern Judaism has developed from the former (although the interpretations of the Pharisees in the gospels are polemical, and fail to do justice to Pharisaism at its best),[6] and modern Christianity from the latter. So present-day Judaism and Christianity have become two separate religions, rather than remaining different interpretations of the same one. In the process, Judaism has preserved synagogue and (to some extent) race as normative values, whereas Christianity has abandoned both. Hence, there are profound differences between the two religions in the modern world, but to recognize their common origin is to admit that there may remain points of common agreement to be developed. Better this surely, both for the sake of truth and of potential reconciliation, than, as a Jew, regarding Christianity as a totally misguided form of universalism, or, as a Christian, interpreting Judaism primarily as an unfulfilled tribal religion.

As a matter of fact, our chosen passage raises the question of the possibility of meaningful dialogue acutely. No doubt because Christians have appropriated it to refer to the achievements of Jesus Christ, there is surprisingly little discussion of it in rabbinical writings.[7] A Jew and a Christian will therefore not wisely come to this passage until they have spent some time together in less contentious areas. But come to it at length they must, since one aim of dialogue is to cope with disagreement as well as common ground.

Who is this servant of the Lord, a tragic and noble figure whose sufferings heal the many?[8] For many Jews who have pondered this passage, not least in this troubled century of catastrophe yet restoration to the land of Israel, the servant is the Jewish community, so often persecuted and hounded, yet knowing God and sustained by him. This seems a credible interpretation. A Jew can point to Isa. 49:3, from one of the other servant passages, to show that the servant is there clearly identified as Israel. Those Christian scholars who argue that the word there is a later addition to the original text do seem guilty of special pleading!

Christian interpreters, beginning with some New Testament writers (we have already cited Acts 8:26–40), have identified Jesus as the servant of the Lord. Christians want to equate the redemptive suffering of the servant with the Lord's death at Calvary. Not only theology and spirituality, but also the stirring music of Handel's *Messiah* reinforce this conviction in an English-speaking Christian's breast. Yet the literary devices of that work ought to give the thinking believer pause for thought. The oratorio draws on Old and New Testament texts to point forward to and describe the career and destiny of Jesus. The still potent view in many Christian circles that the Hebrew Bible is chiefly a prophecy of the 'event' of Jesus is one which many Christians now feel unable to share. It seems doubtful whether full justice is done to the Hebrew Bible, even from a confessedly Christian viewpoint, by treating it as a spiritual Old Moore's almanac. So there remains, for such Christians, the problem of how, if at all, the servant passages can be related to the person and work of Jesus.

The Jew could at this point insist that he had the truth of the matter: the servant is Israel. But here, the Christian would want to speak the truth, as he or she sees it, in love. Events in modern Israel cast doubt on the notion that nations will be startled and kings shut their mouth at what they see—a suffering which redeems, and which, if other servant passages are taken into account, is universal in its scope (chapter 49:6). Arguably, whatever the political needs of the state of Israel, modern Israelis have deeply compromised their religious mission by their involvement in Lebanon and the West Bank. It is as if, in the wake of Hitler's 'final solution' of the Holocaust, some Jews have determined that pain and lack of identity and homeland shall never happen to them again, rather than never happen to *anyone* again. The deepest insights of the Hebrew Bible about God's universal love and justice have been ignored. We are back with a vengeance to that encounter between Jesus and a religious lawyer: how far must love go, God's and ours?

History makes it very difficult for a Christian to say this because the church has usually misrepresented Judaism and often persecuted Jews. Any rebuke in modern times can be interpreted as the latest in a long line of anti-Semitic propaganda. Yet we cannot be muzzled by history, or else nothing will ever change. Surely history must teach us, *how* to speak, not silence us. If a Christian feels compelled to raise this issue, he or she must realize his/her religion's sadly compromised dealings with the Jewish people and be prepared to listen in shame and sorrow.

There is another way of handling this passage. Maybe the important question is not *who* is the servant, but rather *how* can a person or people of God obediently serve him. After all, the prophet drew upon many sources to construct his picture of the servant. For example: Isa. 53:7 is reminiscent of Jer. 11:19; features of the god Tammuz can be discerned in 53:2, 10ff.; and the description of a man judged to be the object of divine displeasure, meriting human avoidance, 53:1ff., calls Job to mind, 30:5, 10. But the servant is not Jeremiah, a dying and rising god, or Job. Nor is he the king, the prophet himself, or any other individual figure whose influence has been seen in the servant songs and particularly in the passage under discussion.

The *vocation* of God's people was, it seems to me, in the forefront of the prophet's mind. The people of God had disobeyed him: calamity and exile was their punishment. How then could they make redemptive use of their humiliation and pain? The prophet interpreted his past to give hope to the exiled Jews of his day that suffering and sin were not the end of the story. Bravely and faithfully borne, they could effect healing for themselves and for others.

To be sure, the prophet was, in this view, equating the servant with Israel. But Israel's vocation was uppermost in his mind. And it seems extraordinary and telling to me that he did not hesitate to borrow from "pagan" religions to help draw his picture of the servant. Indeed, is it not from Tammuz that biblical notions of the redemptive possibilities of death and resurrection find a point of origin? Jew and Christian, both monotheists, might ponder this suggestion together!

What kind of God did the prophet believe in, who makes weal and creates woe, who is destroyer and savior? He is the God, constant in his grace and judgment, who spoke of old to Abraham, and continues to tell his will, who showed his might in the first exodus, and will bring about an even more impressive restoration of his people to their land (51:1–3; 43; 14–21).

If it is a true insight that God is constant in his grace and judgment, then the servant passage(s) can speak to both Jews and Christians in their varied histories. Maybe each can describe historical events and personal experiences, moments when the truth about redemptive suffering, most movingly described by the prophet, has become true for them. Certainly, if suffering, within the constancy of God's grace and judgment, can result in healing and restoration, then, for the Christians, the Scripture at this point speaks supremely of Jesus. Equally, the Scripture here speaks to the Jews of their people's tragic, faithful, and brave history, of Hitler's "Final Solution" and of Jewish repossession of the Promised Land.

Neither of these interpretations is necessarily wrong. If God's constancy means, among other things, that the suffering of his servants can heal them and others, then both the crucifixion of Jesus and modern Jewish history are arenas in which servanthood can be discerned, and authenticated by faithful living. Equally, of course, if a Christian or Jew claims servanthood without embodying it, or else denies its importance as a part of the life of faith, this raises questions about his/her integrity or understanding of Scripture.

A Jew and a Christian may not get this far in their reading together. To travel further would be even more difficult, not least because the Christian will want to say things about God's involvement in the sufferings of Jesus which would not meet with his/her partner's assent. But if the Christian began with a different proposition, talking of God's involvement *with* the sufferings of Jesus, rather than *in* them, perhaps even here, fruitful conversation could take place.

If a *Sunni* Muslim were to join in the conversation, at this stage he or she might want to ask, "Have Jews and especially Christians made too much of the possibility that suffering is redemptive?" When a Christian and a Muslim read the Scriptures together, there is not the difficulty of (as in our first passage) a common Scripture interpreted by divergent histories. Instead, equally divisive, there are accounts of common heroes, differently understood. Let us imagine two partners, Christian and Muslim, discussing these words from the Holy Qur'an, 4:15ff., which describe a list of ways in which Jews have not kept faith with God:

> ...their uttering against Mary a mighty calumny, and for their saying, 'We slew the Messiah, Jesus son of Mary, the Messenger of God'—yet they did not slay him, neither crucified him, only a likeness of that was shown to them. Those who are at variance concerning him surely are in doubt regarding him; they have no knowledge of him, except the following of a surmise; and they slew him not of a certainty—no indeed; God raised him up to Him; God is All-Might, All-Wise.[9]

Many figures from the Hebrew Bible and the New Testament turn up in the Qur'an, but stories about them are differently told, and point up different morals and meanings.

For Christians, these differences are most sharply focused in the Qur'anic descriptions of Jesus.[10] To be sure, he is regarded as the Messiah, but that title or function is emptied of any meaning that Christians would attach to it. The plain fact is that Jesus is a relatively unimportant figure in the Qur'an, not at all portrayed in ways consonant with New Testament assessments of him. Christians need to admit and struggle with their Lord's role in the Qur'an as a member of the supporting cast in a different presentation of the drama of salvation. Jesus is mentioned in only 15 of the Qur'an's 114 chapters, and in 93 of its 6226 verses! For all the honor that Muslims accord him, not only is he radically reinterpreted, but also, if all the Qur'anic references to him had never been recorded, the substance of orthodox *Sunni* Islam (and, indeed, of *Shiah* Islam) would remain the same.[11] In the Qur'an, Jesus serves to confirm Muslim convictions that certain prophets were sent to particular communities, preaching monotheism and judgment. He was prophet to the Jews, as Moses was to the Egyptians, and so forth. He is one such example, not as important as, say, Abraham, still less Muhammad himself.

Perhaps at an early stage of dialogue, the Christian and the Muslim can agree to avoid discussing passages about Jesus for the while. Some Christians will see this as a kind of betrayal, or as a complete "watering down" of what guides their religious journey. I think that, so long as one keeps at the center of one's conversation the kind of God Jesus revealed him to be, there is no reason why the Christian cannot, for some time, talk about God without mentioning Jesus.

Let us assume that the Christian and Muslim have reached the stage of being able to discuss the aforementioned Qur'anic passage without their talks breaking down because of the issues raised. The Muslim might first of all assure the Christian that to call Jesus the son of Mary implies no taunt about her wantonness. In fact, the beginning of our passage criticizes Jews for spreading this 'mighty calumny.' Nevertheless, Jesus is the son of Mary, and not the son of God. The Christian will want to know why, and may be told:

> He (God) is God, One,
> God, the Everlasting Refuge,
> who has not begotten, and has not been begotten,
> and equal to Him is not anyone. (*Surah* 112).

The Muslim finds repugnant any notion that God is involved sexually with a woman and denies that he is one of three. So does the Christian, who could amaze the Muslim by telling him so. The language of Christian belief and devotion is analogical, poetical. It uses words, often paradoxically, to describe unutterable mysteries. Muslims have misunderstood, in part because Christians have misrepresented or carelessly described their own religion. How often Christians have turned trinitarianism into tri-theism and given the impression that Jesus is the physical son of God!

Both Muslims and Christians are monotheists. But careful reflection on the meaning each gives to God's unity will point to profound differences. These surface in our passage. God thwarts the evil determination of the Jews to kill the Messiah. Quite how, the passage does not make clear. The Arabic words translated by "Only a likeness of that was shown to them" are very difficult to understand. Do they mean that Jesus' likeness was given to another, perhaps to Judas Iscariot or Simon of Cyrene? Or do they mean that the Jews' intention to kill Jesus seemed to have been carried out, but that the appearance of death was an illusion since God raised Jesus to himself? If so, this could lead to a fascinating conversation about the meaning of resurrection. Or does the passage deny, not the death of Jesus, but rather, that the Jews crucified him? In fact, the ambiguity and unknowability of the verses' meaning tell us a great deal about Muslims' reflections on God's ways in his world. He is answerable only to himself, his will (and certainly not his need to communicate it) is his main attribute. If the implication of the passage is that God does not want the Messiah killed (is it?), all we may deduce is that this is so. God does not have to provide reasons for his actions. Christians would say (more clearly than Muslims would), that God's actions reveal his nature.

The crucifixion is a sign, not of three gods' inability to act coherently, but of the one God's loving involvement with his creation and of his power which works through weakness to overcome evil.

Muslims read in the Qur'an about the signs of God. These are things in the world which tell the pagan or remind the forgetful of God. Perhaps, then, the Christian can ask the Muslim whether these signs, many of them quite commonly observed: water, cattle, fruit, birds, and so on, in any way tell of God's character as well as his demands. And maybe the Christian can go on to suggest that, for him or her, Jesus is *the* sign of God in and to his world, the focus for Christians of God's nature and will.

Other implications of this passage will lead to even greater divisions between Christian and Muslim. Although it rebukes Christians, implying that if they cannot agree among themselves, they must be following a surmise and not hard knowledge, for the Christian this will not be convincing. For him/her the Qur'an is valueless as an accurate record of Jewish and Christian history. The New Testament is not a compendium of exact historical information (*pace* Muhammad and many others, including many Christians, it was never intended to be such), but because it is closer in time to the events it describes, it gives a proximate and credible account of the 'event' of Jesus, and is an authentic witness to his impact upon some of his earliest followers. From a historian's point of view, the Qur'anic accounts of Jesus are only an interesting quarry from which to unearth the influences of unorthodox Christians upon the mind of a remarkable seventh-century Arab. The Muslim will be shocked by this assumption that the Qur'an is to be attributed to the prophet Muhammad, since an orthodox believer deems it to be actually the word of God, conveyed to the prophet by the angel Gabriel. So there is an *impasse*. The Muslim believes his/her scripture to be precisely the word of God and is disinclined to let the Christian question its literal truth. Moreover, he or she might presuppose that the New Testament is not worth reading because, as is widely assumed among Muslims, Christians have added spurious material to their holy book, whose teachings are to be found undistorted in the Qur'an. The Christian believes that the word of God is a human being, Jesus, who is misunderstood and trivialized in Muslim belief.

It is difficult to see how such division can be overcome. So be it. There are profound differences between religions, some of them deeply divisive, and it does no service to truth and to meaningful human relations to paper over the cracks.

If a Jew were to join this conversation he or she would point up an even deeper divide. The passage is one of several in the Qur'an which condemn the Jews for their faithlessness. No doubt this can be explained as arising out of Muhammad's troubled dealings with Jews. But the orthodox Muslim's conviction that the Qur'an is *God's* word, not his prophet's, with its usual accompanying assumption that the word has an eternal reference and authority, has had a disastrous impact on Jewish/Muslim relations in the modern world.

I recall an occasion when I was talking to Muslim villagers in Pakistan. They had never been near Israel, nor met a Jew and were very angry with me when I told them that I had visited Israel. At the time, we were discussing our passage. One young man then quoted Surah 5:85 to me, to convince me that Muslims and Christians should show solidarity against Jews:

> Thou wilt surely find the most hostile of men to the believers are the Jews and the idolaters; and thou wilt surely find the nearest of them in love to the believers are those who say, 'We are Christians';...

To be sure, issues between Israelis and Palestinians in modern times have muddled waters, but these words from the Qur'an show the waters to have been already troubled! In such circumstances, suggesting that the Jews are in a special relationship to God by being *ahl-ul-kitab*, people with a book, and that they were well treated by Muslims in earlier times when Islam's temporal power was great, is not heard, or at least, not seen to be convincing.

"How do you read?" The encounter between Jesus and the lawyer shows the scope for *intra*-religious disagreement about the meaning of Scripture. But it also shows how holy writ can come alive with new and renewing power. Similarly, friends across the boundaries of faith may find agonizing divisions. We are back to the need for *friends* to dialogue, not strangers. Friends can cope with the pain of disagreement, will keep together, and will assuredly find blessing too.

Certainly, those who read the Scriptures together should do so in awe, wonder, and expectation. Those who do so with serious intent, believe that God speaks to human beings through holy writ, often with unexpected and troubling impact, but always for the good of those who wait upon him. We read, not primarily as scholars, and certainly not as polemicists, but as pilgrims. We abide in the hope that God will speak to us according to our common and individual needs and his will for us.

Notes

1. M. H. F. Forward, "Pilgrimage: Luke/Acts and the World of Religions," *King's College Theological Review*, London, Vol. 8/1, Spring 1985, 9–11.
2. Still the best account of what *logos* Christology meant and means in multi-faith societies is the relevant chapter in A. C. Bouquet, *Christian Faith and Non-Christian Religions* (Nisbet, 1959). And note the comment of C. F. D. Moule, *The Birth of the New Testament* (London: A and C Black, 1962): "The Epistles to the Colossians (i.15ff.) and to the Hebrews (i.1ff.) both contain a 'logos-doctrine' in all but the actual term" (167).
3. Contained in W. G. Oxtoby, *Religious Diversity* (New York: Harper and Row, 1976), 22–40. Page 31 is particularly helpful.
4. The conserve-ing (better this ungainly word, than the misleading, conservative) role of religions as systems is illuminatingly described in J. Bowker, *Licensed Insanities* (London: Darton, Longman and Todd, 1987), 112–143.
5. These words are from W. B. Yeats' poem, *He Wishes for the Cloths of Heaven*. Thomas Dunhill's (1877–1946) setting of it to music adds a poignant dimension to their meaning.
6. A helpful presentation is that by W. D. Davies, *Introduction to Pharisaism* (Philadelphia: Fortressa, 1967).
7. See the helpful discussion by U. Simon, *A Theology of Salvation* (London: SPCK, 1953), 198ff.
8. There are any number of helpful commentaries on our passage. As well as these, helpful if somewhat dated is C. R. North, *The Suffering Servant in Deutero-Isaiah* (Oxford: OUP, 1956).
9. Translations of the Qur'an quoted in the text are by A. Arberry, *The Koran Interpreted* (Oxford: The World's Classics, 1964).
10. The best introduction for the general reader to the issues involved is that by G. Parrinder, *Jesus in The Qur'an* (London: Sheldon Press, 1976).
11. Jesus plays a central role in the *Sufi* or mystical traditions of Islam and in popular but not entirely orthodox views about his role in future days.

9

ECUMENISM AND THE PROBLEM OF RELIGIOUS LANGUAGE

Francis Xavier D'Sa

ANY TRADITION, even a religious tradition, is primarily transmitted through language. For tradition becomes tradition only after it has entered the realm of language.[1] And meaning, the life-blood of language, lives on only in a language. As fish cannot live out of water, so no real meaning can exist outside of language. For as Hans-Georg Gadamer puts it, "language is the real medium of human being, if we only see it in the realm that it alone fills out, the realm of human being-together, the realm of common understanding, of ever-replenished common agreement, a realm as indispensable to human life as the air we breathe."[2] It might therefore be of some help to the study of religion and ecumenism to reflect on the nature of language in general and of religious language in particular.

In this essay I shall argue that what is expressed in language is always and necessarily partial and tentative, that therefore expressions of absolutistic claims in religious traditions have to be *interpreted* differently, and that ecumenism or an ecumenical attitude is a hermeneutic necessity for a correct self-understanding of all religious traditions.[3] I shall begin with the revelatory nature of Reality, and then point to the fragmentary character of human understanding. It will become clear that in spite of the 'all-disclosive' nature of Reality, human beings can *grasp* only an aspect of this disclosure; that humans cannot focus on the whole of Reality but only on certain aspects of it. I shall argue that only these aspects find their expressions in language, and that language, incapable of describing the whole event of understanding in detail, merely highlights some points of reference in the event. I shall further argue that religious language possesses the same characteristics as ordinary language; but that, in addition, it is able in and through these characteristics to transmit the claims and the appeal that Reality makes on us.

In this way the specificity of religious language as well as its inability to contain absolutistic claims will become clear. In light of this I examine the absolutistic claims of Christianity and indicate how they can be meaningfully interpreted today. In conclusion, I shall suggest that the uniqueness of Christian revelation can be upheld not by rejecting or downgrading the claims to uniqueness of other faith traditions but by acknowledging the complementarity of all religious traditions, since all uniqueness is ultimately grounded in the unique Mystery of which every revelation is only a partial manifestation.

Disclosure of Reality

One of the most obvious (and therefore probably one of the most overlooked) facts is the disclosure of Reality on all sides at all times and at all levels. The truth of Reality consists essentially in its continual self-disclosure. What this implies is that what we call Reality (all that *is*) exposes itself fully and completely without any intermittence.[4]

To be is to be present, "to be-fore us," to appear, to become manifest; hence being present ("being there") is not to be interpreted in a univocal manner. Being present happens in a variety of ways depending on the kind of entity in question. Further, presence of one kind can make us blind to other kinds of presence, to say nothing of the concealing side of Reality.[5] However, the gap between the disclosure of Reality and our grasp of it is due not merely to the concealing side of Reality. Human understanding itself is to a great extent responsible for this.

All Understanding Is Partial

There are two senses in which our understanding is partial. In the first sense, partial refers to our "prejudices" which are operative in us and which make us partial to selected aspects of Reality's disclosure. In the second sense, partiality refers to the fact that our understanding can never be exhaustive and total; but that it is incomplete and open-ended. It is always "on the way" to understanding.[6]

By prejudices are meant not so much the psychological prejudices in the pejorative sense of being prejudiced but in the sense rehabilitated by Gadamer.[7] Prejudices refer to our pre-understanding that is formed and shaped by our respective traditions in and through the meanings that are operative in them. Each tradition is really a world of meaning in which both the individual and the society as a whole relate and function.[8] We view and do everything in and through such living meanings.

The other sense in which our understanding is partial lays stress on a different and, for our purposes, more important aspect of the understanding process; namely that all understanding is essentially incomplete and basically open-ended. Whatever is understood is understood, in spite of our best efforts, partially, never exhaustively. This is so because understanding means getting an answer to a specific question. The question is usually implicit and non-thematized. Nevertheless it directs our search in a specific direction without which no understanding would be possible and because of which our understanding is focused but fragmentary.

Understanding is possible because of the question that is posed. If no question is posed, no understanding is possible. Reality in its disclosure makes manifest its claims, and only those claims are heeded which answer our question. If there were no quest, we would be gaping, not perceiving, hearing, listening. "Being there" in the midst of the inexhaustible disclosure of Reality we can respond to the claims of Reality only in as much as our antenna has been tuned by our pre-understanding to a particular sphere. Our understanding is in fact the outcome of a piecemeal process. Consequently all understanding is continually "on the way," never definitive, much less exhaustive.

Does this mean then that our understanding is never "objective"? In a context such as ours, it is best to avoid the subjective-objective kind of language. However, if we insist on using it, we could state the following: if by objective we mean something more than our own prejudices and projections, then understanding is surely objective; but it is not objective in the sense that our understanding is unaffected by our pre-understanding.

Positively put, understanding is both an appropriation and an approximation. It is an appropriation because our understanding happens piecemeal and not exhaustively. It is an approximation, not an "apprehension" of the thing because we enter the realm ("openness") of Reality from a specific point of view only. From the vast panorama of Reality's inexhaustible disclosure, a questioning being picks up only that aspect which corresponds to his search. The disclosure of Reality impinges on us and we pick up only that which answers our question, because our understanding is circumscribed by all that we have understood previously.

But if this is so, how can we ever understand things we have never known before? When it is asserted that understanding is limited by what has been understood before, what is meant is that understanding occurs in as much as that which is to be understood corrects, confirms, challenges, or qualifies what has been understood. Understanding occurs *in as much as* the thing to be understood is understood as having something to do with what has been understood before. Reality is one continuous whole; and every part is connected with every other part, and since there are leaps neither in Reality nor in understanding, understanding of Reality occurs through connections and interconnections with what has been previously understood. If the thing to be understood were totally unconnected with what has been understood before, no understanding could ever take place.

The Event of Understanding

Understanding—namely, the process in which the question shaped by the pre-understanding is answered by the disclosure of Reality—is an event. Understanding is not just gaping but begins as an active search for an answer to a specific question, and ends in the fulfillment of this search. This is an event because understanding is not a mere addition to the stock of our information; understanding affects our whole being. Not only the extension of our understanding but also its intensity determines the degree of our being affected. Due to this "affection" our very being is revised and recreated; and our vision of ourselves, however dim and non-thematic, undergoes a change, and our values and attitudes are transformed to the degree in which we are affected. This is the significance of the event of understanding.

Moreover, in this process our pre-understanding too is revised. Here we have the famous hermeneutic circle. Every act of understanding is determined by the pre-understanding and in turn transforms the pre-understanding itself. The whole affects the part and the part revises the whole.[9]

Event and Language

The event of understanding does not stop there but goes on to become word. Its impact on the knower is verbalized and expressed in language. Our whole being is revised and our language is affected by this; we then begin to speak in accordance with this "affection." Event becomes word as it enters the realm of language.

Speaking of an event might create the impression that it is an independent entity or process. This is far from being the case. The event, though a "whole," is in reality an integral part of the whole cosmos. Hence, when we speak of an event, we are really referring to an aspect of Reality. Understanding is a piece-meal process which concentrates on such aspects called "events." This narrowing down is what is known as the first "closuring."[10] Language speaks of definite events, but through them it is capable of evoking the whole of Reality. Unable to *grasp* the whole disclosure of Reality, language concentrates on aspects and through them responds to the wholeness-claims of Reality.

There is, however, a second closuring through language. If the first closuring concentrates on certain *aspects of Reality*, the second closuring zeroes in on certain *aspects of the event*. For language does not describe the event in its totality; it picks and chooses aspects that outline the event. In this both the piece-meal nature of the process of understanding and the specifying function of language ("saying something about something") are instrumental. Understanding focuses on an event of Reality (first closuring) and language picks and chooses some aspects of this event (second closuring).[11] Let us take the following example:

> With what can we compare the kingdom of God, or what parable shall we use for it? It is like the grain of mustard seed, which, when sown upon the ground, is the smallest of all the seeds on earth; yet when it is sown it grows up and becomes the greatest of all shrubs, and puts forth large branches, so that the birds of the air can make nests in its shade (Mark 4:30–32).

If we limit our discussion just to the process through which the mustard seed goes till it grows up into the greatest of all shrubs, we realize how sketchy the description is. What is an extremely complex process is merely outlined with the help of a few phrases. The first closuring takes place when it is the mustard seed that is spoken of, and the second closuring is achieved by merely hinting at the whole process of growth. Now these are not two separate closurings. Our understanding closured by our pre-understanding is further narrowed down in our linguistic expression. Paradoxically, the linguistic expression *as* text enjoys "semantic autonomy," turning the closuring into a door to the house of interpretation.

From Language to Event

The linguistic expression of a significant event leads back to the event usually through the path of interpretation. A linguistic account of an event, however sketchy and inadequate, is pregnant with innumerable possibilities which are grist to the mill of interpretation. Though not all linguistic accounts of events are equally "heavily" pregnant, a linguistic account as such admits of a plurality of interpretations.[12] However, the worth and the validity of an interpretation are to be gauged from their ability to lead back to the Meaningfulness which gave birth to the original event.

For this to occur, of course, some knowledge of the circumstances of the historical event is a great help. Though this in itself does not deserve the importance that is sometimes accorded it by some historico-critical exegetes (who appear to be under the illusion that this is the real meaning of the text), it is nonetheless not a matter that one can afford to neglect with impunity. To my mind, the importance of the search for and the study of the historical context derives from the fact that it can greatly assist in identifying the "semantic axes," the real thrust of the text.[13]

Having discovered the thrust of the text which refers to the event, an interpreter attempts to make the thrust relevant to the situation of the reader. It is not the historical event of the Exodus, for example, that is to be made relevant to the modern reader; rather it is the Exodus interpreted as an event of liberation that is of relevance to all. An interpretation tries to show that this liberative thrust is of significance even to today's readers and their world.[14]

The Language of Religion

If by religion we mean the communitarian search for Meaningfulness, then the language that emerges from, and at the same time embodies, such Meaningfulness is religious language. In such an understanding of religion, Meaningfulness is an important point of reference. It will therefore not be out of place to say a word about it here.

Meaningfulness manifests itself when human beings respond to the call of Reality and thus discover the truth of Reality. That is why Meaningfulness is ultimate, immediate, and holistic. Ultimacy refers to the obvious and unquestioned horizon against which something becomes meaningful. Immediacy excludes mediation, and, in our context, it means that what is meaningful is so in and by itself without any intermediary. Finally, holism implies that no area is left out, but that every dimension is included. A meaningful experience is holistic in two ways: first, it is a total whole which makes sense by itself; and, second, such an experience affects not just this or that aspect but the whole person and in some ways the whole (cosmic) community.

The effects of Meaningfulness are important since they validate the authenticity of a meaningful occurrence. The effects are dual: the centripetal, which concentrates on the internal freedom of persons and the centrifugal, which sees to the welfare of all.

A religious experience, when it is foundational, founds a tradition where such experience is preserved, proclaimed, and structured in such a manner that it is institutionalized and routinized.

However, the language of Meaningfulness (i.e., the language of religion) is always symbolic, dogmas and doctrines not withstanding. Symbolic language is the language of myth and metaphor, parable, and prophecy. In religious language, to use Heidegger's terminology, the ontic points to the ontological, or, in Panikkar's words, the symbol manifests, makes present, the symbolized.[15]

It is important to grasp the full import of this. The language of pragmatic practice pretends to inform us how things function, even though this is always done approximately and not exhaustively. Symbolic language on the other hand tells us what a meaningful experience is like.[16] This is so because symbols have to do with Meaningfulness; thus only symbolic (poetic) language, the language of metaphors, is an appropriate "way" to Reality.[17] "Object"-language concentrates on information and description but symbolic language, because it communicates the claim of Reality, has to do with the truth of Reality.[18]

Consequently, symbolic language cannot be the language of absolutes, of "either/or" or of exclusive claims. Absolutes and exclusive claims belong to the sphere of the logical and the mathematical where definitions are of the essence and precision is the goal. In the realm of symbols where the concern is about the call of and response to Reality, precise information can neither be required nor acquired.

Religion and Religions

Religion derives from and leads to Meaningfulness. When a religious experience is sufficiently foundational it attracts followers and forms *a* religion, that is, a religious tradition which is *a* way to religion as described above. In course of time a religious tradition develops its doctrines and dogmas, its rites and rituals through which it preserves, proclaims, and routinizes its foundational experience. Religions, or religious traditions, are the outcome of foundational experiences.[19]

The attracting potential of a foundational experience is so enormous that it can fulfill the thirst for Significance, not only of the original founder or founding community but of all those who are open to it.[20] From such a foundational experience arises a whole *Weltanschauung*, a complete set of attitudes and values, and above all an integrated belief-system. This is due to the fact that Meaningfulness is a totality. However, because of our finitude, our experience of Meaningfulness is partial and episodic, neither exhaustive nor definitive. It is not exhaustive because human beings are parts of a larger community on whom they depend for their experience of Meaningfulness. It is not definitive because of human fallibility.

The Absolute Character and Uniqueness of Christian Revelation

Christians have argued for the absolute character of Christian Revelation both eloquently and elaborately, but they seem to have done this in the monadic world of Christendom.[21] In spite of the fact that lately Christianity has taken note of the existence, and in some cases, of the powerful following of some of the world religions, Christian theologians do not always appear to be aware that all their arguments in favor of the absolute and unique character of Christian revelation could, *mutatis mutandis*, be applicable with equal force to these religious traditions too. Besides, theologians often overlook the fact that almost all the major religions lay claim to one or another type of absolutism.[22] Christian theologians have still to formulate their arguments in favor of the absolute and unique character of their religious traditions while taking into account the absolutistic claims of other world religions and the fact that neither understanding nor language is capable of sustaining absolute claims which can stand scrutiny.

Sometimes it is argued that it is neither Christianity nor its theologians that claim uniqueness for their revelation. It is revelation itself that proclaims its absolute and unique character.[23] Such an argument presupposes that divine revelation hands over to us a deposit of clear-cut, unambiguous beliefs which are intelligible to all peoples of all cultures and all times without the help of any interpretation; it presupposes that divine revelation can fully and adequately be grasped by human beings and fully and adequately expressed in human language. Clearly such claims are arbitrary, even irrational, ignoring as they do the human condition.

First of all, even the fullness of divine revelation cannot do away with the finitude and fallibility of human beings, for to do so would be to do away with the fact of their being human. The human condition implies finitude and fallibility.

Second, divine revelation, in spite of its fullness and inexhaustibility, is received by finite and fallible human beings whose grasp and expression of it are anything but absolute and unique.

Finally, words like absolute and unique, as employed in language, mean neither absolute nor unique. Absolute means non-conditioned and non-conditional. The word absolute denies the state of being conditioned. Unique means only relatively unique, and though sometimes it is actually intended to mean absolutely unique, it *cannot* mean that since in human experience there is nothing that is absolutely unique; and if there were anything absolutely unique it would be for human beings as good as nonintelligible. Similarly, there is in human experience nothing that is nonconditional; on the contrary, everything that is understood is understood as conditioned and as conditional. Above all, contexts from which absolutistic claims are deduced are usually proclamatory, not philosophical treatises.

Exclusive and absolute uniqueness cannot be rationally defended. On the other hand a case can be made for relative uniqueness. Exclusive uniqueness believes that one tradition alone possesses normative uniqueness, whereas inclusive uniqueness holds that religious traditions are all relatively unique in some form or another and that they need not necessarily exclude one another.[24]

Along these lines we could say that Christian revelation, like other revelations, is relatively and inclusively unique. Like a mountain that is seen from different perspectives, the mountain of Meaningfulness is experienced from uniquely different perspectives. No view is perfectly identical with others; no view is totally unconnected with the others; no view is more right than the rest; each has its specificity and vantage point and none can be taken as the stand to measure the others. To know the mountain one has to know it from different angles; other than this there is no way of knowing it. There is no mountain for us apart from the perspectives, though the mountain is not the sum of its perspectives. The perspectives are the viewers' experiences of the mountain.

Christian revelation as one of the many perspectives can claim to be unique, relatively unique. However, even relative uniqueness is not given *ipso facto* when one lays claim to it. A tradition has to present its credentials by manifesting in its values and attitudes, its commitment and beliefs, the aspects of internal freedom and external commitment to the welfare to all.[25]

The Wider Ecumenism

A major hurdle in the path of the Christian as well as the wider ecumenical enterprise is the fact that every tradition tends to make absolutistic and exclusivistic claims, without taking into serious consideration the unique claims of the other traditions. Because they neglect to reflect on the nature of human understanding and language, they are prone to interpret their Scriptures and traditions as if they were informative-descriptive statements.

By now it should be obvious that no absolutistic claims can be upheld in the human realm. Even when linguistic expressions tend to appear absolutistic there remains the further task of interpreting them, first from the context—which is usually proclamatory[26]—and second, from the standpoint of the nature of language and understanding. Interpretation that is based on blind loyalty to one's tradition is of course suspect from the start. It has to be undertaken in a context where the claims of all the religious traditions are taken seriously and the characteristics of human understanding and language are not ignored.[27] If this is done, then it will be seen that the concept of relative uniqueness will fit in here very appropriately.

There is, however, a further point to be considered in this context. The differing claims to uniqueness have somehow to be related. It is difficult to maintain these diverse claims if they are totally unrelated to each other. If relative uniqueness is to make sense in each case, there has to be some sort of organic interconnectedness between the claims. Such interconnection has to be seen both from the side of Meaningfulness as well as from the side of the religious traditions. In the final analysis all uniqueness is grounded in Ultimate Meaningfulness. Uniqueness is possible only if a religious tradition derives from ultimate Meaningfulness. Otherwise the validity of such a tradition cannot be upheld.

Given this common source of all the traditions, it follows that the different perspectives of the mountain of Meaningfulness must be organically interconnected. However varied and diverse the views of the mountain may be, they are still views of the same mountain. Or to change the metaphor, the different parts of the human body are organically interrelated not only because they together form one body but because the whole organism is animated by one and the same Spirit. Hence identity-in-difference, as the characteristic of all uniqueness, has to be the hermeneutic principle that discovers the interrelatedness of all traditions belonging to the same body and animated by the same Absolute Spirit.

Finally, the path that leads to the discovery of interrelatedness is a dual one: the study of the specific symbolism of each tradition as expressed in its rites and rituals, in its beliefs and doctrines *and* the *communicatio in sacris mythis* of these traditions. Study should be such that it should lead to openness, openness to the Myth of the other traditions. It is only when we enter into the Myth of these traditions that we are able to understand,

stand under the spell of these traditions.[28] This need not, however, mean that the traditions have to give up their specific character. On the contrary, complementarity will highlight the specificity of each tradition.

Conclusion

It might appear that I have given undue importance to the role of language and have overestimated its contribution to the field of ecumenism. As I see it, language plays a far more important role in our lives than is commonly realized. It is so pervasive that we are hardly aware of its unique mode of being. The general tendency is to consider language as a mere tool. As a matter of fact the tool-aspect of language is only one aspect which is more often than not misunderstood. For language is not like any other tool which after use we can set aside.[29] Rather it is such that all understanding expresses itself only in and through language. Without language, understanding cannot express itself. No understanding can take place without language, and without understanding there is no language.[30] Language is the expression of what we understand. The understood finds expression in language. Hence Gadamer's dictum: "Being that can be understood is language."[31]

However, language and understanding are different, and that difference is fundamental, as fundamental as the symbolic difference between symbol and symbolized reality.[32] The symbols are the expression and the symbolized reality is the expressed. The main function of the symbol is to lead to and express the symbolized reality.

Applying this to symbol-language and the symbolized reality of Meaningfulness, it should be clear that the symbol-language of religion purports to lead to Meaningfulness; and that doctrines about uniqueness and absoluteness cannot be part of such symbol language, and that therefore they cannot really belong to divine revelation.

Given the nature and function of religious language, I am suggesting that an ecumenical attitude is the only sensible way of looking at religious pluralism, and this not from any strategic considerations. The one-sided view of the mountain of Meaningfulness that each tradition (rightly) proclaims has to be (equally rightly) complemented by the other views of the mountain as proclaimed by the other traditions. Such complementarity will necessarily correct exaggerated claims made by the religious traditions. More importantly, traditions will realize not only what they do not have and where they need to be complemented, but also what they have always had in their tradition but have for one reason or another consistently overlooked.

Notes

1. Hans-Georg Gadamer, *Truth and Method* (London: Sheed and Ward, 1975), 351. "The relation between language and understanding is seen primarily in the fact that it is the nature of tradition to exist in the medium of language, so that the preferred object of interpretation is a linguistic one."
2. *Philosophical Hermeneutics*, translated and edited by David E. Linge (Berkeley: University of California Press, 1977), 68.
3. In the following paper I shall be using expressions like absolutistic, absolute, unique, and uniqueness to mean normative for all. If normativeness is exclusive it will mean that there is no other revelation that is accepted or acceptable as normative; if it is inclusive or relative it means that other traditions are accepted or acceptable as also normative.
4. See in this connection M. Heidegger's brilliant essay, "On the Essence of Truth," *Existence and Being* (London: Vision, 1949), 319–351, esp. 333ff.
5. *Ibid.*, esp. 340.
6. See M. Heidegger, "The Way to Language," *On the Way to Language* (New York: Harper & Row, 1971), 111–136.
7. Gadamer, *Truth and Method*, 245ff.
8. For example, a person brought up in a materially highly developed region of the world will have a pretty superficial understanding of cow dung as compared to the understanding of it in members of the rural areas of India. In the first case it will probably be taken as a mere label for an entity connected with a biological function of a cow; but in the second case it is a word for something connected very closely with the necessities of life in the rural regions of India.
9. See Gadamer, *Truth and Method*, 258 ff., esp. 261–262.
10. The closuring is due to the selectivity produced by our pre-understanding. See Gadamer, *Truth and Method*, 235ff.
11. See J. Severino Croatto, *Biblical Hermeneutics. Towards a Theory of Reading as the Production of Meaning* (New York: Orbis Books, 1984), 32f. and 40f.
12. See R. Panikkar, "The Texture of a Text. Response to P. Ricoeur," *Point of Contact* 5 (1978), 50–64.
13. J. Severino Croatto, *Biblical Hermeneutics*, 58.
14. *Ibid.*, 60–65.
15. See Joseph J. Kockelmans, "Ontological Difference, Hermeneutics, and Language," in *On Heidegger and Language*, edited and translated by Joseph J. Kockelmans (Evanston: Northwestern University Press, 1972), 195–234, esp. 206ff. Also R. Panikkar, *Myth, Faith & Hermeneutics* (New York: Paulist Press, 1979), 6f.
16. See P. Ricoeur, *Interpretation Theory. Discourse and the Surplus of Meaning* (Fort Worth: Texas Christian University Press, 1976), 68.
17. *Ibid.*, 45–69.
18. See Ernesto Grassi, *Renaissance Humanism. Studies in Philosophy and Poetics* (Binghamton/New York/Center for Medieval & Renaissance Texts and Studies: State University of New York, 1988), 121ff.
19. Foundational experiences are to be distinguished from personal experiences in that the former have a reservoir of meaning which, when contrasted with the latter, is almost inexhaustible. See Croatto, *Biblical Hermeneutics*, 39f.

20. Because the reservoir of meaning of foundational experiences is as it were inexhaustible, such experiences appeal to peoples of all times and cultures, provided they are open to them. Usually "Scriptures" embody foundation experiences.
21. See P. Knitter, *No Other Name? A Critical Survey of Christian Attitudes Toward the World Religions* (London: SCM Press, 1985), esp. Part II, "Christian Attitudes Toward Religious Pluralism," 63–167.
22. *Ibid.*, 4–6.
23. *Ibid.*, 82ff.
24. *Ibid.*, 219ff.
25. Ultimately the only truth that will be generally acceptable will be that which produces in persons and peoples internal freedom and external commitment to the welfare to all.
26. Contexts in which proclamation is made are certainly not philosophical, and therefore it would be unwise to draw ontological conclusions from them. Proclamation-language is basically religious language and hence its concerns are religious and not ontological.
27. See R. Panikkar, "Faith and Belief. A Multireligious Experience," *The Intrareligious Dialogue* (New York: Paulist Press, 1979), 322–334; F. X. D'Sa, "Konfession und Dialog," *Neue Zeitschrift für Missionswissenschaft* 43:2 (1987), 108–124; and *Gott, der Dreieine und der All-Ganze. Vorwort zur Begegnung zwischen Christentum und Hinduismus* (Düsseldorf: Patmos, 1987), 125–129.
28. Panikkar, "Witness and Dialogue," *Myth, Faith and Hermeneutics*, 232–256.
29. See Gadamer, "Man and Language," *Philosophical Hermeneutics*, 62f.
30. *Ibid.* "The University of the Hermeneutical Problem," 3–17, esp. 15f.
31. See Gadamer, *Truth and Method*, 432.
32. Panikkar, *Myth, Faith & Hermeneutics*, 6f.

10

EXTRA ECCLESIAM NULLA SALUS

CRITICAL REFLECTIONS FROM BIBLICAL AND AFRICAN PERSPECTIVES

Joseph Osei-Bonsu

ONE MAJOR FACTOR that does not promote good relations between Christianity and the other world religions is the traditional Christian maxim *extra ecclesiam nulla salus* ("outside the church there is no salvation"). If we take the world today, there are 4.8 billion people living on the earth. Of these about 1.4 billion are officially Christian—nearly one-third of the world's population. Then there are 723 million Muslims, 583 million Hindus and 274 million Buddhists.[1] In addition to these there are the adherents of the various African Traditional Religions (for whom, to my knowledge, no reliable figures have been given), as well as devotees of other smaller religions and those who do not profess any religion.

The rigid application of the traditional maxim would mean that in our world today at best only one-third of the world's present population will attain salvation and the remaining two-thirds or more who are not Christians will not be saved.

It is my purpose in this paper to examine the traditional Christian maxim *extra ecclesiam nulla salus* to see whether it is supported by biblical evidence and to interpret it from an African perspective. In order to understand the meaning and implications of the traditional saying it will be necessary to start with a brief history of the axiom.

A History of the Axiom

The axiom[2] can be traced to the image of the Ark of Noah, used in 1 Pet. 3.20, to speak of salvation brought about by baptism. The image of the Ark of Noah occurs in the following context (1 Pet. 3:18–21):

> For Christ also died for sins once for all, the righteous for the unrighteous that he might bring us to God, being put to death in the flesh but made alive in the spirit; in which he went and preached to the spirits in prison, who formerly did not obey, when God's patience waited in the days of Noah, during the building of the ark, in which a few, that is, eight persons, were saved through water. Baptism, which corresponds to this, now saves you, not as a removal of dirt from the body but as an appeal to God...through the resurrection of Jesus Christ.[3]

We should observe that whereas 1 Pet. 3:20 states positively that there is salvation *inside* the ark, i.e., in the Church, it does not say that there is salvation *only* in the ark; neither does it add the negative statement that there is *no salvation outside the ark*.

The Patristic Use of the Image

The image of the Ark of Noah was adopted by a number of Church Fathers, starting with Ignatius of Antioch (d. ca. 110). Ignatius was concerned with a particular problem—schism. For him schismatics, those who had severed relations with their bishops, cannot be saved.[4] He was not discussing the question of the fate of those outside the Church, i.e., non-Christians.

For Irenaeus (d. 202), bishop of Lyons, the Church is the only place where the Holy Spirit and all grace can be found. Thus those who do not hasten to the church cannot be saved.[5]

Clement of Alexandria (d. ca. 211) simply identified salvation with the Church. He said: "To follow Christ is salvation" and God's "decision is the salvation of human persons and this is called the church."[6]

For Tertullian (d. after 220) the flood of Noah's time was a type of baptism and the ark was a figure of the church.[7] The axiom received its negative formulation for the first time from Origen (d. ca. 253). He stated categorically: "Let no one fool himself; outside of this house i.e., outside of the church, no one is saved; for if someone goes outside, he becomes responsible for his own death."[8]

Cyprian (d. 258), bishop of Carthage, more than any of the Church Fathers, was responsible for the rigorous interpretation of the saying. He stated that "whoever goes out from the gathering, that is, whoever withdraws from the Church, will be guilty, that is, the fact he will perish will be imputed to himself."[9] For him the Church was the assembly of the elect and the saved, and so if anyone left it, that person was doomed to perish. He wrote that one cannot have God as one's Father unless one also has the Church as one's mother.[10] He concluded that "there is no salvation outside the church."[11] Cyprian concluded from this axiom that baptism given by heretics outside the Church was invalid, and that martyrdom outside the Church was useless: "Even if such men are killed in confession of the name, that stain is not washed away, not even by blood...He cannot be a martyr who is not in the Church."[12]

Augustine of Hippo also insisted that membership of the church was *sine qua non* for salvation: "Whoever is separated from this Catholic Church—however much he believes that he is living laudably—will not have life but the anger of God rests upon him; the reason is this offense alone: he is sundered from the unity of Christ."[13]

Even more rigorous than Augustine was Fulgentius of Ruspe (d. 533) who followed the teachings of Augustine:

> Hold most firmly and do not doubt that not only all pagans but all Jews, heretics, and schismatics who terminate the present life outside the Catholic Church will go into eternal fire "which was prepared for the devil and his angels."[14]

Medieval and Reformation Times

The medieval Church also regarded the Church as the only place where salvation was possible. Thomas Aquinas retained the traditional teaching, though he said that in some cases an implicit faith was enough for salvation. On the subject of the salvation of Gentiles, he said that those Gentiles could be saved who had "implicit faith in divine providence and... believed that God is the deliverer of men according to ways pleasing to himself and according to what he revealed to those knowing the truth."[15]

The most weighty document in the history of the axiom was the bull *Unam Sanctam* (Nov. 18, 1302) of Pope Boniface VIII:

> Faith urges and constrains us to believe in and to embrace the one holy, catholic, apostolic church, and we firmly believe and absolutely confess this [church] outside of which there is neither salvation nor forgiveness...To be sure at the time of the flood there was one ark of Noah, a type of the one church...We read that outside the ark all living creatures were destroyed.[16]

The Council of Florence (1442) also stated that pagans, Jews, heretics, and schismatics would not be saved unless they were joined to the Church.[17]

The major Reformers did not differ from the medieval Church in believing that outside the Church there is no salvation. Though they had different views of the Church, they held to the doctrine in its essentials.[18] Luther, for example, said: "Whoever would find Christ must first find the Church...outside the Christian Church there is no truth, no Christ, and no salvation."[19] Elsewhere he says:

> I believe that no one can be saved who is not part of this community and does not live in harmony with it in one faith, word, sacrament, hope and love; and no Jew, heretic, pagan, or sinner will be saved with it unless he is reconciled and united with it and conformed to it in all things.[20]

Calvin stated that "beyond the pale of the Church no forgiveness of sins, no salvation, can be hoped for, as Isaiah and Joel testify (Isa. 37:23; Joel 11:23)."[21]

The Nineteenth Century

Pope Pius IX retained the traditional teaching but he added a qualifier when he said:

> Those who are in invincible ignorance of our most holy religion but who carefully observe the natural law and its precepts which God has written in the hearts of all men, who are ready to obey God and to lead an honest and upright life, can through the power of the divine light and grace attain eternal life.[22]

The First Vatican Council (1869–1870) expresses a similar sentiment when it says:

> ...it is a dogma of faith that outside the church no one can be saved. And yet those who are invincibly ignorant of Christ and his church must not for this reason be condemned to eternal punishments, for they are not bound by any fault in this matter in the eyes of the Lord, who wishes all men to be saved and to come to a knowledge of the truth and who does not deny grace to him who does what is within his power to attain justification and eternal life.[23]

It is noteworthy that for Cardinal Newman[24] the Church's intervention was not necessary in every case of salvation. Karl Adam[25] was of the view that God's grace can touch people without the mediation of the Church.

The Second Vatican Council (1962–1965)

The Second Vatican Council does not use the expression "outside the church there is no salvation," though it talks of the necessity of the church for salvation.[26] In the *Dogmatic Constitution of the Church*, Article 16, the Council says:

> Those also can attain to everlasting salvation who through no fault of their own do not know the gospel of Christ or His Church, yet sincerely seek God and, moved by grace, strive by their deeds to do His will as it is known to them through the dictates of conscience.

On the major world religions the Council says:

> The Catholic Church rejects nothing which is true and holy in these religions. She looks with sincere respect upon those ways of life, those rules and teaching which, though differing in many particulars from what she holds and sets forth, nevertheless often reflect a ray of that Truth which enlightens all men.[27]

Our survey shows that from the patristic times up to the nineteenth century, with the exception of a few theologians like Aquinas, Newman and Karl Adam who thought that in some cases an implicit faith was enough for the salvation of non-Christians, or that the Church was not required in every instance of salvation, the consensus was that non-Christians, including Jews, would have no share in salvation. In Pius IX and Vatican I we begin to have an official modification of the traditional axiom. Vatican II went even further in not using the adage and showing a more liberal attitude towards the non-Christian religions.

With this we may compare the more rigorous stance of the (Protestant) Frankfurt Declaration of 1970:

> ...the adherents of the non-Christian religions and world views...must let themselves be freed from their former view and false hopes in order to be admitted by belief and baptism into the body of Christ (paragraph 6).

Elsewhere the statement says: "in him (i.e., Christ) alone is eternal salvation promised to them."

The Biblical Evidence

Having briefly traced the history of the axiom, we shall now look at the biblical evidence and see if it teaches that non-Christians will not be saved. We shall begin with the Old Testament and see what the attitude of the Old Testament was towards the Gentile nations, whether it regarded them all as damned or not. This will be followed by an examination of the New Testament evidence on the question of non-Christians and salvation.

The Old Testament Evidence

According to the Old Testament, pagans were under the wrath and judgment of God. If they wanted salvation they had to be converted to the God of the Jews. Against this background the Jews generally had nothing positive to say about pagan religions and culture. On the contrary there were denunciations of pagan religions and practices.

However, there are a few passages where Yahweh is presented not only as the God of the Jews but also of the Gentiles and where the Gentiles are offered a share in God's salvation. It was sometimes recognized that Yahweh, the God of Israel, was the one God of all humankind. The covenant that God made with Noah and his descendants was seen as a universal covenant of God the creator with all living creatures (Gen. 9:8). The enumeration of all the peoples of the earth that follows the story of Noah (Gen. 10) underscores the universal character of the covenant. Another covenant is made with Abraham by whom "all the families of the earth will bless themselves" (Gen. 28:14).

Relevant in this connection is the Book of Jonah, which is generally regarded as a parable or at least didactic fiction. Its purpose was to provide a mirror for the writer's contemporaries to see themselves as they really were—people who were not willing to admit that God's love is not limited to the Jews but that it extends to all humankind. They failed to see that if the Gentiles repented, God's threats against them could be set aside in the same way as divine threats against Israel could be (Jer. 18:8). The book is a satire against the narrow nationalism and intolerance of the Jews who thought that as the chosen people salvation was theirs alone. The book is the rejection of the "Old Testament version of the doctrine 'outside the Church no salvation' understood without qualification and so excluding even those who are joined to the Church at least in desire."[28] The story of Jonah is also the author's way of protesting about the refusal of the Jews to take up the mission to be "a light to the Gentiles" urged by Deutero-Isaiah (Isa. 41–42; 49:6).

There are other passages where we find a positive attitude towards the nations. The classic passage for this is Isa. 2:2–4:

> It shall come to pass in the latter days that the mountain of the house of the Lord shall be established as the highest of the mountains, and shall be raised above the hills; and all the nations shall flow to it; and many people shall come and say: "Come, let us go up to the mountain of the Lord, to the house of the God of Jacob; that he may teach us his ways and that we may walk in his paths." For out of Zion shall go forth the law, and the word of the Lord from Jerusalem. (cf. Mal. 4:1–4; Isa. 18:7; Jer. 3:17; 16:19; Isa. 45:18–25; 60:1f.; Zeph. 3:8–11; Hag. 2:6–9; Zech. 2:10–13; 14:16).

These passages state that the nations will make a pilgrimage to Zion in the last days when they will see the glory of Yahweh. In all these passages Israel is the center of attention. The nations come to see Yahweh's glory through Israel. The idea of the eschatological pilgrimage of the nations is found in some intertestamental Jewish writings—Tob. 13:13; Sib. Or. III, 716f., 772f.; Test. Ben. 9:2; 1 En. 10:21; 48:5; 53:1; 90:33; Ps. Sol. 17:31; IV Ezr. 13:12f.

The New Testament Evidence

1. Matt. 8:11 (par. Luke 13:28) states: "Many will come from east and west and sit at the table with Abraham, Isaac, and Jacob in the kingdom of heaven, while the sons of the kingdom will be thrown into the outer darkness." This statement was made by Jesus after the pagan centurion had demonstrated such faith as Jesus said he had not found even in Israel. The "many" (*polloi*) here are clearly the Gentiles, for they are contrasted with the "sons of the kingdom," that is, the Jews (Matt. 11:19). These passages challenge the privileged position of the Jews, for the Gentiles will be included in the kingdom.

2. There are passages that pronounce woes on Galilean towns (Chorazin, Bethsaida, Capernaum; cf. Matt. 11:20–4; 10:15; Luke 10:13–15; 10:12) and state that certain pagan towns (Tyre and Sidon, Sodom and Gomorrah) will fare better at the judgment than these Galilean towns. In the Old Testament Tyre and Sidon were regarded as the epitome of pagan sin and pride (Ezek. 26–28) and Sodom and Gomorrah as the place where the most heinous pagan sins were committed. Yet it is said that at the judgment these cities will fare better than the Galilean towns mentioned.

3. There are three passages speaking about the sign of Jonah (Mark 8:11–12; Matt. 12:38–42; Luke 11:29–32). In these passages it is said that whereas the people of Nineveh repented at the preaching of Jonah, the people of Jesus' generation did not repent of their evil ways. It is said that the Gentiles (the people of Nineveh and the queen of the South) will judge the Jews at the judgment—a startling reversal of Jewish expectation.

4. In the parable of the sheep and goats (Matt. 25:31–46) the phrase "all the nations" (*panta ta ethne*) in v. 32 refers either to the Gentiles or to all peoples, rather than to Christians. Both Jews and Gentiles will be judged by the Son of Man, not according to their origin, but solely on the basis of whether they practiced neighborly love or not.

5. Mark 10:45 and parallels speak of the Son of Man giving his life as a ransom for many. In this passage "many" (*polloi*) probably reflects a Semitism which can mean "all."[29] If this is the case, then the Gentiles are included. With this we may compare 2 Tim. 2:6 which speaks of Christ "who gave himself as a ransom for all." Similarly, in Mark 14:24 and parallels, the blood of Christ is shed for "many," i.e., for all.

6. In Mark 12:2f. since the workers in the vineyard are the Jews (cf. Isa. 5:1–2), the "others" who are given the vineyard in the end must be the Gentiles.

We shall now look at a few Lucan passages since, among the evangelists, Luke seems to have a more universal view of salvation history. In the infancy narrative, Simeon praises God for giving him the opportunity to see the salvation made ready for all peoples (*panton ton laon*) and the revelation for "the nations" in Jesus himself (2:30-32). The note of universalism, first heard here, is heard again in 3:6 where in quoting the words of the prophet Isaiah (40.3) with reference to John the Baptist's presence in the desert, Luke adds v. 5 with its statement that "all flesh shall see the salvation of God." "All flesh" refers to all humankind. This latter verse is not found in Mark.

Luke traces the genealogy of Jesus, not merely to David or Abraham, as in Matthew, but to "Adam, the son of God" (3:23–38). In doing this Luke wanted to show "the organic relation of Christ to all humanity"[30] and that "his mission was ultimately to all mankind."[31]

In Luke's version of the parable of the great banquet (14:15–24) he differs from Matthew (22:1–10) in the mentioning at the end a double sending-out of servants into "streets and lanes of the city" (to bring in Jews after the invited guests had declined the invitation) and then into "highways and hedges" beyond the town (to bring in non-Jews).[32]

In the prologue to the Fourth Gospel, there is the reference to the coming of Christ into the world, "the true light which enlightens every man" (John 1:9). This would seem to indicate that Christ in some way unknown to us enlightens all human beings, and this would include non-Christians, if we are to give the weight to the phrase "every man" i.e., "every human being."

In Paul there are some passages which show that non-Jews are also included in God's offer of salvation. In Rom. 2:10 he says that there will be "glory and honor and peace for every one who does good, the Jew first and also the Greek" (i.e., the Gentile). Paul goes on (v. 11) to say that this is because "God shows no partiality." His election of the Jews does not mean that they enjoy an exclusive right to his favor. Paul continues in verses 14 –15:

> For when Gentiles who have not the law do by nature what the law requires, they are a law to themselves, even though they do not have the law. They show that what the law requires is written on their hearts, while conflicting thoughts accuse or perhaps excuse them on the day...when God judges the secrets of men.

Paul means that the Gentiles can sometimes do the things that the law requires. Since they do not have the Torah, they fulfill the requirements of the law by following the dictates of their conscience. In this manner they show the effect of the law written on their hearts.

In a few places Paul makes some effort to excuse pagans for their lack of faith in the one true God. He says that God has "in past generations allowed all the nations to walk in their own ways" (Acts 14:16); he has overlooked "the times of ignorance" (Acts 17:30). At Lystra Paul says that God did not "leave himself without witness" to the pagans, as he had given testimony to himself in the world of nature by providing good things for humankind and filling their hearts with gladness (Acts 14:17).

At Athens Paul discovers a religious desire, and in the worship of an unknown god, he perceives an obscure, unconscious awareness of God. They had not been forsaken by God in their superstition and idolatry because "he is not far from each one of us, for 'In him we live and move and have our being'; and even some of your poets have said, 'For we are indeed his offspring'" (17:27).

We conclude this section by citing 1 Tim. 2:4 where God's universal salvific will for humankind is explicitly stated. The passage speaks of God our Savior "who desires all men to be saved and to come to knowledge of the truth."

Perhaps at this point we may cite Acts 10:34 where Peter says the following words after hearing about the vision of the pagan Cornelius: "Truly I perceive that God shows no partiality, but in every nation any who fears him and does what is right is acceptable to him." This passage would seem to suggest that there may be people who may not know of Christ but who nevertheless may be acceptable to God on the basis that, following the dictates of their conscience, they fear God and do what is acceptable in God's eyes.

In the light of the foregoing it cannot be maintained that the Bible takes a completely negative attitude of exclusive intolerance towards other religions. God is regarded as the God of all humankind and not just of Jews or Christians. God wills all people to be saved. It is incorrect to maintain that in those passages that show a positive attitude to the Gentiles the New Testament has only Gentile Christians in mind. Even though Christ commanded the disciples to go and preach the good news to all nations and all creation (cf. Matt. 28:19ff., Mark 16:15f.), it cannot be maintained that the New Testament passages that speak positively of the Gentiles assume that the whole world would have been evangelized by the time the Son of Man comes to judge the world. There is no evidence of this.

We must now deal with two passages that pose special problems with regard to the question of the salvation of non-Christians. These passages are John 14:6 and Acts 4:12. The former passage says (with reference to Jesus): "I am the way, and the truth and the life. No one comes to the Father, but by me." The latter passage says: "There is salvation in no one else, for there is no other name under heaven given among men by which he must be saved."

With regard to the Johannine passage some have questioned whether the Fourth Gospel records the actual words of Jesus. If it does not, the exclusive claim made there will have to be reevaluated. But even granting that the words of John 14:6 are the *ipsissima verba Jesu*, do they imply that non-Christians cannot be saved? Do they imply that one has to become a Christian before one can be saved? The passage may be saying that salvation is possible only through Jesus. Jesus is the only way to the Father. By his death and resurrection Jesus has become the avenue of salvation, the way to the Father. But since Jesus is not identical with the Christian Church it seems to me that it is possible that one may benefit from the salvific work of Christ without being a member of the Church. Since Christ died for all humankind, and not just for Christians, the salvation inaugurated by his death cannot be limited to Christians only. The same may be said of Acts 4:12.

Reflections from an African Perspective

As an African Christian, or more specifically, as a Ghanaian Christian addressing this issue, I cannot help but reflect on the destiny of the millions of Africans who lived both before Christ and after Christ, who died without knowing him. After the death and the resurrection of Christ it took centuries before Christianity came to Africa south of the Sahara. Even today there are millions in Africa on whom Christianity has made little impact. It is not that they have not heard of Christianity; many of them have, but it has not made any deep impression on them just as many of us Christians have heard of Hinduism, Buddhism, Islam, etc, but these religions have not impressed us deeply enough to make us abandon our Christian religion.

Now these people who follow the African Traditional Religions do believe in God. If I may take the Asante of Ghana as an example, those among them who follow the traditional religion have a concept of God. God's existence for them is axiomatic, as evidenced by the saying, "Obi nnkyere akwadaa Nyame," meaning "No one need to show God to the child."[33] This God is believed to be the creator of the world and to be immortal, omnipotent, dependable, etc.[34] Even if there are lesser gods who feature in the cult of the Asante, they are not worshipped. Worship is reserved only for God, or the Supreme Being. The lesser gods and the ancestors are not worshipped; they are venerated.[35] A high ethical code is observed by the adherents of this religion. It is believed that failure to observe this will result in punishment by God.[36] As a result many of them lead lives that put Christians to shame. In their daily lives many of them show brotherly and sisterly love in a way that sometimes makes one wonder whether they are not more Christian than many of us who are officially Christians.

I do not believe that if such people die—at least those among them who try to lead good lives in accordance with the dictates of their conscience—they will be sent to hell just because they were not members of the Christian Church. Even though they do not have the Law or Christianity, they do what the Law or Christianity require. They show the effect of the Law or of Christianity written on their hearts. What I have been saying about the devotees of the African Traditional Religions also applies to the adherents of the major world religions who strive in their various ways to serve God.

Conclusion

The adage *extra ecclesiam nulla salus* is not biblical. It is an inference made on the basis of 1 Pet. 3:18ff. but the inference is incorrect. Whereas the passage states that there is salvation within the ark i.e., the Church, it does not say that salvation is possible only in the ark; neither does it say that salvation is not possible outside the ark. It cannot be maintained that in the Bible we have an entirely negative attitude towards Gentiles and non-Christians. God is presented as the God of all humankind. God's universal salvific will is clear from 1 Tim. 2:4. We believe as Christians that Christ died for all humankind. Thus all people, Christians and non-Christians, should in principle benefit from the salvific work of Christ. The Logos who enlightens all human persons and who died for all can in ways unknown to us bring non-Christians to the Father. In this he is assisted by the Spirit who blows where he will.

As far as the traditional axiom is concerned, I think its use should be abandoned. It cannot be taken literally and does not do justice to the biblical evidence. As J. P. Theisen says,

> The content of the axiom in its historical genesis was itself unfaithful to the message of Christ. Consequently its very content and formulation must be retired from the theological scene. What is involved here is more than the reformulation or reconceptualization of a dogmatic statement of the past. It is the abandonment of an adage that in its literalness never was a dogmatic position.[37]

Notes

1. See H. Küng, ed., *Christianity and the World Religions* (Garden City, New York: Doubleday & Co. 1986), xiii.
2. For the history of the axiom, we draw on the excellent work of J.P. Theisen, *The Ultimate Church and the Promise of Salvation* (Collegeville, Minnesota: St. John's University Press, 1976).
3. Translation from the *Revised Standard Version*, as in all subsequent biblical citations.
4. Cf. the *Epistle to the Philadelphians*, 3, 2–3. *Early Christian Writings. The Apostolic Fathers*. Translated by Maxwell Staniforth (Baltimore: Penguin Books, 1968), 112.
5. *Against Heresies*, Bk. 3, chapt. 24, I (J. Migne, *Patrologiae cursus completus. Series Graeca* (Paris, 1857ff.), 7,966. (Henceforward cited as *PG*).
6. *The Tutor* Bk. I, chapt. 6 (*PG* 8, 281).
7. *Homily on Baptism*, translated and edited by Ernest Evans (London: SPCK, 1964), 19.
8. *Homilies on Joshua*, 3, 5. (*PG* 12, 841f.)
9. *Letter 69, 4, Corpus Scriptorum Ecclesiasticorum Latinorum* (Vienna: C. Gerold's Son, 1866ff.), 3,753. (Henceforward cited as CSEL).
10. *The Unity of the Catholic Church*, 14 (Corpus Christianorum). Series Latina (Turnhout: Brepols, 1953ff.) 3,253 (Henceforward cited as CC).
11. *Letter 73, 21* (CSEL 3, 795).
12. *The Unity of the Catholic Church*, 6, 14 (CC 3,259).
13. *Letter* 141, 5 (CSEL 41, 238).
14. *On Faith, to Peter*, Chapt. 37. J. Migne, *Patrologiae cursus completus. Series Latina* (Paris, 1844ff.) 65, 703f.).
15. *Summa Theologiae*, II–II, q.2, a.7, and 3.
16. Denzinger-Schönmetzer, *Enchiridion Symbolorum et Definitionum de Rebus Fidei et Morum*. Ed. by H. Denzinger and A. Schönmetzer, 33rd ed. (Barcelona: Herder, 1965), 870 (Henceforward cited as DS).
17. DS 1351.
18. Cf. J. P. Theisen, *Ultimate Church*, 28ff.
19. *Kirchenpostille 1522, D. Martin Luthers Werke, Kritische Gesamtausgabe* (Weimar, 1883ff.) Vol. 10, I, 1, 140.
20. *Eine kurze Form der zehn Gebote, eine kurze Form des Glaubens, eine kurze Form des Vaterunsers 1520, WA* Vol. 7, 219.
21. *Institutes of the Christian Religion*, Bk. 4, Chapt. I, sect. 4. Transl. H. Beveridge (Grand Rapids, Michigan: W.B. Eerdmans 1966), Vol. 2, 283.
22. DS 2865–2867.
23. *Schema constitutionis dogmaticae de Ecclesia Christi Patrum examini propositum. Acta et Decreta Sacrorum Conciliorum Recentiorum Collectio Lacensis*, Vol. VII (Freiburg: Herder, 1980), col. 569.
24. Cf. "A Letter Addressed to His Grace the Duke of Norfolk (Dec. 27, 1874) on the occasion of Mr. Gladstone's Recent Expositions," in *Certain Difficulties Felt by Anglicans in Catholic Teaching*, Vol. II (London: Longmans, Green and Co., 1896), 335.
25. Cf. J. King, *The Necessity of the Church for Salvation in Selected Theological Writings*

of the Past Century (Washington, D.C.: Catholic University of America Press, 1960), 160–168; 347.

26. See Theisen, *Ultimate Church*, 37ff.
27. *Declaration on the Relationship of the Church to Non-Christian Religions*, Article 2.
28. P. F. Ellis, *The Men and Message of the Old Testament* (Collegeville, Minnesota: Liturgical Press, 1962), 458.
29. Cf. J. Jeremias, *The Eucharistic Words of Jesus* (London: SCM 1966), 179ff. Cf. also S. G. Wilson, *The Gentiles and the Gentile Mission in Luke-Acts*, Society of New Testament Studies, Monograph Series 23 (Cambridge: Cambridge University Press, 1973), 7f.
30. W. Manson, *The Gospel of Luke* (London: Hodder and Stoughton, 1930), 35.
31. G. B. Caird, *St. Luke* (London: Pelican Gospel Commentaries, 1963), 77.
32. J. A. Fitzmeyer, *The Gospel according to Luke*, I–IX (Garden City, New York: Doubleday & Co., 1981), 190.
33. See P. Sarpong, *Ghana in Retrospect* (Ghana Publishing Corporation, Accra-Tema, 1974), 9.
34. See Sarpong, *Ghana in Retrospect*, 10–11; K. Asare Opoku, *West African Traditional Religions* (FEP International Private Limited, Jurong, Singapore, 1978), 27–29.
35. See Asare-Opoku, *West African Traditional Religions*, 5; Sarpong, *Ghana in Retrospect*, 33ff.
36. See Asare-Opoku, *West African Traditional Religions*, 152ff.
37. J. P. Theisen, *The Ultimate Church*, 1153–1154.

PART III

THE WIDER ECUMENISM AND CONTEMPORARY CHRISTIAN THEOLOGY

11

SOME CHRISTOLOGICAL IMPLICATIONS OF RECOGNIZING THE JEWISHNESS OF JESUS

Marcus Braybrooke

TO RECOGNIZE THAT Jesus was a faithful Jew is to understand Christianity in a new light. For centuries, Christians have affirmed the significance of Jesus Christ by contrasting him with and setting him over against Judaism. The Church claimed that Jesus was the Messiah foretold in the Old Testament. The Jews not only failed to recognize him, but were held to be responsible for his death ('deicide'). In punishment, the Jews, who were often spoken of as 'children of the devil,' were exiled by God from the Land of Promise.

The horrors of the Holocaust have gradually awoken Christians to the evil consequences of anti-Jewish teaching. It is widely agreed that it is historically, morally, and theologically wrong to hold the Jews guilty of the death of Jesus. Historically, he suffered crucifixion, which was a Roman penalty. It is known that Pilate was a cruel ruler and anyone who was said to claim to be a king was likely to be in trouble. By the time the Gospels were written, Christians wanted to gain legitimacy in Roman eyes and seem to have shifted the blame for Jesus' death on to the Jews. Some Jews opposed Jesus, and the high priests, who may have felt their vested interest would be threatened by trouble with the Romans, may have been involved in a plot to get rid of him. Yet other Jews mourned and lamented over him. Those who became his first disciples were, of course, all Jewish.[1] Morally, it is wrong to hold a whole people guilty of the supposed wrongdoing of their ancestors. Theologically, the Second Vatican Council and other Church Synods have affirmed that God's Covenant with his people has never been broken.[2] In this century, Jewish people have returned to the Land of Promise.

Yet, if the old dogmatic anti-Judaism is fading, much historical and critical writing on the New Testament still seeks to affirm the significance of Jesus by contrasting him with Judaism. Indeed, there is a tendency to locate his divinity at the point where he differs from the religion that nurtured him. For example, Bousset, who has had considerable influence on subsequent German New Testament scholars, admitted some formal similarities between Jesus and his contemporaries, but denied any similarity on essentials. "In the one case we have mere exposition of the Scriptures, in the other a living piety. There the parables are designed to illustrate the distorted ideas of a dead learning...Here the parable was handled by one whose soul was set...upon the real."[3] Others have suggested that Jesus' intimate sense of God as Father (abba = 'Daddy') is unique, but the evidence does not seem to support this.[4]

Such an approach often belittles and distorts Judaism. A misleading contrast is made between Law and Gospel, and the New Testament caricature of the Pharisees is taken at face value. Instead, as John Pawlikowski writes, "the basic link between Jesus and Judaism must be sought in his sharing of the revolutionary vision of Pharisaic Judaism."[5]

Jesus in a Jewish Milieu

Unravelling the evidence and seeing Jesus in a Jewish milieu is complex. First, because our knowledge of Jesus is mediated by the early Christian community. The Gospels reflect their concerns and indeed their polemic against Jews who did not believe in Jesus. Further, because any reconstruction of the historical Jesus is so tentative, it is unsafe to base claim for him by contrasting him with his contemporaries.[6]

A second reason why it is difficult to see Jesus in a Jewish milieu is that Rabbinic Judaism was codified from the second century C.E. "Many rabbinic debates reflect the new situation which existed after the destruction of Jerusalem and the temple in the year 70, when Judaism had to adapt to a totally new situation." Even so, as Michael Hilton and Gordian Marshall go on to say, "The oral transmission of rabbinic ideas was very important and the rabbinic texts clearly reflect much earlier material."[7] We can have a general picture of Pharisaic Judaism, but detailed arguments about influence or primacy are likely to be unhelpful. We also know, through the discovery of the Dead Sea Scrolls and other material, that Judaism in the first century C.E. was far more varied than is suggested by the Gospels or Josephus. This may be seen, for example, in the growing tendency to place the Fourth Gospel in a Jewish rather than a Hellenistic milieu.[8]

Covenant and Torah. Judaism needs to be understood in terms of the Covenant. God promised to Abraham that he would bless his descendants. God rescued the people of Israel from slavery in Egypt and chose them to be His own people. The Torah was given by God to those whom He by grace had chosen for His own. To obey the Torah was to affirm the covenant and to accept God's promise. It was the loving response to God's gracious act of rescue and his choice of Israel to be his own. Too often Christians have pictured the Law as a burden rather than as a delight. The influence of Luther and the way Paul has often been interpreted are reflected in the hymn "Rock of Ages," which has the lines, "Not the labours of my hands, Can fulfill thy Law's demands...."

This needs to be compared with Psalm 119 where the Psalmist says, "I love your commandments more than gold, more than the finest gold" (v.127) or "Lord how I love your law, it is my mediation all the day long" (v.97).

E. P. Sanders and others have shown in detail that to regard Judaism as a religion of legalistic works and righteousness "is based on a massive perversion and misunderstanding of the material."[9] God chose Israel. Obedience to the Torah shows a reliance on God's fidelity, not a concern to win His favor. The debates about atonement show that there was a means by which the penitent sinner could be restored to a right relationship to God, a relationship established by God's mercy and maintained by the individual's obedience and repentance and by God's forgiveness.[10]

The Pharisees. The Pharisees' understanding of Covenant and Torah was essentially the same. Pharisaism was a lay movement which took seriously the obligation laid upon Israel as a whole to be a 'holy nation' before God. Cultic purity was not just for priests at the Temple, but for all God's people. Taking the call to holiness seriously, the Pharisees sought to apply the law to contemporary life and here disagreed with the Sadducees, the high priestly party, who stuck to a literal and often out of date interpretation.

The Torah was the major source of information on ordering the cult—the Temple worship—but it also shows the way of life that God expected. It was, however, seldom precise enough to show the exact behavior required, while, of course, life changes and laws have to be reapplied to new circumstances. Therefore there grew up a cumulative reinterpretation and application of the Torah. Some of it was based on interpretation of a passage of Scripture; some of it takes the form of a pronouncement by a rabbi, and in addition there are stories which illustrate the teaching. In interpreting the Law, the Pharisees were guided by two principles. One was to build a fence around the Torah; the other was to make explicit what was implicit or unsaid. Professor John Bowker suggests that "the people welcomed the assistance of the Hakamim (the learned) in alleviating the strictest interpretation of Torah and in defending their traditional ways."[11]

The Pharisees also stressed table fellowship (*Haburah*), to belong to which a person had to undertake certain obligations of cultic purity and way of life. The aim was to regard the whole world, not just the Temple, as the sanctuary where God dwells. Inevitably these rules separated the Pharisees from ordinary people, in the way Masons or vegetarians may separate themselves. There is no evidence, however, that they expected everyone to obey those self-chosen rules nor that they thought the common people were excluded from salvation.[12]

There were sharp differences among the Rabbis, for example, between Hillel and Shammai, and it seems there were also sharp differences among the Pharisees. Yet, "more important than the divisions were the far greater unities of methods, beliefs, and intentions which they held in common, and which differentiated them as a whole from, for example, the Sadducees or the communities on the shores of the Dead Sea."[13] There also appears to have been growing criticism of extremist elements, who appear to have been known as *perushim*, who stressed that the detailed interpretation of Torah was the only way to holiness. The criticism of these extremists in rabbinic sources is similar to criticism of them made in the Gospels.[14]

Jesus and the Pharisees. Such criticism should not disguise the fact that Jesus was close to the Rabbis in his teaching, calling upon all Israel to acknowledge the rule of God. "As we carefully examine the ministry of Jesus," writes Pawlikowski, "certain parallels between him and the Pharisaic movement become evident. On any number of occasions he is seen in the process of teaching the oral Torah, reinterpreting the Hebrew Scriptures in a manner more in line with the social setting in which he found himself. His general ministerial stress with its emphasis on teaching and healing without question falls into the general pattern set for the authentic rabbi.... The early Jerusalem church...shows great similarities to the synagogue model advocated by the Pharisees. He likewise appears to have participated in Pharisaic-type fellowship meals, instituting the Christian Eucharist at the final one he attended. In the area of doctrine the resemblances continue. Emphasis on love, on the *Shemah*, on the themes summarized in the Beatitudes and on the Resurrection indicate the presence of a strong Pharisaic spirit in the life of Jesus. In particular Jesus' stress on his intimate link with the Father picks up on a central feature of Pharisaic thought."[15]

It seems that he did not observe the usual rules about ritual purity and table fellowship, which would have surprised the Pharisees. Further, where there was evident personal faith and repentance, even among sinners, Jesus seems not to have been too concerned about the detailed requirements of the Law. Bowker suggests that among the Pharisees "there were those who emphasized that the yoke of the Law was easy and burden light, ...(to whom) the first imperative was to encourage people to set themselves within the intention of keeping the covenant, after that the details could be added as a constantly extending act of love towards God."[16] For others, the whole Law was meant to be kept and the details were as important as the general spirit. Jesus, Bowker suggests, made the extreme deduction from the first view that "the first and only step to be taken is in the direction of God. Thus his *kelal*, or summary, of Torah is the love of God and love of one's neighbor as oneself."[17]

Whereas Jewish teaching saw repentance as a pre-condition for forgiveness, Jesus appears to have offered sinners inclusion in the kingdom while they were still sinners. He seems to have believed that the initiative in seeking for the sinner was taken by God, who sought for the lost sheep and welcomed the lost son. He also may not have required of the sinners repentance as normally understood. His companions would therefore, at least technically, remain sinners. "It seems to be the case," writes E. P. Sanders, "that Jesus offered the truly wicked—those beyond the pale and outside the common religion by virtue of their implicit or explicit rejection of the commandments of the God of

Israel—admission to *his* group (and, he claimed the kingdom) *if* they accepted him."[18]

Yet, despite possible differences of emphasis, as E. P. Sanders argues, "We *know* of no substantial dispute about the Law, nor of any substantial conflict with the Pharisees."[19] Jesus did not reject the Mosaic dispensation, Sanders says, but he no longer regarded it as final, because a new age was dawning.[20]

Eschatological expectation, not disputes about the Law, seems to have been the key point on which Jesus and his followers differed from his contemporaries. He did not attack the Covenant and Torah, but his conviction that a new age was dawning gave him a new perspective on Judaism.

Eschatology. Speculation about the end of the world was a significant part of Pharisaic teaching, but it was the absorbing concern of the Essenes, the community which withdrew to the Dead Sea. Whereas the Pharisees tried to be holy within society, the Essenes rejected society and were hostile to other Jews. They lived a strict ascetic life and saw themselves as Sons of Light struggling with the Sons of Darkness.

Eschatological expectation was varied and far from clear cut, just as Christian pictures about the Second Coming are imprecise. There was a general belief that this present age would give way to a new age of peace, righteousness, and justice, when the faith of the righteous would be vindicated. The new age would be preceded by a period of deep distress, 'the Messianic Woes.' Some hoped for a universal salvation that would include the Gentiles and there was hope for a general resurrection. Jerusalem would remain central in the new age. There is not much literature about Messianic expectations and this has probably been given greater emphasis by Christian scholars than it deserves.[21] The Messiah would be a descendant of David, who would lead God's people. Some expected the end to be ushered in by a decisive act of God, others like the Zealots expected a political revolution.

Jesus' Preaching of the Kingdom. Jesus seems to have been convinced this new age was dawning with his ministry. Whereas the early Church preached about Jesus, his own message was that 'The kingdom of God is at hand.' Sanders, in his book *Jesus and Judaism*, focuses on the Cleansing of the Temple. He rejects the view that Jesus was objecting to the dishonesty of the money changers or to the trading as such, which was necessary for the sacrificial cult. Jesus was not just demonstrating against an abuse, but threatening the Temple itself, as is implied by the charges brought against him at his trial. The Cleansing, Sanders argues, was a symbolic prophetic action. The driving out of the animals signified the end of the sacrificial system. The overturning of the tables foreshadowed the Temple's destruction. This, Sanders says, was in line with Jewish eschatological expectation. The coming of the 'new age' would mean 'a new temple.' In the Temple Scroll, God says, "I shall sanctify my sanctuary with my glory: I shall cause my glory to dwell upon it until the Day of Blessing, when I myself shall create my sanctuary, establishing it for myself forever, like the covenant which I made with Jacob at Beth-El."[22]

Besides the expectation of a new Temple, there was also the expectation that the Twelve Tribes of Israel would be restored. This gives significance to Jesus' choice of twelve disciples.[23]

There is some disagreement about their names, but not about their number—and the number twelve had to be maintained after Judas' suicide. It was also expected that in the new age, the outcasts of Israel would be gathered in.[24] This would give added point to Jesus' emphasis on going to the sinners and outcasts. There was a further expectation that the in-gathering would include the Gentiles.[25] This was not part of Jesus' own ministry, but explains why for Paul the conviction that Jesus was the Christ and his commission to preach to the Gentiles belonged together. In the new age, too, the Torah takes on a different significance.

Jesus, it seems, believed that with his ministry, a new age was dawning. This points also to a self-consciousness and awareness of a special vocation. His contemporaries recognized that he spoke with authority, and the Cleansing of the Temple also raised the question of authority. This became the key issue. In words attributed to the disciples who journeyed to Emmaus on Easter Day, "We hoped that He was the One who would deliver Israel."[26]

The Early Christians' Belief in Jesus. Those who believed that God had raised Jesus from the dead, believed that the new age had indeed dawned. Increasingly, in the light of the Resurrection, they focused attention on Jesus himself rather than his message of the kingdom. The Gospel material is shaped by this concern, so it is impossible to be sure how Jesus himself understood his role in the coming kingdom. Critical study suggests that most of the titles used for Jesus in the Gospels derive from the early Christian community. Frances Young has summarized widely accepted conclusions of critical study in this way. "(a) The titles and concepts were there to be used before the early Christians adopted them—that is, they can be found in non-Christian documents and with non-Christian interpretations; (b) that by their application to Jesus they were filled with new content, and new interpretations became inevitable as a new combination of once distinct concepts were made; (c) the combination was probably the result of believers searching for categories in which to express their response to Jesus, rather than Jesus claiming to be these particular figures; and (d) each block of writings in the New Testament has its own emphases and combinations, that is, its own christological picture."[27]

Did Jesus Claim a Title for Himself?

Conzelman argues that Jesus did not use the titles, 'Son of God,' 'Messiah,' or even 'Son of Man.'[28] "How then did Jesus regard himself?," he asks. "The answer cannot be given by a christological concept. It must come through a demonstration of how Jesus associated the announcement of the kingdom of God with himself as a sign. Of course christology is implied here. It will have to be developed after Easter."[29] In a similar vein Raymond Brown writes, "If Jesus presented Himself as one in whose life God was active, He did so not primarily by the use of titles, or by clear statements about what He was, but rather by the impact of His person and His life on those who followed Him."[30]

Those who first developed a christology were Jews. Their understanding of Jesus had to make sense in terms of their Jewish faith and categories of thought, even if these were transformed by belief that the kingdom was dawning. Other titles, such as Son and Lord, when they were taken over by Gentile Christians, used to Hellenistic ways of thinking, acquired a different meaning.

Messiah. Because of Christian claims that Jesus was the long-awaited Messiah, overmuch attention has been given to contemporary Messianic expectation, giving it an exaggerated importance. It seems clear that Messiah was not a divine figure and that Jesus did not fit Messianic expectations.

"By origin," Conzelmann writes, "the 'Messiah' belongs to the nationalistic type of Jewish eschatology. 'Anointed' is a designation of the king in the Old Testament. Thus from the beginning the Messiah is no supernatural figure, but a human savior. Of course, over the course of time the different types of hope coalesce, and with them the ideas of the savior. The figure of the Messiah is accentuated until it becomes transcendent. But basically Messiahship always remains alien to apocalyptic thought...For a savior only fits into the restoration of the earthly kingdom of Israel, and not into the kingdom of God which comes from above. So in Judaism, Messiah and kingdom of God are not conceptually linked, the idea that the Messiah brings in the kingdom of God is missing."[31] Similarly Allan Brockway writes, "The activity of Jesus bears little resemblance to the Jewish picture of the Messiah. The history of the Church does not bear out any claim that Jesus initiated the messianic age." In the New Testament, 'Christ' becomes a name and links Jesus' death to the work of salvation. "To equate the concepts," Brockway continues, "does violence to the Jewish hope for the Messiah, it hinders if it does not block the Church's proper development of cogent christologies."[32]

Jesus was not the 'Messiah' whom Judaism expected, and therefore the negative conclusion that the Jews rejected their Messiah is invalid. It is also improbable that Jesus himself claimed to be Messiah. The title is used seven times in Mark's Gospel. It is used as a title in the opening verse of the book. It is used in the saying about a cup of water (9:41, but compare Matt. 10:42), in mockery (15:32), in the apocalyptic in chapter 13, and in the dispute over Davidic sonship (12:35).

The two most interesting occasions when the term is used are Peter's confession (8:30) and the question of the high priest (14:62). Of the former, Nineham writes, "The story is not so much intended to describe faithfully what happened on the first occasion when Jesus was recognized as Messiah as to show what is essentially involved and demanded whenever such a recognition takes place."[33] The latter verse (4:62) raises the very difficult questions about the historicity of the accounts of the trials of Jesus, which seem to defy almost all known Jewish rules of procedure. Again to the evangelist it seems that the theological content of the passage was what mattered, not the historicity.[34] It seems unlikely that Jesus claimed to be the Messiah. If he did so, he would have needed radically to reinterpret contemporary understanding of Messiahship.

Certainly, quite early Christians used the title Christ of Jesus, but some contemporary writers question whether he was indeed 'Messiah,' in terms of Christian expectation. For such writers, the manifest evil in the world belies the claim that Jesus is Messiah—and it is said that Christians have ignored this reality either by thinking the kingdom was expressed in the Church, as St. Luke does, or by spiritualizing and interiorizing the idea of redemption.

Paul van Buren speaks of the tremendous cover-up which had occurred before Christianity was even one hundred years old. "What it had not accomplished, including such minor details as the end of the human suffering, sickness, injustice, oppression and torture, death, much of it horrible...—all such details were simply scaled down in value in the mythological scenarios as being of only transient concern. After all, with eternal life won, why care about actual human life? The more triumphalist the mythological interpretation of Easter, the more Christianity could calmly ignore the world which it claimed that God so loved."[35]

Gregory Baum, Monika Hellwig, and Rosemary Reuther all say that any Messianic notion in Christianity must be understood in a future sense. "What Christianity has in Jesus," says Rosemary Ruether, "is not the Messiah, but a Jew who hoped for the kingdom of God and who died in that hope."[36] Any Messianic claims for Jesus are proleptic or anticipatory. There is therefore considerable ambiguity about the claim that Jesus was Messiah. The Jewish 'no' to Christian claims that he was Messiah may be seen as faithfulness to their own understanding of Messiahship and as a necessary corrective to any tendency of Christians to spiritualize redemption.

Son of God and Lord. In a similar way, the use of the term 'Son of God' by Gentile Christians is radically different from its use by Jewish believers. In the Old Testament, both Israel and the king are called 'Son of God.' The use of the title in Mark's Gospel seems clearly the work of the evangelist. It is used in the opening verse of the Gospel (1:1), used of Jesus at his Baptism (1:11), used by those possessed with demons, who were thought to have supernatural insight (5:8), and used at the transfiguration (9:8). The title is used also at the trial by the high priest who, on behalf of the Jews, rejects its use for Jesus (14:62), whereas the Roman centurion, a Gentile, at the foot of the cross confesses "Truly this man was the (or a) Son of God" (15:39).

To the first believers, who were Jewish, Jesus' sonship would have been understood in moral, not physical, terms. The idea of his miraculous conception introduced a Hellenistic understanding of the term.[37] "We need, therefore" says Pawlikowski summarizing Monika Hellwig, "to change our attitude toward the statement 'Jesus is Son of God' and 'Jesus is divine' from simple equation to interpretation."[38]

The use of the title Kyrios, Lord, shows even more clearly the change from the primitive community to Hellenistic Christianity. The Aramaic cry *maranatha* comes from a community which waits in hope. Kyrios or Lord Jesus is "an acclamation and proclamation."[39] Its use derives either from the pagan environment in which Kyrios was used as a designation of God or from the Septuagint.

Son of Man. There has perhaps been more discussion of the term 'Son of Man' than of any other title. It is the title most commonly put on the lips of Jesus in the Synoptic Gospels. Sometimes it is used as a way of speaking of himself. "The Son of Man has nowhere to lay his head" (Matt. 8:20). At other times, it is used in predictions of his suffering and death. "He began to teach them that the Son of Man had to undergo great sufferings..." (Mark 8:31). The third use is with reference to when "the Son of Man comes in the glory of his Father and of the holy angels" (Mark 8:38). Geza Vermes argues that "there is no evidence whatever, either inside or outside the Gospels, to imply, let alone demonstrate, that the son of man was used as a title... The only possible, indeed probable, genuine utterances are sayings independent of Daniel 7 in which, in accordance with Aramaic usage, the speaker refers to himself as the son of man out of awe, reserve or humility."[40]

It seems then that we have to speak with great caution about the claims that Jesus made for himself. We do not have the evidence to speculate about his self-understanding, and it is doubtful whether he used for himself any of the titles applied to him by New Testament writers. It has been suggested above that he believed a new age was dawning, which he was called to proclaim. The cleansing of the temple, the choice of twelve disciples, the miracles, the welcome to publicans and sinners may be evidence of this belief. He spoke of the boundless generosity of God and called on people to live as His children, happy in His protection and subject to His rule. Like Martin Luther King, he may have had a premonition of the fate that awaited him in Jerusalem. Christology is an attempt to convey the significance he has for those who believe in him and who through him have discovered new life and a new relationship to God. A particular form of confession of faith is not, however, required by Our Lord himself, as far as we can reconstruct his life and ministry.

To those who first believed in him, he made God present in a new way. They spoke of his being raised by the Father as similar to the deliverance from Egypt and the revelation at Sinai. The believers read the Scriptures in a new light and found in them confirmation of their faith. They applied to Jesus titles drawn from their Jewish heritage. Yet it is clear that there is no single consistent Christology in the New Testament. Rather, different writers used whatever language they could to convey the significance of Jesus to them. The New Testament does not impose on future generations a single orthodox Christology. That comes later, when after the Councils of the Church, the Emperors hoped to find in Christianity a cohesive faith to bind together their scattered subjects.

Christological Developments in the Gentile Church

As the Church became increasingly Gentile, the titles used for Jesus emphasized his divine status. Jewish believers saw in him the presence of God and the herald of the kingdom. As Gentile Christians emphasized his divinity, so they separated him from Judaism. Yet, while the Christological developments of the Councils of the Gentile church may have been partly responsible for the increasingly negative view of Judaism, they can also be seen as authentic developments, attempting to affirm in ways appropriate to their historical circumstances the presence of God in Jesus Christ.

The Creeds were, however, as Frances Young points out, culturally conditioned. Patristic discussion of christology was conducted within the framework of contemporary philosophical discussions.[41] They become problematic therefore when they are regarded as for all time the expression of Christian belief, when many of the presuppositions and thought-forms of the Church of the Fathers are no longer accepted today. To stress the substantive union of Father and Son may be misleading when we think in dynamic terms rather than in terms of substance. Terms like 'person' have acquired today a different meaning from that given to them when the Creeds were formulated.[42] The effect has been to focus attention on the divinity of Jesus as the object of Christian worship, rather than seeing him as the Way to the Father. This separates Jesus of Nazareth from his historical Jewish milieu.

If we see the language of the Creeds as historically conditioned, this also allows us to see them as expressing the significance of Jesus to those who believe in him, rather than as ontological statements. As John Hick has written, "It seems reasonable to conclude that the real point and value of incarnational doctrine is not indicative but expressive, not to assert a metaphysical fact but express a valuation and evoke an attitude."[43]

Conclusion

Many Christians today do not share the philosophical presuppositions of the Church Fathers. Critical historical study of the New Testament and Jewish milieu suggests that, unwittingly, the Church Fathers misread the Gospel evidence. As those who today affirm God's presence in Jesus Christ, we share the underlying affirmation of the Fathers and the Creeds and stand in the tradition of faith which they proclaimed. We are not, however, bound by their formularies. Particularly we need to develop a Christology for the Jewish/Christian reality, recognizing that Jesus was a faithful 'Son of the Covenant,' who was close to the Pharisees, and recognizing also that God's Covenant with Israel continues.

In his attempt to do this, Paul van Buren has made two fundamental decisions. The first is that every proper Christological statement, however 'high,' will make clear that it gives the glory to God the Father. For Jesus leads us to the Father. Second, every proper Christological statement will make clear that it is an affirmation of the Covenant between

God and Israel.[44] For God, who is present in Jesus Christ, is faithful to his promises to Israel.

Many Christians in their emphasis on Jesus Christ seem almost to forget the Father. As John Bowden has written in a recent study, "The symbols of Jesus and the Christ...occupy too prominent a place in Christianity. They have accumulated too much power; so much power indeed that in many contexts the figure of Jesus has come to eclipse that of God."[45] As a result, Jesus is used to separate Christians from other believers in God and is used to justify an attitude of superiority towards Jews, women, people of other faiths, and races. We have to affirm what Jesus means to us, without denying the affirmations made by others. For, as Friedrich-Wilhelm Marquardt has said, "We will only have Christian anti-Judaism behind us when theologically we will have succeeded in making positive sense of the Jewish 'no' to Jesus."[46]

Those who are seeking to develop a Christology for the Jewish/Christian reality wish to affirm that, in Donald Baillie's phrase,[47] "God is in Christ," without denying that God is with his people Israel.[48] Further, they affirm the recognition of His presence in other communities of faith, enabling Christians to witness to their experience of God's saving and gracious activity in Jesus Christ while eagerly seeking to listen to and learn from the witness of others to their knowledge of the One True God.

Notes

1. Luke 23:27 and 23:48. See E. Rivkin, *The Death of Jesus.*
2. See *Stepping Stones to Further Jewish-Christian Relations* and *More Stepping Stones to Jewish-Christian Relations*, ed. Helga Croner (Stimulus Books, 1977 and 1985).
3. Quoted by E.P. Sanders, *Jesus and Judaism* (London: SCM Press, 1985), 18. See also Charlotte Klein, *Anti-Judaism in Christian Theology* (Philadelphia: Fortress Press, 1978).
4. Hans Conzelmann, *An Outline of the Theology of the New Testament* (London: SCM Press, 1969), 103–104.
5. John Pawlikowski, *Christ in the Light of the Christian-Jewish Dialogue* (Ramsey, N.J.: Paulist Press, 1962), 134, 89ff.
6. Detailed arguments will be found in any critical introduction to the New Testament, e.g., W. D. Davies, *Invitation to the New Testament.*
7. M. Hilton and G. Marshall, *The Gospels and Rabbinic Judaism, A Study Guide*, 6.
8. See Raymond Brown, *The Community of the Beloved Disciple* (New York: Paulist Press, 1979).
9. E. P. Sanders, *Paul and Palestinian Judaism* (London: SCM Press, 1977), 59.
10. *Ibid.*
11. John Bowker, *Jesus and the Pharisees* (Cambridge: Cambridge University Press, 1973), 31. *Hakamim* is the term used by later rabbis to refer to their predecessors and Bowker identifies them with the Pharisees.
12. E. P. Sanders, *Jesus and Judaism*, 188ff.
13. Bowker, *op. cit.*, 32.
14. *Ibid.*, 38.
15. Pawlikowski, *op. cit.*, 92–93.
16. Bowker, *op. cit.*, 32, and Sanders, *Jesus and Judaism*, 206. See also Hilton and Marshall, *op. cit.*, 17ff.
17. Bowker, *op. cit.*, 64.
18. Sanders, *Jesus and Judaism*, 210.
19. *Ibid.*, 292. See also Michael Cook, "Jesus and the Pharisees," *Journal of Ecumenical Studies*, 15, 3 (1976), 132–147.
20. Sanders, *Jesus and Judaism*, 123ff.
21. L. Grollenberg, *Unexpected Messiah How the Bible can be Misleading* (London: SCM Press, 1986), 56.
22. The Temple Scroll. (llQ Temple 29, 8–10), see Sanders, *op. cit.*, 85.
23. Matt. 19:28.
24. Isa. 44:21.
25. Isa. 56:6–8; Zech. 2:11, 8:20–22.
26. Luke 24:21.
27. Frances Young in *The Myth of God Incarnate*, ed. John Hick (London: SCM Press, 1977), 15.
28. Conzelmann, *op. cit.*, 129.
29. *Ibid.*, 140.
30. Pawlikowski, *op. cit.*, 113, quoting Raymond Brown, "Does the New Testament

call Jesus God?" *Theological Studies* 26, No. 4 (Dec, 1965), 546.
31. Conzelmann, *op. cit.*, 73.
32. Allan Brockway, *Learning Christology Through Dialogue With Jews* (Geneva: WCC, 1965), 4.
33. D. E. Nineham, *Saint Mark* (Penguin, 193), 227.
34. *Ibid.*, 398ff.
35. Paul van Buren, quoted by Pawlikowski, *op. cit.*, 12.
36. Rosemary Ruether, *Anti-Defamation League Bulletin* 30, (May 1973) 4., quoted by Pawlikowski, 26.
37. Conzelmann, *op. cit.*, 76–82.
38. Pawlikowski, *op. cit.*, 10.
39. Conzelmann, *op. cit.*, 82.
40. Geza Vermes, *Jesus the Jew* (Fontana: Collins, 1976), 186. See also N. Perrin, *Rediscovering the Teaching of Jesus* (London: SCM Press, 1967).
41. Frances Young, *op. cit.*, 23.
42. G. L. Prestige, *God in Patristic Thought* (London: SPCK, 1959).
43. John Hick, *The Myth of God Incarnate*, 178.
44. Paul van Buren in an unpublished paper.
45. John Bowden, *Jesus: The Unanswered Questions* (London: SCM Press, 1988), 182. See also, 196–198.
46. Quoted by J. Schoneveld, *The Quarterly Review* Vol 4, No. 4 (Winter 1984), from Friedrich-Wilhelm Marquardt, "Feinde um unsretwillen: Das judische Nein und die christliche Theologie," in Peter von der Osten-Sacken ed., *Treue zur Thora; Beitrage zur Mitte des christlich-jüdischen Gesprachs; Festschrift fur Günther Harder zum 75. Geburtstag*. 2nd ed. (Berlin: Institut Kirche und Judentum, 1979), 174.
47. D. M. Baillie, *God Was in Christ* (London: Faber, 1961), 106ff.
48. Pawlikowski's book gives several examples. See also Eugene B. Borowitz, *Contemporary Christologies: A Jewish Response* (New York: Paulist Press, 1980).

12

ARE THERE OTHER 'SAVIORS' FOR OTHER PEOPLES?

A DISCUSSION OF THE PROBLEM OF THE UNIVERSAL SIGNIFICANCE AND UNIQUENESS OF JESUS THE CHRIST

Peter C. Phan

IN RECENT INTERRELIGIOUS dialogues between Christianity and other world religions the question has often been raised whether Christians can and must recognize that there are, besides Jesus the Christ, other saviors, such as Gautama the Buddha and Muhammad, who may be equal or even superior to Jesus. The question is often couched in terms of the uniqueness of Jesus: Is Jesus so unique among the religious figures of history as to rule out any other possible mediator of salvation? Can and should Christians continue to affirm that Jesus the Christ is normative for all peoples in their relationship with God, that is, "ultimately decisive, definitive, archetypal for humanity's relation with God?"[1]

Answers given to this question can be grouped into three types: exclusivistic, inclusivistic, and pluralistic.[2] The exclusivistic type affirms that only in Jesus can true revelation and salvation be found, the Christ event being constitutive of any authentic encounter with God, always and everywhere.[3] The inclusivistic type affirms the uniqueness of Jesus without denying that God's saving presence may also be operative in other founders of religions. Proponents of this view, however, insist that Christ includes other religions either by being present in them anonymously or by fulfilling them. Jesus remains, if not constitutive of, at least normative for, all religious experience.[4] Finally, the pluralistic type affirms that Jesus is unique, but his uniqueness includes and is included by other potentially equal religious figures. It views Jesus as neither constitutive of nor normative for authentic religious experience, but as ***theocentric***, that is, as a ***universally relevant*** manifestation, incarnation, and sacrament of God's revelation and salvation in history.[5] Jesus may have universal relevance but not uniqueness.

Sometimes the question of uniqueness is raised not so much of Jesus as of Christianity. The issue then is whether Christianity as a historical religion is the only true religion. Again, for exclusivists, Christianity is the only one true religion founded by Jesus himself, other religions being nothing but human attempts at self-salvation deformed by errors, superstitions, and vices. Inclusivists would hold that while their religions may be ways of salvation, Christianity is the best religion, divinely authenticated as the surest means of access to God and intended to absorb and fulfill other religions. Pluralists would view Christianity as one of the many religions, equally valid and mutually complementary.

The pluralist stance is represented by its proponents as the most radical view of the relationship between Christianity and the non-Christian religions and as the most productive strategy for interreligious dialogue. Often the metaphor of crossing the Rubicon is used to illustrate the decisive and irreversible nature of the move from inclusivism to pluralism.[6]

In this article I would like to evaluate some of the grounds for the pluralistic stance. I will begin by summarizing succinctly the three basic reasons that have been proffered by the pluralists for crossing the Rubicon. Next, on the basis of these arguments I will focus on the issue of the uniqueness of Jesus and Christianity. Finally, I will make some reflections on the task of interreligious dialogue by which not only the universal significance of Jesus but also his uniqueness can be preserved.

I

In a recent work edited by Paul F. Knitter, *The Myth of Christian Uniqueness: Toward a Pluralistic Theology of Religion*[7] proponents of the pluralist stance elaborate the reasons why the "myth" of Christian uniqueness must be reexamined. This myth, so these proponents claim, has come to connote "the uniqueness, definitiveness, absoluteness, normativeness, superiority of Christianity in comparison with other religions of the world."[8] It is this myth that they reject, and in so doing they believe they have to cross over from the shores of exclusivism and inclusivism to pluralism. The three reasons or "bridges" that force them to do the crossing are historical consciousness ("the historico-cultural bridge"), the reality of God as Mystery beyond all forms, transcending every conceptualization of it ("the theologico-mystical bridge"), and the existence of immense sufferings allegedly caused by the myth of Christian uniqueness ("the ethico-practical bridge").

Historical consciousness, "the ever more impelling awareness of this historico-cultural limitation of all knowledge and religious beliefs, and the difficulty, if not the impossibility, of judging the truth claims of another culture or religion on the basis of one's own,"[9] makes the claim for Christian uniqueness totally indefensible. Gordon Kaufman argues that every theology is an imaginative construction of what he calls the four structural categories of worldview, namely, God, world, humanity, and Christ. Given the move from the classicist mentality to the thoroughgoing historical consciousness in our times, it is no longer possible, according to Kaufman, for a contemporary theology to claim that "its assertions were directly and uniquely authorized or warranted by divine revelation"; rather its construal of the fourfold categorical structure of the worldview is nothing more than a "human imaginative response to the necessity to find orientation for life in a particular historical situation."[10]

Therefore the past claims of Christianity to be the "only" or the "highest" form of religion must be abandoned. John Hick proposes that the claim to superiority is an empirical issue and therefore must be settled by an examination of the facts. But in this test Christianity would fail, just as any other religion would, since "...it seems impossible to make the global judgment that any one religious tradition has contributed more good or less evil, or a more favorable balance of good and evil, than the others.... But as vast complex totalities, the world traditions seem to be more or less on a par with each other. None can be singled out as manifestly superior."[11] Lastly, Langdon Gilkey, in explicating the implictions of pluralism for theology, agrees that no religious tradition is universal and can serve as the absolute norm for all the others. Nevertheless, frightened by the specter of relativism and convinced of the absolute obligation to resist evil, he suggests that relativism can be overcome by the commitment of prophetic praxis. In praxis the absolute manifests itself in relative situations, the unconditioned in the conditioned complexities of life.[12]

The theologico-mystical case for pluralism is built on the realization that God is an incomprehensible Mystery that cannot be adequately represented by any religion or any theological system. The incomprehensibility of God demands religious pluralism and forbids any one religion to claim having the "only" or "final" word. Wilfred Cantwell Smith, making use of the notion of "idol" as an image, declares that each religion is an "idol" of God in this sense of the word, just as theologies are conceptual images of God. But, to claim one's "idol" as exclusive and final is "idolatry." The various religions are particular "idols" of God; but, says Smith, "to mistake them, however, for God himself, or mistakenly to elevate any one of them to some divine status, is to commit the fallacy of looking at the window rather than through it to God and giving to it the honor, dignity, deference, due only to God."[13] Stanley J. Samartha, speaking from his multi-religious culture, affirms that God as Mystery provides the ontological basis for tolerance: "The nature of Mystery is such that any claim on the part of one religious community to have exclusive or unique or final knowledge becomes inadmissible."[14]

Raimundo Panikkar, in an extremely suggestive essay,[15] divides Christian history into five periods (witnessing, conversion, crusade, mission, and dialogue) corresponding to the three symbolic rivers (the Jordan, the Tiber, and the Ganges). The first period is nurtured by the waters of the Jordan, the following three periods by the waters of the Tiber, and the last and contemporary period by the waters of the Ganges. Again, distinguishing three attitudes (Christianity, Christendom, and Christianness) he suggests that Christianity is close to the spirituality of the Jordan, Christendom to that of the Tiber, and Christianness to that of the Ganges. Dialogue and Christianness imply pluralism: "Pluralism adopts a nondualistic, advaitic, attitude that defends the pluralism of truth because reality itself is pluralistic—that is, incommensurable with either unity or plurality."[16] Panikkar's understanding of pluralism is so radical that he refuses to say that there are many saviors, which is a nonpluralistic assertion; rather, he affirms that there is an all-embracing myth, a Mystery called the Christ or the Christic principle which is expressed in various religions so that no one religion can make an exclusive claim for itself.

Seiichi Yagi, a Japanese New Testament scholar, suggests that what the New Testament calls "the Risen Christ" or "the Son of God" is nothing but the primary contact of God with each human being, "the divine-humanity, Logos incarnate, oneness of the divine and the human at the depth of every human being (self)."[17] There is therefore no basic difference between any one of us and Jesus except that Jesus was awakened to the primary contact of God so thoroughly and completely that he became the model for other selves.

The third and last argument for crossing the Rubicon to pluralism is based on the confrontation with human sufferings and the need to put an end to such outrages. The need to promote justice requires a new attitude toward other religions. From her feminist perspective Rosemary Radford Ruether argues that there is a parallelism between Christianity's claim to superiority and sexism: "The idea that Christianity, or even the biblical faiths, have a monopoly on religious truth is an outrageous and absurd religious chauvinism....True revelation and true relationship to the divine is to be found in all religions. God/ess is the ground of all beings, and not just of human beings."[18] In a similar vein Marjorie Hewitt Sochocki maintains that to hold up Christianity or Christ as the norm for all other religions is just as exploitative as is the attempt of sexism to make male experience the universal norm for humanity. For her, the norm for judging the truth and value of the religions is not simply doctrinal but historical and ethical. One must ask of the religions whether they bring about justice, that is, whether they contribute to the fundamental, physical well-being of humanity (food, water, shelter, work, and community), to human dignity and recognition in the human community, and to self-development and self-determination within the context of community.[19]

The theme of justice is carried on by Aloysius Pieris in his essay "The Buddha and the Christ: Mediators of Liberation."[20] He shows that on the level of interpretation there is a parallel between the Christian attempt to divinize Jesus (christology) and the Buddhist attempt to install Gautama as the cosmic lord (buddhology). The claims that Jesus is the Christ and that Gautama is the Buddha are, however, kerygmatic affirmations that cannot be demonstrated rationally but only by means of praxis in favor of justice. Jesus himself shows that he is the medium of salvation by means of the cross, the symbol of his twofold ascesis: his struggle to be poor and for the poor. Christianity's claim to uniqueness would be an empty boast unless its adherents continue this double ascesis.[21]

Lastly, on the basis of liberation theology, with its hermeneutics of suspicion, its preferential option for the poor and the nonperson, its understanding of praxis as the origin and confirmation of theory or doctrine, its retention of the primacy of orthopraxis over orthodoxy, Paul F. Knitter suggests that the claim to uniqueness of any religious figure and religion can be settled only by asking how much they bring liberation to the poor and the nonpersons, that is, how much they contribute to God's kingdom of justice: "The perspective on *Soteria* given by any one mediator is always open to clarification, completion, perhaps correction by the viewpoints of other mediators. So again, the absolute, that which all else must serve and clarify, is not the church or Christ or even God—but rather, the kingdom and its justice."[22]

II

So far I have summarized the three arguments of pluralists for rejecting the myth of Christian uniqueness: historical consciousness, the absolute transcendence of the divine Mystery, and the struggle for justice. I have drawn attention to the fact that the use of the term "Christian uniqueness" is ambiguous: it refers both to the uniqueness of Jesus and to that of Christianity. None of the authors we have studied has explicitly identified Jesus with Christianity, but in their critique of the myth of Christian uniqueness they tend to glide from Christianity to Jesus as though the two were identical. Paul F. Knitter, for instance, in his critique of Hans Küng's inclusivistic stance represented in his *On Being a Christian*,[23] says: "I suspect that, like many Christians today, he stands before a theological Rubicon. To cross it means to recognize clearly, unambiguously, the possibility that other religions exercise a role in salvation that is not only valuable and salvific but perhaps equal to that of Christianity; it is to affirm that there may be other saviors and revealers besides Jesus Christ and equal to Jesus Christ. It is to admit that if other religions must be fulfilled in Christianity, Christianity must, just as well, find fulfillment in them."[24]

This imperceptible slippage from Christianity to Jesus, whether intentional or not, is, in my opinion, the Achilles' heel of the pluralist stance, for, and this is my contention, while it is not possible to claim that Christianity is unique in the sense of definitive, absolute, normative, and superior to other religions, it is legitimate to claim that Jesus is the only Christ and Savior. Furthermore it is my thesis that it is not necessary to abandon the claim of the uniqueness of Jesus to achieve the goal of interreligious dialogue. These points will be substantiated in what follows, but first let us attend to the distinction between Jesus and Christianity and hence between the claim to uniqueness of Jesus and that of Christianity.

That Jesus is neither Christianity nor Christendom nor even Christianness, to use Panikkar's categories, is rather obvious.[25] The New Testament explicitly recognizes this distinction when it speaks of Jesus the Christ as the head and the church as his body, the former as the shepherd and the latter as the sheepfold, the former as the vine and the latter as its branches. While the Pauline and Johannine writings often stress the intimate union between Jesus and his followers, there is never an ontological identification of the two. Such identification, furthermore, makes no sense from historical and sociological standpoints. Jesus is an individual, historical, once-and-for-all entity, whereas Christianity, with its social organization, its dogmas, its liturgy, its discipline, is a collective and ongoing reality. From the theological standpoint, the distinction is absolutely vital: Christians believe in Jesus the Christ; they do not believe in the Church, in Christianity, and much less in Christendom![26]

If Jesus is not identical with Christianity, then the claims to uniqueness for Jesus and for Christianity are two different claims. They may be connected but are not the same. Not only are they claims for two different realities, their epistemological status is different and therefore cannot be validated in the same manner. The claim that Jesus is the only Christ is a claim of faith, a "kerygmatic affirmation," to use Aloysius Pieris's term, as is the claim that Gautama is the only Buddha; whereas the claim that Christianity is the only true religion, superior to other religions, is based, or at least has traditionally been based, on empirical evidences. The claim of faith, as we shall see, can and must be validated on its own criteria, whereas the claim of superiority for Christianity, as John Hick has rightly suggested, must be tested by an examination of the facts.

It is precisely the distinction between Jesus and Christianity, between the claim to uniqueness for Jesus and that for Christianity, that enables some Catholic theologians to be critical of Christianity, as a historical religion, and to recognize that non-Christian religions can be authentic ways of salvation, and not merely that there is a general revelation in them, as most mainline Protestant theologians, such as Paul Althaus, Emil Brunner, Paul Tillich, Wolfhart Pannenberg, and Carl Braaten, are willing to concede. Inclusivists such as Karl Rahner, Hans Küng, Walbert Bühlmann, Arnulf Camps, Lonergan, Richard McBrien, and H. R. Schlette are sharply critical of Christianity as a sociopolitical and religious institution and yet continue to affirm the normativity of Jesus precisely because they maintain a radical difference between Jesus and Christianity.[27]

Hans Küng, for instance, has affirmed quite emphatically:

> I am a Christian because I...with confidence and in practice trust that the God of Abraham, Isaac (Ismael), and Jacob has acted not only in the history of Israel (and Ismael), and has spoken through the prophets, but has bestowed self-revelation in an incomparable, and for me a decisive, manner in the life and work, suffering and death, of the Jew Jesus of Nazareth....He is, therefore, according to the words of the Gospel of John, for us *the* truth, and *the* life!

> This means, in a self-critical address to Christians: Christians *do not believe in Christianity*. Christianity as a religion—with its dogmatics, liturgy, and discipline—is like every other religion, a highly ambivalent historical reality; Karl Barth was completely right in emphasizing that point. From this it follows that it would be untenable to maintain that Christianity is the "absolute religion" as Hegel still thought he could do; as a religion, Christianity appears in the history of the world just as relatively as do all other religions.[28]

If the distinction between Jesus the Christ and Christianity and between the claim to uniqueness for Jesus and that for Christianity is granted, as I think it must, then the force of the third argument—the ethico-practical bridge—for the pluralistic stance is quite blunted. If exploitation, colonialism, sexual discrimination, religious imperialism, violence, war, and other evils were and are part and parcel of the history of Christianity, as Hick, Ruether, Sochocki, and Knitter have eloquently pointed out and as all Christians must humbly acknowledge, the most that can be said in this regard is that the culprit who must bear responsibility for all these evils is the claim to uniqueness and superiority for Christianity (or better still, Christians), rather than the claim to uniqueness and superiority for Jesus and, of course, much less Jesus himself.

Perhaps it should be noted that religions whose adherents do not make claims to uniqueness and superiority are not free from such terrible misdeeds. This fact suggests that such a history of cruelty and injustice might not entirely be the result of the claim to uniqueness and superiority of a particular religion and might plausibly be explained by the inherent desire of human beings for self-aggrandizement and domination. These remarks are not at all intended to exculpate Christianity or to justify the claim to superiority for it; rather they serve both to underlie the difference between the claim to uniqueness for Jesus and that for Christianity and to show that all the evils deplored by the pluralists as attendant upon the myth of Christian uniqueness are not entirely caused by it. It would be the height of naivete to think that once the claim to uniqueness for Jesus or for Christianity or for any other religion is abandoned, the evils often associated with such claims that marred the history of Christianity and other religions will be significantly reduced and the chance for a successful interreligious dialogue is dramatically increased.

But to return to the claim to superiority and uniqueness for Christianity as a historical religion. Can such claim still reasonably be made? The pluralists' answer is a resounding *No* on the basis of the three basic reasons given above. My response is both *Yes* and *No*. Lest I be accused of clever tergiversation, allow me to explain. First of all, two things must be clear. First, the claim to superiority for Christianity is, as I have said above, an empirical claim, at least that has been the way in which this claim is substantiated by the Catholic Church. Vatican I declares: "To the sole Catholic Church belong all the manifold and wonderful endowments which by divine disposition are meant to put into light the credibility of the Christian faith. Nay more, the Church by herself, with her marvelous propagation, eminent holiness and inexhaustible fruitfulness in everything that is good, with her Catholic unity and invincible stability, is a great and perpetual motive of credibility and an irrefutable testimony of her divine mission."[29] Consequently, the validity of such a claim must be tested by an examination of the facts.

Second, since religions are both "gnostic" and "agapeic" (to use Pieris's terminology), both enlightenment and transformation, the criteria for judging their "truth" must be both doctrinal and praxeological. Religions are "true" if they both teach correct doctrines and transform human lives, if their "verum" and their "bonum" merge together. As Hans Küng puts it: "Insofar as a religion serves humanness, insofar as in its credal and moral doctrines, its rites and institutions, it *fosters* human beings in their human identity, meaningfulness, and value, and helps them gain a meaningful and fruitful existence, it is a *true* and *good* religion."[30]

On the basis of these criteria, the answer to the question whether Christianity can claim uniqueness in the sense of superiority over other religions, can only be *Yes* and *No*. *No*, because *some* of its teachings, both credal and moral, are inadequate or simply wrong. No, also because, empirically, it has not always shown "marvelous propagation," "eminent holiness," "inexhaustible fruitfulness," "Catholic unity," and "invincible stability." Or to put it bluntly, Christianity, or more precisely, some Christians have been (and will always be) arrogant, bloodthirsty, power-hungry or just plain stupid. On the other hand, yes, because, empirically, there are *some* doctrines, both credal and moral, in Christianity that are noble and uplifting and to this extent transformative of human lives, while there are *others* that can be shown to be "truer," more humane and hence more liberative than those taught by other religions on the same subject matter (e.g., social justice). Yes, also because, empirically, there have been (and will always be) *some* Christians who live lives of self-sacrifice and generosity, sometimes perhaps even better than non-Christians, just as there are some non-Christians who live a better life than Christians. Perhaps to some my remarks may seem punctilious and priggish, but the point I am making is that there is no such a thing as Christianity as an abstract whole; rather it is made up of a variety of concrete doctrines and practices, some of which are bad, some good, others superior. And in interreligious dialogue, where truth and honesty are of paramount importance, to declare *in globo* that Christianity (or any other religion for that matter) cannot claim uniqueness and superiority in this restricted sense is surely not the most fruitful move.

But what if the claim to superiority means that Christianity has the fullness of truth, that Christians possess a full and perfect understanding of religious matters? In the light of the utterly ineffable nature of the divine Mystery, of the historically conditioned character of human understanding and language, and of the inherent limitations of the human intellect, only a fool or one totally innocent of all learning would make such a claim. In this sense the second argument of the pluralists (the theologico-mystical bridge) is on the mark. But, of course, no inclusivist has ever claimed that a particular religious or theological system represents an exhaustive and final understanding of God. No contemporary theologian, to my knowledge, has so persistently, almost obsessively, insisted upon the incomprehensibility of God as did Karl Rahner whom Paul Knitter regards as the chief advocate of inclusivism.[31] Besides, there is a strong tradition in Christian theology that has always emphasized the ineffability of God before whom all discourse ends in worshipful silence (the *theologia negativa*). Even Thomas Aquinas repeatedly affirms that we cannot know who God is but only what he is not. Thus the distinction between inclusivism and pluralism evanesces on *this score*.

The decisive difference then between inclusivists and exclusivists lies not in the claim that Christianity is unique or superior (which claim can or cannot be made depending on the particular issue at hand), but in the claim that Jesus is the only Savior and Christ and hence the norm or criterion against which the claim of others to be saviors must be measured. It is my thesis that such a claim about Jesus is *ultimately* a faith claim or a kerygmatic affirmation. Of course, when Christians affirm that Jesus of Nazareth is the Savior (or Messiah, Christ, Lord, Son of God, God), they do not do so voluntaristically but on the basis of their experience of who Jesus was and what he taught and wrought for them. There are signs that Jesus performed (e.g., miracles), his message (i.e., the coming of God's rule), his behavior (e.g., his forgiveness of sins and his special love for sinners and the downtrodden), the way he spoke of and related to the God of Abraham, Isaac, and Jacob (e.g., the Abba invocation) his active presence after his death, all this (and many other things) addresses the minds of Christians, in Newman's words, "both through the intellect and through the imagination; creating a certitude of its truth by arguments too various for direct enumeration, too personal and deep for words, too powerful and concurrent for refutation."[32] Though through what Newman calls the "illative" sense Christians can arrive at one complex act, both of inference and assent, of affirmation of the lordship of Jesus, nevertheless the claim of Jesus' messiahship and divinity is in the last analysis an affirmation of faith. Such an affirmation, though neither irrational nor unreasonable, transcends the limits of reason, has its own internal logic, and cannot be validated by an empirical examination of the facts. Furthermore, according to Christian faith and theology, a real assent to such a claim cannot be made unless the person is moved internally by divine grace and the Holy Spirit. In the last part of this essay I will discuss how this faith claim is to be handled in interreligious dialogue.

Paul F. Knitter has argued at great length that the abandonment of the claim of Jesus' uniqueness (read: superiority, normativeness, and perhaps even divinity) is neither contradictory to New Testament christology, nor inconsistent with contemporary christologies, especially transcendental and process christologies, nor inimical to faith in Jesus' resurrection, nor, finally, destructive of a total, personal commitment to Jesus.[33] This is not the place to engage in a full evaluation of Knitter's arguments. But three observations will be made in this regard.

First, granted that early New Testament christology is dialogal, pluriform, and evolutionary; and granted that the context in which the New Testament claim of Jesus' uniqueness was made is classicist, eschatologico-apocalyptic, and minoristic; and finally, granted that the language in which this claim was couched is confessional and not philosophical, still it must be admitted that the meaning intended by the early Christians in their proclamation of Jesus as Lord, Savior, Son of God, God (the cognitive or metaphysical content of their confession of faith) cannot be determined by means of psychology or sociology of knowledge or by an analysis of literary language alone. The meaning of a statement is not identical with its causes, its intended purposes, or its *de facto* effects.[34] Even if the language form of a statement is "love language, caressing language" (Kristen Stendahl), still a metaphysical truth may be asserted thereby, just as myth, despite its literary form, affirms something about the real. If there is some metaphysical truth in the early Christians' claim of Jesus' uniqueness, as Knitter himself seems to concede,[35] can it be dismissed simply because it is allegedly imperialistic to affirm it in an interreligious dialogue?

Second, to Knitter's question of why the complete actualization of the incarnation is to be limited to only one human being (i.e., Jesus) if transcendental and process theologians hold that Jesus is the full realization of what is the *potential*, the God-given, goal of all human beings,[36] two replies may be given. First, Christian theology never denies that other human beings can be "divinized"; the whole patristic doctrine of *theosis*, in particular that of Irenaeus, Athanasius, and Gregory of Nyssa affirms precisely that. Each in his own way affirms that God is made human so that humans be made God. The only difference—a vital one—is that we all are made divine by grace or by participation, as Gregory of Nyssa puts it, whereas Jesus is divine by nature. Thus, there is no difficulty in affirming that there can be and indeed *are* other "incarnations," as long as these incarnations are participation in the Incarnation of God in Jesus. Second, as to why the Incarnation took place only once, the answer is that if the Incarnation of God in Jesus is the *self-identity* between the Jew Jesus and the Logos (these two statements are faith claims), then it is metaphysically and psychologically difficult to see how there can be more than one Incarnation of God in *this* sense. There would be what might be called an "ontological schizophrenia" of the Logos himself.

This brings me to the third remark concerning the possibility of a total and personal commitment to Jesus even if one abandons the claim of Jesus' "uniqueness." Knitter's argument for such a possibility revolves around the analogy of total and faithful commitment to one's spouse, even though one well knows that there are other persons in this world equally as good, intelligent, beautiful as, and even better than, one's spouse.[37] His argument would be well taken if commitment to Jesus were simply of the same order as that of a person to his or her spouse. It is true that Christians should develop love, fidelity, and devotion to Jesus, but Christian faith, practice, and worship have consistently affirmed the possibility and necessity of offering adoration (*latria* and not simply *dulia*) to Jesus himself, since the "person" of Jesus is believed to be none other than the divine Logos. This aspect of the Christians' relationship with Jesus must honestly and openly be acknowledged in any interreligious dialogue and not belittled or ignored.[38] One may want to argue that this adoration is misguided or simply wrong, but one ought not surreptitiously to suggest that it is equivalent to spousal fidelity and commitment.

III

If the claim of Jesus' uniqueness is a faith affirmation, ought it to be made in an interreligious dialogue? Does such affirmation not hinder or even render interreligious dialogue altogether impossible? The answer to these questions depends of course on what one understands by the nature and aims of interreligious dialogue. A lot has been written on what interreligious or interfaith dialogue should be and accomplish.[39] In this final section I shall not bore the readers with another list of ground rules for a successful interreligious dialogue and with an elaboration of the necessity of "crossing over" to and "coming back" from other religions (to use John Dunn's phraseology) or of dialogal dialogue (Panikkar) in order to understand other faiths and religions.

My aim is a very modest one: to see whether the Christian partner in an interreligious dialogue should abandon the claim of Jesus' "uniqueness." Paul F. Knitter believes that he or she should: "...No matter how much truth and good one recognizes in another religion, if one enters the dialogue convinced that by God's will the final, normative, unsurpassable truth for all religions resides in one's own religion, this is *not* a dialogue between equals."[40] If by "one's own religion" is meant Christianity, then, of course he may be right, as I have indicated above. It is worth repeating that Christianity as an abstract entity does not exist; there are only particular Christian doctrines, Christian institutions, Christian practices and so on, some of which are extremely bad, good, better, or excellent in comparison with the doctrines, institutions, and practices of other religions. The same thing should be said of any other religion vis-à-vis Christianity.

But, assuming that by "one's own religion" is meant the claim of *Jesus*' uniqueness, does it follow that the partners in dialogue cannot function as equals if the Christians were to make that claim? Let us recall here my thesis that the claim of Jesus' uniqueness is a faith claim, a kerygmatic affirmation. Such claim has a certain reasonable basis, but ultimately it is a faith statement, especially if by "uniqueness" is meant Jesus' lordship and divinity, and therefore cannot be "proven" to an outsider with "objective" arguments. Now, if one of the ground rules of interreligious dialogue is that no one partner can and should step outside of his or her religion and suspend his or her own religious experience and beliefs—the phenomenological *epoche* applied to interreligious dialogue[41]—then I can hardly see how a believing Christian can abandon the claim of Jesus' uniqueness.

What a Christian partner can and must do, when the question of Jesus' uniqueness comes up for discussion, is to explain to others what the claim means and does not mean,[42] how there may be reasonable arguments to support such a claim, how there may be a *homology* between Buddhahood and Christhood,[43] and how the claim is ultimately a faith statement. Very probably, the Buddhist partner would do the same for the claim that Gautama is the Buddha, and the Muslim partner for the claim that Muhammad is the Prophet. It is likely that the Christian, the Buddhist, and the Muslim come away from their dialogue with a better understanding of what they mean by affirming in faith that Jesus is the Christ, Gautama the Buddha, and Muhammad the Prophet, and with a better understanding of the reasons why the others make such a claim for their religious founders. But there is no reason why each of the partners should abandon his or her faith claim prior to and/or during the dialogue, nor is there any ground for saying that Jesus or Gautama or Muhammad achieves a greater degree of uniqueness as the result of the dialogue. If, as Panikkar affirms,[44] the aim of the interreligious dialogue is understanding and communication in order to bridge the gulfs of mutual ignorance and misunderstanding between the different cultures of the world, and not to win over or convert the other, or to come to a total agreement, or to found a universal religion, then I think that our model of dialogue has achieved its aim. There is, of course, the possibility that any of the partners may be converted as the result of the dialogue and abandon the claim of uniqueness, but such an abandonment happens *after* the dialogue, and does not precede it as a condition for its possibility.

Finally, is the claim of Jesus' uniqueness a sign of arrogance, destructive of universal justice and peace? I must confess I fail to see the logic of the following statement of Tom Driver's: "The immoral factor in the 'scandal of particularity' today is its insistence upon a once-and-for-all Christ in a relativistic world.... It precludes Christianity's ability to affirm that all people have a right to their place in the sun.... If the incarnation of God in finite humanity can occur but once, the religious value of all other human history is nil."[45] I hope that what I have said above and, most of all, the history of Christian mission will be sufficient to show that Driver's affirmation is an unfortunate exercise in *non sequitur* reasoning.[46]

Moreover, and this is much more important, it is a historical fact that whenever Christian individuals rose up in defense of the poor, the oppressed, the hungry, the nonpersons against the abuses of secular and ecclesiastical powers (one can think of Francis of Assisi, Luther, Martin Luther King, Mother Teresa and countless others), they never felt the need to abandon their faith claim of Jesus' uniqueness. Rather they derived their inspiration, nurtured their strength, prolonged their patience, and sometimes vented their holy anger against the oppressive systems from a deeper understanding of what Jesus the Lord meant for them. It is precisely a true and vital understanding of this claim that made them reject all arrogance, exclusivism, and dogmatism in relation to others.

John Cobb, Jr., in trying to understand the source of his own personal growth from exclusivism to universalism, writes:

> The question now is, Where have I learned these things? There are many answers: home, school, church, books, friends. But when I press the question more deeply, I must come back to the fact that it is from the Christian story that I have learned them, primarily from the Bible. And when I ask how in fact I understand the Bible, I must confess that I read it in terms of a center that is Jesus. My impulse to live out of a story larger than the one that is historically interconnected with Jesus comes from Jesus.[47]

My conclusion, then, is that in interreligious dialogue it is neither necessary nor warranted (and perhaps also ill-timed) to cross the theological Rubicon. Unwarranted because the "uniqueness" of Jesus is central to the Christian message, and unnecessary because interreligious dialogue is not best served by abandoning such a claim of Jesus' uniqueness.

Notes

1. Hans Küng, *On Being a Christian* (New York: Doubleday, 1976), 123.
2. For critical surveys of these views, see Alan Race, *Christians and Religious Pluralism: Patterns in the Christian Theology of Religions* (Maryknoll, N.Y.: Orbis, 1983); Paul F. Knitter, *No Other Names? A Critical Survey of Christian Attitudes Toward the World Religions* (Maryknoll, N.Y.: Orbis, 1985); and Gavin D'Costa, *Theology and Religious Pluralism: The Challenge of Other Religions* (Oxford: Basil Blackwell, 1986). Knitter's book has been the object of a theological symposium published in *Horizons* 13 (Spring 1986).
3. Proponents of this view are mostly fundamentalist and conservative evangelicals and pre-Vatican Catholics. One of the most famous theologians holding this view is of course Karl Barth, for whom, "religion is unbelief." See Paul F. Knitter, *No Other Names?*, 75–96.
4. This view is proposed somewhat differently by mainline Protestants and Catholics. Protestant theologians such as Paul Althaus, Emil Brunner, Paul Tillich, Wolfhart Pannenberg, Carl Heinz Ratschow, and Carl Braaten admit the existence of a general revelation of God in history and therefore in non-Christian religions, but they tend to deny that these religions are ways of salvation. On the other hand, Catholics such as Karl Rahner (his famous theory of "anonymous Christianity"), Hans Küng (who rejects Rahner's theory), and Walbert Bühlmann affirm that non-Christian religions can be ways of salvation. See Knitter, *No Other Names?*, 97–144.
5. The foremost proponents of this pluralistic view are Knitter (see his *No Other Names?*, 145–231), Gordon D. Kaufman, John Hick, Langdon Gilkey, Wilfred Cantwell Smith, Stanley J. Samartha, Raimundo Panikkar, Seiichi Yagi, Rosemary Radford Ruether, Marjorie Hewitt Sochocki, Aloysius Pierius, and Tom F. Driver. Their views were discussed at a meeting at Claremont Graduate School, Claremont, California, March 7–8, 1986; and their essays have been published in a volume edited by John Hick and Paul F. Knitter, *The Myth of Christian Uniqueness: Toward a Pluralistic Theology of Religions* (Maryknoll, N.Y.: Orbis, 1987). Other theologians were invited to discuss their views, among whom were John B. Cobb, Jr., Schubert Ogden, and David Tracy. These, though ardent advocates of interreligious dialogue, felt however that the pluralist move is either unwarranted, unnecessary, or ill-timed. See *ibid.*, viii. Since this work is often cited, it will henceforth be abbreviated as *MCU*.
6. See Knitter, "Hans Küng's Theological Rubicon," *Toward a Universal Theology of Religion*, ed. Leonard Swidler (Maryknoll, N.Y.: Orbis, 1987), 224.
7. See note 5.
8. MCU, p. vii.
9. *Ibid.*, ix. Leonard Swidler affirms that historical consciousness deabsolutizes the

notion of truth: truth is deabsolutized insofar as it is made to be historical, praxis-oriented, perspectival, and interpretive. This historical consciousness is corroborated by the sociology of knowledge, the limits of language and hermeneutics. Truth is now seen as dialogic and relational. See *Toward a Universal Theology of Religion*, 7–13.

10. *MCU*, 12. Kaufman's essay, entitled "Religious Diversity, Historical Consciousness, and Christian Theology," is found in 3–15.
11. *Ibid.*, 30. Hick's article, entitled "The Non-Absoluteness of Christianity," is found in 16–36.
12. See "Plurality and Its Theological Implications," *ibid.*, 37–50.
13. *Ibid.*, 59–60. Smith's essay is entitled "Idolatry in Comparative Perspective" and is found in 53–68.
14. *Ibid.*, 77. Samartha's essay, entitled "The Cross and the Rainbow: Christ in a Multireligious Culture," is found in 69–88.
15. "The Jordan, the Tiber, and the Ganges: Three Kairological Moments of Christic Self-Consciousness," *ibid.*, 89–116.
16. *Ibid.*, 109.
17. *Ibid.*, 130. Yagi's article, "'I' in the Words of Jesus" is found in 117–134.
18. *Ibid.*, 141. Ruether's essay is entitled "Feminism and Jewish-Christian Dialogue: Particularism and Universalism in the Search for Religious Truth" and is found in 137–148.
19. See *ibid.*, 154–156, Sochocki's essay is entitled "In Search of Justice: Religious Pluralism from a Feminist Perspective" and is found in 149–161.
20. See *ibid.*, 162–177.
21. See *ibid.*, 174–175. Pieris's article is found in 162–177.
22. *Ibid.*, 190. Knitter's essay, entitled "Toward a Liberation Theology of Religions," is found in 176–200.
23. Hans Küng rejects Rahner's theory of "anonymous Christianity" but maintains that Christianity is the necessary critical analyst for all other faiths. Without Christ's revelation, religions, according to him, cannot really understand and appropriate the salvation at work within them; they would be caught in their "unhistoricity, circular thinking, fatalism, unworldliness, pessimism, passivity, caste spirit, a social disinterestedness." *On Being a Christian* (New York: Doubleday, 1976), 110. Küng modified his views somewhat in his later works. See his "What is True Religion: Toward an Ecumenical Criteriology," in *Toward a Universal Theology of Religion*, ed. Leonard Swidler (Maryknoll, New York: Orbis, 1981), 231–250 and his latest book *Christianity and the World Religions: Path to Dialogue with Islam, Hinduism and Buddhism* (New York: Doubleday, 1986).
24. *Toward a Universal Theology of Religion*, 225.
25. See *MCU*, 104–107. It is interesting that Panikkar does not ground the three "attitudes" of Christendom, Christianity, and Christianness in the historical Jesus. Implicitly there is recognized a distinction between Jesus and the three attitudes. However, for Panikkar, Jesus as the historical person is not decisive at all; rather what is normative is Christianness, the mystical core of the Christian religion (as opposed to its social and sacramental aspects) which may be called the christic principle. See his personal credo stated in *ibid.*, 113–114 and his brief reply to the charge that he ignores the scandal of the incarnation and the historical process of redemption.

26. In objection to my statement, it could be pointed out that some ancient creeds, e.g., the old Roman Creed, state that: "Credo...in Spiritum sanctum, santam ecclesiam...." and therefore that the Church is an object of faith. In reply, it may be noted that already ancient commentators made a distinction between faith in the Holy Spirit and faith in the Church. Rufinus, for example, insisted that the preposition *in* referred to the Holy Spirit only. He contended that one believes *in* a divine person, whereas when the object of belief is created realities, it is more accurate to say we believe them rather than *in* them. Similarly, Faustus of Rietz affirms that we believe that the Church exists, but that we do not, in the proper sense, believe in the Church. For this discussion and references to these two authors, see J. N. D. Kelly, *Early Christian Creeds* (London: Longmans, 1952), 152–153.
27. For Rahner, see his *Foundations of Christian Faith* (New York: The Seabury Press, 1978), 142–175, 311–321; for Küng, see note 23; for Bühlmann, see *God's Chosen Peoples* (Maryknoll, N.Y.: Orbis, 1983); for Camps, see *Partners in Dialogue: Christianity and Other World Religions* (Maryknoll, N.Y.: Orbis, 1983); for Lonergan, see *Method in Theology* (New York: The Seabury Press, 1979), 101–124; for McBrien, see *Catholicism* (Minneapolis: Winston, 1981), 269–271, 290; for Schlette, see *Towards a Theology of Religions* (London: Burns and Oates, 1966).
28. *Toward a Universal Theology of Religions*, 247.
29. Vatican I's Dogmatic Constitution *Dei Filius*, chapter III. The English text can be found in J. Neuner and J. Dupuis, eds., *The Christian Faith in the Doctrinal Documents of the Catholic Church* (New York: Alba House, 1981), 43.
30. *Toward a Universal Theology of Religions*, 242. It must be noted, however, that for Küng "soteriological effectiveness" (John Hick's phrase), that is, the *humanum* as a general ethical criterion, is only one of the three mutually complementary criteria. The other two criteria are fidelity to the original or canonical witness (e.g., of the Bible or the Qur'an) and fidelity to the spirit of Jesus himself. The second criterion is a general religious criterion, whereas the third is the specifically Christian one. I find Küng's criteriology more adequate than those proposed by Sochocki (justice) and Knitter (orthopraxis).
31. See his *No Other Names?*, 125–130.
32. *An Essay in Aid of a Grammar of Assent* (Westminster, Md.: Christian Classics, Inc., 1973), 492. On the illative sense, see *ibid.*, 341–383.
33. See his *No Other Names?*, 171–204. Knitter proposes what he calls a "theocentric christology" which permits a "relational uniqueness" to Jesus. Later, in response to criticism that theocentrism is inherently imperialistic since a particular (probably, Western) concept of God is imposed as normative, Knitter suggests, on the basis of liberation theology, that one should move from theocentrism to "kingdom-centrism" or "soteriocentrism." See "Toward a Liberation Theology of Religions," *MCU*, 187. In the same article he affirms "The perspective on *Soteria* given by any one mediator is always open to clarification, completion, perhaps correction by the viewpoints of other mediators. So again, the absolute, that which all else must serve, is not the church or Christ or even God—but rather, the kingdom and its justice" (*ibid.*, 190). It seems rather odd that in making this move Knitter does not seem to realize that the use of categories such as kingdom and justice (especially, kingdom, which is monarchical and male!) is also imperialist. After all, what constitutes the justice of God's kingdom? Marjorie Hewitt Sochocki is very much exercised by such a question and shows commendable sophistication in commending the notion of

justice as the norm of religious truth. See her "In Search of Justice: Religious Pluralism from a Feminist Perspective," *ibid.*, especially 156–160. The whole issue, it seems to me, turns on the question of whether to affirm the truth in a dialogue is *ipso facto* a sign of cultural imperialism.

34. See Gerald O'Collins, *Fundamental Theology* (New York: Paulist Press, 1981), 167–168.
35. See footnote 43 of chapter 9, *No Other Names?*, 261 and *MCU*, 196.
36. See *No Other Names?*, 192.
37. See *ibid.*, 185, 201.
38. It is interesting to note that for Charles Hartshorne only that which is "unsurpassable" is "worshipful." It would be inconsistent to worship someone who is not above everyone or everything else. In this connection it may be useful to bring up the issue of the sinlessness of Jesus. Can a person as savior be a total savior if he or she personally needs redemption and is actually saved from his or her own personal sins? If so, then the person who saves this sinful savior would be the "real" and "ultimate" savior. Perhaps the question of whether there are "other" saviors should be examined in this light. Did Gautama and Muhammed need to be "saved" ("enlightened") even while they themselves "saved" others through their teaching and examples? At any rate, it is interesting that the New Testament already contains statements regarding Jesus' sinlessness, even though he is said to be made unto sin. See, for instance, 2 Cor. 5:21.
39. See, for example, Swidler's latest decalogue of dialogue in "Interreligious and Interideological Dialogue: The Matrix for All Systematic Reflection Today," *Toward a Universal Theology of Religion*, 13–16; Paul Knitter, *No Other Names?*, 205–223; Raimundo Panikkar, *The Intrareligious Dialogue* (New York: Paulist Press, 1978), 25–37.
40. "Hans Küng's Theological Rubicon," *Toward a Universal Theology of Religions*, 228.
41. See *No Other Names?*, 207–208; Panikkar, *The Interreligious Dialogue*, 39–52. Such an *epoche*, when applied to religious dialogue, Panikkar rightly contends, is psychologically impracticable, phenomenologically inappropriate, philosophically defective, theologically weak, and religiously barren.
42. For a brief statement of what the claim of Jesus' uniqueness means and does not mean, see Hans Küng, "What is True Religion?," *Toward a Universal Theology of Religion*, 245–249.
43. By "homology" is meant not that the two notions are analogous, i.e., partially the same and partially different, but that they play equivalent roles and occupy homologous places within their respective systems. See the extremely informative article by Aloysius Pieris, "The Buddha and the Christ: Mediation of Liberation," *MCU*, 162–177.
44. See *The Intrareligious Dialogue*, xxvii.
45. *Christ in a Changing World: Toward an Ethical Christology* (New York: Crossroad, 1981), 58, 60, quoted with approval by Knitter in *No Other Names?*, 164.
46. For a much more nuanced assessment, see the testimony of a veteran of missionary work, Richard Henry Drummond, *Toward a New Age in Christian Theology* (Maryknoll, N.Y.: Orbis, 1985), 199–202.
47. "Toward a Christocentric Catholic Theology," in *Toward a Universal Theology of Religion*, 92.

13

KARL BARTH AND THE WIDER ECUMENISM

Donald W. Dayton

KARL BARTH, it may be argued, towers above 20th-century Protestant theology and has had a pervasive influence far beyond the boundaries of Protestantism. Even those who have sought to evade his influence and articulate alternative positions have quite often had to do that in direct dialogue with him. This is perhaps especially true with regard to Barth's position on the question of the relationship of Christianity to the other religions of the world—the issue of "the wider ecumenism." Barth's position is often interpreted through its popularization by Dutch missiologist Hendrick Kraemer in *The Christian Message in a Non-Christian World*, a volume prepared for the Tambaran Conference of what has since become the Commission on World Mission and Evangelism of the World Council of Churches.[1] In this volume, largely rooted in Barth but qualified by a slight dose of Emil Brunner, Kraemer stressed Barth's contrast between revelation and religion to argue that the "true religion" is to be found "only in God's revelation in Jesus Christ" and that other faiths are "all in error."

More recent treatments of this question have taken Barth as the primary illustration of an "exclusivist" position to be avoided in the search for a more positive Christian attitude toward the world's religions. Thus Alan Race, in *Christians and Religious Pluralism: Patterns in the Christian Theology of Religions*, develops a tripartite typology in terms of "exclusivism," "inclusivism," and "pluralism."[2] In elaborating this typology Race takes Barth's thought to represent "the most extreme form of the exclusive theory." Similarly Roman Catholic Paul F. Knitter in *No Other Names?* has taken Barth as his primary example of the "conservative evangelical" position of exclusivistic "Christocentrism" to be overcome by his own proposal of a "theocentric Christology" more amenable to dialogue with other religions.[3] Knitter offers a more extended analysis of Barth in his earlier (1972) doctoral dissertation at Marburg published as *Toward a Protestant Theology of Religions*, a study of the work of German Protestant theologian Paul Althaus on this question.[4] In this volume Knitter follows Althaus in using Barth and Troeltsch to mark out the "Scylla and Charybdis for any Christian theology of the religions" (p. 37). Knitter accepts the label of Althaus to describe Barth's position as "Christomonist"—a "narrow, restrictive, exclusive understanding of the reality of Christ, which bans all extra-Christian reality into the realm of meaninglessness and godlessness" (p. 23).

I will make no effort to minimize the exclusivistic tendencies that follow from Barth's "Christocentric concentration" in both the method and the content of his theology, but I do think that these readings of Barth are remarkably unsympathetic to his fundamental intention and fail to grasp some of the countervailing themes in Barth that do provide some basis for a greater engagement with non-Christian religions than these interpretations imply. I am especially intrigued that Knitter would use Barth as an example of the "conservative evangelical" approach to the world religions because such "conservative evangelicals" have always been troubled by Barth's "universalistic tendencies" that have seemed to them to erode any real need for the revelation in Christ. Thus I will explore three themes in Barth that seem to me to qualify the reading given above: (1) the extent to which Barth's condemnation of "religion" includes the "Christian religion" and from one angle at least thereby puts all the world's religions on the same level—and that the resulting subtle dialectical character of Barth's thought on this question is often insufficiently grasped by his critics; (2) the extent to which Barth's Christology is revelationally "exclusivistic" but soteriologically "inclusivistic" and "universalistic"; and (3) Barth's late statement on the issue in his articulation of the relation of "the Light and the lights" in such a way as to allow something less than the total condemnation of all religious experience outside of Christ.

The Abolition of Religion

The key text that has been repeatedly used to understand Barth's attitude toward non-Christian religions is paragraph 17 (81 pages, but usually designated as a "paragraph" in the structure of Barth's work) in the *Church Dogmatics* entitled in the English translation "The Abolition of Religion." As Herbert Hartwell points out in *The Theology of Karl Barth: An Introduction,*[5] this is in many ways an unfortunate translation that misses precisely the ambiguity and dialectic that is present in this section. The word translated as "abolition" is the German *Aufhebung*, a notoriously difficult word to render into English (as has been illustrated in Hegel studies and elsewhere). Hartwell suggests that the title should be rendered "The Abolition and the Exaltation of Religion" because both ideas are present in the section; and Barth is deliberately playing on the ambiguity in the German word.

Barth is notoriously difficult to interpret—among other reasons because of the dialectical character of his thought in which what appears to be stated absolutely at one point will be qualified later in a manner difficult to reconcile with the first point. This is especially true in this paragraph. The three subsections of the paragraph are entitled (1) "The Problem of Religion in Theology," (2) "Religion as Unbelief," and (3) "True Religion." Some interpreters, in addition to missing the dialectic of this paragraph, have also failed to grasp the precise nature of the contrast that Barth is making between "religion as unbelief" and "true religion." In the first place this contrast is *not* primarily between Christianity and the non-Christian religions. Barth is struggling with the 19th century tendency to interpret *Christianity* in anthropocentric and naturalistic terms and in light of a common human "religious" orientation or *a priori*. Barth's answer to this tendency was to emphasize revelation and the movement from above to below in such a way as to block all movement from below to above. The contrast in this paragraph is thus first of all between "revelation" given from above by the Living God as active subject and "religion" as human achievement and self-justification.

Barth is quite explicit that his condemnation of religion includes from at least one angle Christianity as well as other forms of religious life and activity. At this point Barth is a good Calvinist, understanding the human mind, and even the Christian mind, as an active *fabrica idolorum*. Barth's primary concern is to attack self-justificatory and idolatrous forms of the Christian "religion" rather than the non-Christian religions, though it is true that for Barth they regularly fall under the same condemnation. When Barth takes up the discussion of "true religion," he is quite clear about this point:

> In our discussion of "religion as unbelief" we did not consider the distinction between Christian and non-Christian religion. Our intention was that whatever we said about the other religions affected the Christian similarly....Therefore the discussion cannot be understood as a preliminary polemic against the non-Christian religions, with a view to the ultimate assertion that the Christian Religion is the true religion.[6]

> On the contrary, it is our business as Christians to apply this judgment first and most acutely to ourselves: and to others, the non-Christians, only in so far as we recognize ourselves in them.[7]

Now of course it is true that when Barth turns to unfold the character of "revelation," it is seen primarily and perhaps even exclusively (carefully here—at least from one angle of the dialectic!) in Jesus Christ. It is here that the usual reading of Barth has its most validity. Christian "religion" can become "true religion" as it is grasped by grace and becomes subject to the revelation in Jesus Christ. Here Barth is "radicalizing" and "actualizing" the Reformation doctrine of justification by faith in response to Divine initiative in such a way as to undercut any form of human initiative or *analogia entis* that can move toward God "from below."

But this radical subjection to the revelation in Jesus Christ is not the whole story or, as we shall see, all that Barth has to say on these questions. This conceptual framework puts the religions (including in some sense the "Christian religion" as well) on the same level as all other forms of human insight, including philosophy, natural theology, culture in general, and so on. It is generally assumed that Barth has no place for any of these, but Barth clearly does not operate on this assumption—as is evidenced by his wide reading and use in his *Dogmatics* of philosophy, history, social science, etc. What Barth takes away with one hand he gives back with the other. The issue is at what point these human achievements are brought into play and whether they are ruled by revelation in Jesus Christ. Thus philosophy or natural theology are wrong as starting points or as a place from which to launch a human movement of self-justification toward God, but they may be caught up in the *Aufhebung* and find themselves (or at least fragments of their insights) in the service of revelation. Thus in theory, at least, there could be, I believe, some role in Barth for the insights of the other religions and their dialogue with Christianity—if they do not presume to replace "revelation" and are brought into subjection to the Living God as revealed in Jesus Christ. But we shall have to explore this theme further, later where Barth takes it up most explicitly.

Barth's Soteriological Universalism

Those who interpret Barth through his particularism and revelational exclusivism sometimes fail to notice or give adequate weight to the countervailing "universalistic" themes that so often bother "traditionalists." In so doing, such interpreters miss one of the most innovative sides of Barth and the unusual dialectical relationship in his thought between the particular and the universal. While the usual tendency of the modern study of religion is to seek a "universal" perspective by the qualification and relativizing of the particular, Barth on the other hand moves to the universal through the particular. This move is especially clear in volume four of the *Church Dogmatics* where Barth develops a cosmic Christology and a soteriology that is strongly "universalistic."

It is beyond the limits of this essay to expound the full shape and originating motives of Barth's Christology. Suffice it to say that Barth is concerned to avoid the tendency of the "infralapsarian" theologies to make the incarnation a contingent response to human sin. His theology is radically "supralapsarian" in that he makes the incarnation and Christology part of the basic intention of God. This move binds creation intimately to redemption and makes Christ both the "Creator" and the "Redeemer" in a profound sense. Creation is the area of redemption from the beginning, and redemption is not an after-thought in response to human sin. From this orientation many of the distinctive themes of Barth follow naturally—particularly those themes that makes his a radically "inclusive" and "universal" Christology.

Thus in volume four of the *Church Dogmatics* Barth is concerned to argue that the covenant of God with Israel from the beginning has a universal dimension and intention that not only is revealed in Jesus Christ but includes the whole human family. In Barth's view the fundamental reality that defines all human life is the actual and effective justification, sanctification, and vocation of all humankind. Though not all live according to this reality none can escape it and fall out of the hand of God. The church in this context—and ontologically true for the whole human race—believes that God has bound himself to humankind in an everlasting covenant. When combined with other themes in Barth (especially in his doctrine of creation that the sexual bipolarity is a testimony that from the beginning humankind is created to be in fellowship and in his ecclesiology that the existence of the church takes precedence over the faith of the individual) these claims move toward a radical doctrine of human solidarity.

We sometimes forget that Barth's theology was forged in the midst of the Nazi threat and fail to see the extent to which the fundamental thrust of his theology is toward forms of human solidarity that were denied by Hitler. This is true especially in the more restricted sense that his theology so binds Jew and Christian together that any form of anti-Semitism, for example, must become self-denigration. Similarly his theology binds all humankind together in a radical solidarity. It is true that this solidarity is defined Christologically—again partially in response to the German Christians' tendency to give the state a certain autonomy rooted in creation outside the Christological determination. This Christ-ocentric focus may be offensive to advocates of other religious, but it should be clearly recognized that it is an "inclusive" and "universal" Christology aiming for a radical human solidarity rather than an "exclusive" Christology that rules out non-Christians and divides the human race ultimately and finally into the "saved" and the "lost." Here, of course, is the offense to more traditional theologies and the major reason that Barth should not be classed as a representative of the "exclusive Christology" of the "conservative evangelicals."

The Light and the Lights

One of the more difficult questions in Barth is whether to discern a fundamental shift between his earlier and his later work. We cannot resolve this question fully here. Those that do find a major shift notice a change in metaphors from the early work (especially his controversial commentary on Paul's epistle to the Romans) where he tended to speak of God as the "wholly other" and revelation as the "tangent" to the circle which has no integral relationship to the world of human experience and can only create the crater left by its impact to a later, more incarnational vision that finds expression in the "inclusive" Christology that we have developed above. This vision is one in which all of reality seems to be lifted up into Christ in such a way that there is a fundamental affirmation of human reality, at least as it is determined by Christ. Barth himself reflected a little on this question of change in an essay entitled "The Humanity of God." There he suggested that he could only utter the "yes" after the "no" had been clearly established. This seems to support the reading that we have given above that much depends on when human experience is brought to bear and for what purposes. For Barth, such human effort can never be salvific, but once that issue is clear and efforts at self-justification are undercut, Barth can gather insights, metaphors, and visions from almost any source.

This issue of fundamental change in Barth has also been debated in terms of his attitude toward the non-Christian religions. Paul Knitter describes the debate up to the publication of his dissertation in an excursus on "Did Barth Change his Verdict on the Religions?." He sides with those who maintain that Barth's position on the religions remains fundamentally unchanged.[8] A few years after the publication in 1974 of Knitter's dissertation, the question was taken up in the annual "Leuenberg" (a retreat center outside Basel) meeting of Barth scholars. The lectures by Dutch theologians Hendrik Berkhof and Hans-Joachim Kraus, and an Old Testament scholar who has moved to occupy the chair of theology that Barth once held at Göttingen, were published in *Theologische Studien* under the title *Karl Barths Lichterlehre*.[9] Here the issue is whether by contrast with the position in paragraph 17 of the *Church Dogmatics* on the "Abolition of Religion" the elaboration of the third Christological theme in paragraph 69 on Jesus Christ as the "Light of the World" reveals a new openness to the non-Christian religions. This issue is often debated in terms of the relationship between the "Light and the Lights."

Paragraph 69 is found in volume IV/3 of the *Church Dogmatics* where Barth deals with the "prophetic" office of Christ—one that brings to the fore the role of Christ as "revealer" or as "the Light of Life." Here we find parallels to many earlier points. Barth's use of rhetoric lends itself to "exclusivisitic" interpretations:

> Jesus Christ is *the* light of life. To underline the "the" is to say that He is the one and only light of life. Positively this means that he is the light of life in all its fullness, in perfect adequacy; and negatively it means that there is no other light of life outside or alongside His, outside or alongside the light which He is.[10]

Barth also makes the point quite clearly that we indicated above—that Christian experience and truth is also brought under judgment along with all other forms of truth:

> Thus the criticism expressed in the exclusiveness of the statement affects, limits, and relativizes the prophecy of Christians no less than the many other prophecies, lights, and words relativized and replaced by it....What it says concerning the importance of all other prophecy which attempts to rival its own is valid only in analogy to, and an consequence of, that fact that first and supremely it is true of the Christian sphere.[11]

But Barth also quite explicitly in this section affirms the other side of the dialectic to say quite clearly that there are other words to which we should attend:

> We recognize that the fact that Jesus Christ is the one Word of God does not mean that in the Bible, the Church and the world there are not other words which are quite notable in their way, other lights which are quite clear and other revelations which are quite real....Nor does it follow from our statement that every word spoken outside the circle of the Bible and the Church is a word of

> false prophecy and therefore valueless, empty and corrupt, that all the lights which rise and shine in the outer sphere are misleading and all the revelations are necessarily untrue.[12]

Barth then goes on to say that the issue is whether these lights are to be put on the same level as the one Word of God in Christ. The "lights" must not displace, transcend, or attempt to encompass the one "Light." But in their proper place they may function as true and real lights. Barth can make this move in part because of the role of Christ in creation and the way in which Creation and Redemption are unified in Christ. But the result is that there are other "lights" in the world that can also be genuinely called "lights" and genuinely reveal and inform—as long as they do not replace the "Light." Here we see quite clearly the other side of the dialectic expressed in the difficult translation of *Aufhebung* cited above in the section on "The Abolition of Religion." Here Barth quite explicitly uses the positive language of "exaltation":

> ...they are taken, lifted, assumed and integrated into the action of God's self-giving and self-declaring to man and therefore to the world made by him. And in the power of this integration they are instituted, installed, and ordained to the *ministerium Verbi Divini*.[13]

The genuine dialectic in Barth is expressed quite clearly in the final lines of the section:

> This... is the critical, but also, since it is genuinely critical, the positive relationship of the light of life to the lights which the God whose saving action is revealed by the one light does not withhold from his creatures as such but gives them in His eternal goodness.[14]

The results of this study are modest. We have not challenged directly Barth's own Christological exclusivism. We have merely argued that he is often misunderstood—that his thought is more subtle and dialectical than is often assumed. I am not sure that Barth himself would have developed his own thought in the direction of dialogue with other religions (indeed, there are signs and incidents that indicate that he did not have much personal interest in these questions), but I do think that it is possible on Barthian premises to have more engagement with other religions than is usually assumed. This is to be sure a modest place, but I believe it to be a valuable place nonetheless.

Notes

1. Hendrick Kraemer, *The Christian Message in a Non-Christian World* (London: 1938).
2. Alan Race, *Christians and Religious Pluralism: Patterns in Christian Theology of Religions* (Maryknoll, New York: Orbis Books, 1982).
3. Paul F. Knitter, *No Other Names?* (Maryknoll, New York: Orbis Books, 1985).
4. Paul F. Knitter, *Towards a Protestant Theology of Religions* (Marburg: N. G. Elwert, 1974).
5. Herbert Hartwell, *The Theology of Karl Barth: An Introduction* (London: Duckworth, 1964).
6. Karl Barth, *Church Dogmatics*, ed. G. W. Bromiley, T. F. Torrance (Edinburgh: T. & T. Clark, 1958), l/S, 326.
7. *Idem*, 327.
8. Paul F. Knitter, *Towards a Protestant Theology of Religions* (Marburg: Elwert, 1974), 32–36.
9. Henrik Berkhof and Hans-Joachim Kraus, "Karl Barths' Lichterlehre," *Theologische Studien*, no. 123.
10. *Church Dogmatics*, IV/3a, 86.
11. *Ibid.*, 91.
12. *Ibid.*, 97.
13. *Ibid.*, 164.
14. *Ibid.*, 164–165.

14

THE UNDERSTANDING OF CHRIST AS FINAL REVELATION

Mary Ann Stenger

WITH TECHNOLOGIES and communication networks connecting us to peoples around the world, we can think in terms of a global community. With increased mobility of peoples, our own neighborhoods have become a microcosm of that community, with cultural and religious diversity. In such a context, any form of Christian imperialism seems offensive and archaic. But the theological issues involved in avoiding Christian imperialism are complex and reach the very center of Christian doctrine.

One such central issue is the understanding of Christ as final revelation and its significance for dealing with religious pluralism. This issue raises the following interdependent questions for discussion: 1) Can the understanding of Christ as final revelation include revelation and truth in non-Christian religions? 2) Does emphasis on the universal of Christ over the particularity of Jesus allow for more openness to non-Christian religions? 3) To what extent is the doctrine of Christ as final revelation diluted by a move to theocentrism in cross-cultural theological discussion? (Christocentrism vs. theocentrism). With these questions defining the issues for our discussion, we will analyze diverse Christian view points and work toward an understanding which is both Christian and ecumenical.

Final Revelation in Jesus as the Christ

Traditionally the Christian belief in Jesus as the Christ as final revelation has been a motivating factor in proselytizing and the primary means of Christian interaction with non-Christian religions. To see Jesus as the Christ as the final revelation can mean seeing other religious traditions as preliminary truths that have been surpassed in Jesus as the Christ. And it can mean that there can be no later revelations, cutting off all revelatory claims after Jesus. Many of us grew up with such a 'Christian' outlook, but today we are uncomfortable with the imperialism of such an approach which often went hand in hand with economic and political imperialism.[1] From a popular, liberal standpoint, some resolve this discomfort by rejecting all efforts at conversion and saying, "To each, his/her own." But if we look at this stance more deeply, we are also dissatisfied with an unthought-out pure relativism.

Is there a way to mediate the difference between the imperialism of an absolutist approach and the indifference of a relativist approach? How can we be open to non-Christian religious persons and still maintain a critical religious stance? How can an ecumenical Christian deal with the claim of final revelation in Jesus Christ? Let us attempt to answer these questions by looking at varying interpretations of final revelation in Jesus Christ and the implications of those views for Christianity's relation to non-Christian religious traditions.

Barth: Critique of Religion by God's Revelation in Christ. For Karl Barth the understanding of Jesus as the Christ as final revelation is based on his emphasis on God's freedom and righteousness in contrast to human self-righteousness and sin. Revelation is God's self-offering, perfectly shown in Jesus Christ, and it cannot be replaced with human knowledge and efforts as found in religion.[2] Barth offers a radical critique of all religions as idolizing human efforts instead of responding to God's revelation. For Barth, it is God's revelation in Jesus Christ which shows all religion to be unbelief and in fact is the abolition of religion.[3] Christianity as well as all other religions stand under this negative judgment.

But through divine righteousness and freedom, God chose to reveal truth to humans through Jesus Christ, thereby making Christianity the bearer of truth and the "true religion."[4] Thus, God's revelation in Jesus Christ both brings truth to Christianity and also judges Christianity and all other religions as idolatrous and unbelieving. To ask if God could have revealed truth elsewhere is to turn toward human concerns and away from God's revelation.[5]

Yet Barth is very clear that he does not intend the affirmation of Christianity as the bearer of truth to lead to self-righteousness or arrogance. Other religions are to be "valued and taken seriously" even though the Gospel can in no way compromise with them or for them.[6] The revelation in Jesus Christ is for all people, even though they may not have recognized it or responded to that revelation.[7] The light of Christ can be reflected both inside and outside the church.[8] But those who do not come into the light of Christ are condemned by their own unspiritual lives, not because God had pre-ordained them to condemnation. God through Christ offers reconciliation and salvation to all people, but without Christ all religious efforts are futile.

For Barth, then, final revelation in Jesus Christ means that God has acted for all humans in and through Jesus Christ. The testimony to that revelation (especially in Scriptures) rules out other revelatory claims. Since this revelation puts all humanity and thereby all religions under judgment and critique, Christianity is seen as under the same judgment as non-Christian religions. Barth does include non-Christians in God's plan of salvation but only if they convert to Christ.

On a theoretical level, Barth may be able to claim that he has preserved his respect for non-Christian religions and has avoided an arrogant imperialism. But on a practical level, his theory seems to lead toward just that kind of imperialism and self-righteousness. When Barth says that Christianity can be called the bearer of true religion through Christ, it is difficult to see the subtle differences between that claim and a claim of superiority for Christianity, especially when those claims are acted on in the world. His interpretation of the centrality of final revelation in Christ is too narrow to be fully open to non-Christians.

Rahner: Christian Inclusivism with Anonymous Christians. Like Barth, Rahner wants to retain the centrality and absoluteness of final revelation in Christ. But he also is more concerned about including rather than condemning non-Christians. The basis of this more inclusive stance is his belief in the universality of Christ's redemption. He therefore develops the idea of "anonymous Christian" to do justice to the Christian view that salvation cannot come apart from the theistic God and Christ and to include the possibility of supernatural salvation and faith for non-Christians.[9]

In "Christianity and the Non-Christian Religions," Karl Rahner accepts Christianity's self-understanding as the absolute religion, intended for all people, which cannot accept any other religion as equal to itself.[10] Similarly to Barth, the basis of this is rooted in God's own action for humans in Christ.[11] But Rahner states more strongly that non-Christian religions do contain supernatural elements of grace because of God's gift in Christ.[12] A non-Christian can be called an anonymous Christian because their experience of grace is rooted in Christ.

Such a position may satisfy the Christian's concern to love one's neighbor and avoid an imperialistic condemnation of non-Christians. But like Barth, Rahner's inclusiveness is rooted in God's gift in Christ rather than any quality in non-Christian religions themselves. To a non-Christian, this may appear as a somewhat more subtle and therefore more offensive claim of Christian superiority. Any positive religious value in their traditions is seen as coming from Christ, not from the religious and spiritual actions set forth by their own scriptures and leaders. Again as with Barth, on a practical level, Christian inclusivism fails to take the non-Christian seriously on his or her own terms.

Tillich: Paradox in Final Revelation as Criterion. Paul Tillich's discussions of final revelation and universal revelation provide another example of Christian inclusivism, but the concepts of paradox used in his analysis can be developed more universally. When Tillich focuses on the concrete content of the Christ or the Cross, he retains the traditional sense of Christian superiority. But his formal abstractions of meaning from those events need not be tied to the specific Christian content.

In the *Systematic Theology*[13] Tillich defines revelation as "the manifestation of what concerns us ultimately" (ST, I, 110). Such manifestation is always a concrete event for someone in a particular situation of concern (ST, I, 111). Tillich does not accept a general revelation, but he does affirm the ***universal possibility*** of revelation. Because every person and thing participates in the ground, meaning, and power of being-itself, anything can bear revelation (ST, I, 118).

This view of revelation has significant implications for developing an inclusive ecumenical understanding. Krishna, Buddha, and Mohammad, like all beings, participate in the ground of being and can express it through revelation. The universal possibility of revelation is not tied to a Christian context, even though Tillich develops it from Christianity.

"Final revelation" is a specific form of revelation, in Tillich's view, not just the last genuine revelation. It is "the decisive, fulfilling, unsurpassable revelation, that which is the criterion of all the others" (ST, I, 133). That criterion, based in Jesus as the Christ or the New Being, is that "a revelation is final if it has the power of negating itself without losing itself" (ST, I, 133). Jesus' sacrifice to himself as the Christ is particularly seen in the Cross; the negation of Jesus on the Cross is his affirmation as the Christ.[14]

Jesus as the Christ is the final revelation, but because of the grounding of all in the power of being-itself and the transforming power of the New Being (ST, II, 167), other events outside Christianity can be revelatory of that power. Also, Tillich accepts the possibility of divine self-manifestation in other ways before and/or after our history (ST, II, 101). And in "The Significance of the History of Religions for the Systematic Theologian," Tillich suggests other possibilities of transforming revelation. What happened in the Cross in a symbolic way "also happens fragmentarily in other places, in other moments, has happened and will happen even though they are not historically or empirically connected with the cross."[15]

The paradoxical content of the criterion of final revelation relates to the paradoxical structure of all revelation which occurs in any unity of the ultimate with the finite.[16] A finite symbol of the ultimate is both conditioned and yet points to and bears the unconditioned. But even more, this paradox of final revelation involves the negation of ultimacy which is yet an affirmation of ultimacy. The negation of ultimacy for Jesus on the Cross is yet the affirmation of ultimacy for Jesus as the Christ.

As with Tillich's affirmation of the universal possibility of revelation, so also his paradoxical criterion of final revelation can provide a basis for judging final revelation outside the Christian tradition. Many non-Christian symbols and ideas involve a paradoxical unity of the conditioned and the unconditioned, the finite and the ultimate. And some may even involve the paradoxical content of negation/affirmation specified in Tillich's criterion of final revelation.[17] Thus, the move to abstract formal meaning from specific content allows more openness to non-Christian traditions and may prevent the absolutization of the concrete itself.

Hick: Absoluteness of Christ for Christians. John Hick has called for a switch from a Ptolemaic understanding of religion to a Copernican viewpoint. Often, this discussion has focused on the center of all religious as the Real, with salvation in any religion as the transformation of the person from self-centeredness to Reality-centeredness.[18] Christianity, then, is just "one of a number of worlds of faith which circle around and reflect that Reality."[19] Religious truth and moral goodness can be found in all the major religious traditions.[20]

Hick's emphasis on one divine center does not mean that he has abandoned the significance of Christ for Christians. But he has moved away from the traditional view of universal finality in Christ. He applauds those modern Christologies which judge the Christ event historically, seeing the historical Jesus as an exemplification of a specific religious quality and as one who leads others to respond to that truth.[21] Such Christologies cannot argue historically for absolute truth in Jesus even though they do assert the absoluteness of Christ for Christians.

Hick prefers metaphorical to literal understandings of the incarnation. Viewed metaphorically, the incarnation can be understood as one human way of expressing the Christian contact with God's presence, love, and power through Jesus. That view allows the possibility of other ways of salvation outside of Christ while still affirming salvation in Christ.[22]

With such interpretations, Hick accepts the psychological absoluteness of Christ for Christians but asks that this not be turned into a claim of objective absoluteness and superiority which rejects all claims from non-Christian religious traditions.[23] His position affirms religious pluralism rather than just including non-Christians into his Christian framework.

Preliminary Comparisons

As we have moved from Barth to Hick, we have seen a move from an affirmation of revelation only in Christ (Barth) to an acceptance of truth in all religions (Hick). Rahner's position is closer to Barth's, but he does affirm more strongly the presence of grace and supernatural action in non-Christian religions than does Barth. Tillich's view is closer to Hick's, but Tillich retains the finality in Christ and a sense of the superiority of Christianity because of the Christ and the Cross.

All of these positions do affirm a center in God, the ultimate/unconditioned, or the Real. For each, that center is the absolute which grounds all truth and all reality. All would also agree on an integral relationship between Jesus Christ and the divine center. But for Barth and for Rahner, Christ is in the center with God; there is no revelation of God apart from Christ. Parts of Tillich's position suggest that he agrees with Barth and Rahner; all reality is grounded in the ultimate, being-itself, and all saving transformation of people is grounded in the New Being manifested in Jesus as the Christ. But to the extent that Tillich's discussion abstracts from the concrete New Being in Jesus Christ and offers more universal, formal meaning for the Cross and the Christ, his ideas can be applied more universally—both inside and outside Christianity. Hick, like the others, retains absoluteness in Jesus Christ, but unlike the others, the absoluteness affirmed is not objective but psychological for Christians. Similarly, he would see other religious truth-claims as psychologically absolute for members of that tradition but not objectively or universally absolute.

Final revelation in Jesus as the Christ, then, may be understood as *inclusive* of non-Christian when it emphasizes the universal significance of the Christ and the Cross for all people. But such inclusion does not take the non-Christian seriously in his/her own terms but simply brings the non-Christian into the "Christian fold." An understanding of revelation which is open to revelation outside the Christian context (such as Tillich's position) is a necessary beginning of genuine openness to non-Christians. But we may also need to move beyond that position to a deeper relativization of the understanding of Christ, such as Hick proposes in his affirmation of pluralism. Such relativization of the doctrine of Christ will involve analyzing the relationship between the historical Jesus and the universal Christ, as well as reconsidering the role of that doctrine within Christian theology.

Universality of the Christ vs. Particularity of Jesus

Even if one affirms the finality of God's revelation in Christ, one may still be able to develop a theology which is open to non-Christian religious traditions by focusing on universal meaning in Christ. How possible it is to focus on the universality of Christ may depend on how the relationship between the Christ and the historical Jesus is understood. Let us now look at some examples of diverse ways of understanding that relationship and their implications for Christianity's relationship with non-Christian religions.

Barth and Rahner: Centrality of the Historical Jesus with Some Universal Significance of the Christ. For Barth, God's revelation in Jesus Christ is directly connected with the historical Jesus' birth, death and resurrection which brought the reconciliation of humans to God. With Barth, there is little separation of the historical Jesus from the universal Christ. It is not just that Jesus is a particular *example* of religious perfection or some other ideal quality. Barth is quite clear that "theology must begin with Jesus Christ, and not with general principles" as if Jesus Christ "were a continuation of the knowledge and Word of God, and not its root and origin, not indeed the very Word of God itself."[24] In Barth's discussions of Jesus Christ, he moves back and forth between references to the historical events in Jesus' life and the reconciliation and liberation for humanity which were achieved through those events. He rejects a formal meaning for Christ and focuses instead on Christ's salvific meaning for the Christian in faith.

But this salvific meaning was meant for all people; all are called into the light of Jesus Christ.[25] Barth speaks of Jesus Christ as the one light of the world but also of reflecting lights both inside and outside the church.[26] True words which reflect the light of Christ can occur in Christian communities but also outside Christian communities—perhaps in other religious or secular settings. The basis for such a view is in Barth's acceptance of the pre-existence of Jesus Christ. God's covenant from the beginning included God's redemptive choice to be unified with humans through Jesus Christ. God wills redemption first, then creation. The universal significance of Jesus Christ then relates to all persons through creation and may be reflected in some particular words which point to God's word in Christ.[27]

The positive side of Barth's position is that it does have a universal, inclusive dimension. Theoretically and theologically, all persons of the world are included as capable of expressing at least a possible reflection of Christ's truth. But Barth is also clear that for someone to reflect the light of Christ, that person must have had some contact with Christ.[28] Thus, Barth's suggested inclusiveness is not an inclusion of non-Christian religions in their own right but only if there is some reflection of Christ's truth. Nor does this inclusiveness imply a tolerance of non-Christian ideas and practices that are not centered in Christ. Practically, Barth's position excludes non-Christians except for some reflections of *Christ's truth* or as witnesses to the *light of Christ*.

Barth's understanding of the universality of Christ is centered in the historical Jesus. He does not see the reconciliation between humans and God occurring through any other person than Jesus Christ. Thus, the universal Christ does not include Gautama Buddha, Amida Buddha, Krishna, or Brahman, etc.

Like Barth, Karl Rahner also affirms the centrality of Jesus Christ, but Rahner allows more inclusiveness based on the universality of Christ. The anonymous Christian is the person who lives in the grace of Christ through faith, hope, and love but who does not explicitly recognize its source in Jesus Christ and who is not explicitly oriented to salvation through Christ.[29] Thus, Rahner is not using the term to refer to every person (universal salvation) but to persons whose beliefs and actions reflect the grace of Christ. It is Rahner's strong acceptance of the universality of Christ's redeeming action that grounds his position on anonymous Christians.[30] His Spirit/Logos christology, i.e., his emphasis on the universal Christ, more than the particular historical Jesus, provides the basis for his inclusion and openness.

Although both Barth and Rahner share an emphasis on the centrality of Christ, Barth shows more focus on the particular event of Jesus Christ while Rahner emphasizes the universal Christ and the wide-spread efficacy of grace-filled salvation through Christ. That difference leads to the differences in degree of inclusiveness of non-Christians. The greater the emphasis on universality, the greater degree to which non-Christians are included in grace and salvation.

Tillich: Centrality of the Universal Christ with Some Roots in the Historical Jesus. Tillich attempts to maintain a dynamic tension between the particularity of the historical Jesus (including the Cross) and the universal meaning of the Christ or the New Being. But his emphasis on the Christ more than the historical Jesus is expressed throughout his theology. When defining the essence of the Christ event, or the meaning of the Cross or setting forth criteria of religious truth, Tillich focuses on the universal meaning derived from the concrete event more than the historical Jesus himself. In fact, he sees final revelation in Jesus as the Christ precisely because the particularities of the finite Jesus are sacrificed to the universal Christ. "The decisive trait in his picture is the continuous self-surrender of Jesus who is Jesus to Jesus who is the Christ" (ST, I, 134).

When Tillich discusses the historical Jesus in relation to the New Being, he is quite clear that historical research about the historical Jesus does not guarantee us the reality of the New Being, nor that Jesus of Nazareth is that person, nor that the biblical details are correct (ST, II, 114–115). Faith and participation in the transforming power of the New Being can guarantee that the biblical picture of Jesus is an adequate expression of that transforming power, but they cannot guarantee that Jesus is the name of the person who is the New Being (ST, II, 107, 115). While it is important to Tillich that some historical reality bear the transforming power of the New Being, he does focus on the certainty of the historical Jesus as such.

Tillich specifically discusses the inter-relationship of particularity and universality in Jesus as the Christ and the significance of that for judging religious truth. Jesus is a particular historical life, but he makes no claims for himself based on his particularity. "What is particular in him is that he crucified the particular in himself for the sake of the universal."[31] Tillich applies this negation of particularities to all religions.

> Religion cannot come to an end, and a particular religion will be lasting to the degree in which it negates itself as a religion....In the depth of every living religion there is a point at which the religion itself loses its importance, and that to which it points breaks through its particularity, elevating it to spiritual freedom and with

> it to a vision of the spiritual presence in other expressions of the ultimate meaning of man's existence.[32]

Once again, Tillich's criterion of religion builds on the paradoxical significance he derives from Jesus as the Christ. He pushes to the depth of the religion, to the underlying spiritual presence and a spiritual freedom which is found by breaking through the finite particularities of religion (parallel to the Christ revealed by breaking through the finite particularities of the historical Jesus). This criterion applies to all religions, including Christianity, out of whose center the criterion is developed. It is important to recognize that Tillich is not advocating a universal religion outside of traditional religions; rather, he is calling people to experience the depth within each living tradition. In that depth, he believes that they will be spiritually free from the finite particularities of their own tradition and therefore open to that possibility in other religious traditions.

In a similar way, Tillich's critique of idolatry develops from the symbol of the Cross but is then applied to all religious symbols. The self-negation of Jesus to himself as the Christ leads to a criterion of a true religious symbol as one in which the finite aspects are transparent to the ultimate, without the finite elements themselves being taken as absolute. When people instead absolutize the finite medium itself, it ceases to be a medium of revelation and becomes an idol. Once again, although developed from the Cross, this critique of idolatry can be applied outside Christianity.

At one point, he uses this criterion to claim the superiority of Protestant Christianity.[33] But it would seem that he has overstated the claim since elsewhere he applies the critique within the Protestant tradition as well as all of Christianity and other traditions. Still, there is little doubt that for Tillich, the Cross and Jesus' sacrifice of himself to himself as the Christ on the Cross did insure the unsurpassability of Christian revelation. Yet, his statement of a Yes and No judgment, that the symbol expresses the ultimate (yes) but also its own lack of ultimacy (no),[34] is not stated in Christian terms and could be applied cross-culturally, even to his own view of the Cross and Christ.

Once again, we see that emphasis on the universality of the Christ and the universal meaning developed from the event of the Christ leads to more openness towards religious truth and spiritual meaning in non-Christian religious traditions. For Tillich, one cannot really separate that meaning and truth from the Cross, from the picture of Jesus as the Christ. But we suggest that these meanings might be developed for application across all religious traditions, without simply imposing a

Christian standard or Christian meaning. We will need to ask to what extent the critique of idolatry and the paradox of negating particularities to reach the infinite depth might be acceptable and applicable across religious traditions.

Christocentrism vs. Theocentrism

Recognizing that the particularity of Christian claims can be a blocking point in dealing with non-Christian religions, John Hick has proposed an understanding which shifts the emphasis to the Real from the Christ. We need to look at the implications of such a shift both within Christianity and in relation to non-Christian religions.

John Hick's call for a Copernican revolution in the Christian attitude toward other religions involves "a shift from the dogma that Christianity is at the center to the thought that it is *God* who is at the center and that all the religions of mankind, including our own, serve and revolve around him."[35] Hick proposes one transcendent, divine noumenon, which transcends all human conceptions of it and a plurality of divine phenomena (God as a personal god, the impersonal Absolute, etc.).[36] This imagery clearly calls into question any Christian claim of superiority over other religious traditions.

But Hick's shift to theocentrism here does not ignore the Christian center in Christ. As we have seen earlier, he allows for a psychological absoluteness but rejects the traditional claim of "objective absoluteness and superiority of our own faith in comparison with all others."[37] He also uses a metaphorical interpretation of Jesus Christ to relativize but retain the incarnation of Christ in relationship to the Real.

Hick is particularly interested in what he calls "degree Christologies" which talk about "the activity of God's Spirit or of God's grace" in varying degrees in human lives.[38] Although the authors of such Christological theories often affirm the superiority of revelation in Jesus Christ, Hick points out that such superiority can no longer be claimed *a priori*. Therefore, Christian claims of revelation are put on the same level with other claims. It is possible to see "God's activity in Jesus as being of the same kind as God's activity in other great human mediators of the divine."[39] By emphasizing God's activity, theocentrism can replace Christocentrism without giving up the central significance of Christ in Christianity.

Hick takes history seriously in emphasizing the diverse human cultural situations in which the different religious images and traditions operate. "It is the variations of the human cultural situation that concretize the notion of deity as specific images of God."[40] This fits with his view that missionary activities (until recently) have often involved spreading the cultures out of which the religious tradition came.[41] Only the Real itself is beyond the metaphors, myths, and cultures which attempt to express that Reality.

Hick's theocentrism is more accurately described as Reality-centeredness, since he does recognize that "God" is not an accurate name for the ultimate in all religious traditions. But Hick does believe that across religious traditions there are many people who "experience life in relation to a limitlessly greater transcendent Reality—whether the direction of transcendence be beyond our present existence or within its hidden depths."[42] With the center in that Reality, religious pluralism can be affirmed in such a way that diverse concepts, images, practices, and forms of religious awareness can be seen as based on and directed toward the Real. These diverse ways are authentic to the extent that they are effective in transforming people from self- to Reality-centeredness.[43]

Hick's approach, then, maintains its openness to non-Christian religions by relativizing all human forms of religion, a move that is also made by Barth's critique of religion and Tillich's critique of idolatry. He affirms pluralism rather than inclusivism by understanding Jesus Christ metaphorically rather than literally and by shifting absoluteness to the Real which is beyond human forms from specific religious conceptions or practices. It is important to note that Hick's pluralism does not come from simply emphasizing universal meaning in Christ but rather from understanding all religious traditions as centered in the one transcendent Real.

Conclusions

From our discussion of Barth, Rahner, Tillich, and Hick, we can clearly see the tension between final revelation in Christ and a desire to be open to truth in non-Christian religions. For those who want to retain the centrality of final revelation in Christ and a close tie to the historical Jesus Christ, openness will most likely be expressed as some form of Christian inclusivism. We can look at Barth's more closed stance or Rahner's more inclusive view, but each is a form of inclusivism, including non-Christians under Christian rubrics. Even most of Tillich's writings, although more open than Barth or Rahner because of his formal abstractions of universal meaning, basically express a Christian inclusivism centered in Jesus as the Christ as final revelation.

Although I am more sympathetic to Tillich's more open position than Barth's more closed stance, I see problems with any form of Christian inclusivism. Such a position fails to take the non-Christian religions seriously, on their own terms. It really dismisses their teachers, Scriptures, prophets, deities, and ultimates as secondary and really irrelevant to Christian truths. With such a position, dialogue is a sharing of ideas but not an openness to new ideas. But if we really engage with another person, we are open to adjusting our ideas.

In fact, both Tillich and Hick have engaged in dialogue with non-Christians, and one can see ongoing shifts in their thought as a result of those conversations. In fact, both make similar moves in their thinking, toward one underlying Reality or depth beneath the particular phenomena of the religions. They, like some others, have found a form of theocentrism as a solution to their acceptance of truths outside Christianity. Such a position has the advantage of allowing individual religions to have their truths but makes all religious truths relative to the one underlying or centering Real or depth.

Such a position does not destroy the acceptance of final revelation in Christ, but it does relativize it in relation to other revelations in non-Christian traditions. Christians can still retain the absoluteness of Christ for them, but they do not assert it in relation to the non-Christian.

One can develop criteria out of one's own tradition and state them in ways that are not tied to the particular tradition (for example, Tillich's criterion of "affirmation in negation"). But the real test of such criteria is not just how they can be in dialogue with non-Christians. Many traditions might agree on Tillich's critique of idolatry or Barth's critique of religion in relation to God's revelation, even though they would not accept the concrete content from which the critiques arise.

Our future, then, is not to abandon our Christian centering in Christ as final revelation but to relate that center finally to ultimacy which is beyond finite expressions and forms. I recognize that there are some who call for an even more radical relativism, seeing each tradition operating within its historical-cultural context, without claiming one underlying absolute. But I see the direction toward ultimacy and truth in all religions as a structural commonality even if we do not agree on the nature of that ultimacy. Consequently, we can only work out of our own traditions and cultures, but we must continue in conversation and dialogue that is based on our common search for truth and transcendence. As we do so, core doctrines like final revelation in Christ are not abandoned but interpreted anew for our present pluralistic situation.

Notes

1. See Rosemary Radford Ruether, *To Change the World; Christology and Cultural Criticism* (London: SCM Press Ltd., 1981), 38.
2. Karl Barth, *Church Dogmatics*, ed. G. W. Bromley, T. F. Torrance (Edinburgh: T. & T. Clark, 1958), I/2, 301–302.
3. *Ibid.*, I/2, 297. (See also I/2, 325–327.)
4. *Ibid.*, I/2, 349–350.
5. *Ibid.*, I/2, 354.
6. *Ibid.*, IV/3B, 875.
7. *Ibid.*, IV/3A, 354.
8. *Ibid.*, If/3A, 112.
9. Karl Rahner, "The One Christ and the Universality of Salvation," *Theological Investigations* XVI (London: Darton, Longman & Todd, 1979), 218.
10. Karl Rahner, "Christianity and the Non-Christian Religions," *Theological Investigations V* (London: Darton, Longman & Todd, 1966), 118.
11. *Ibid.*
12. *Ibid.*, 121.
13. Paul Tillich, *Systematic Theology*, 3 Vols. (Chicago: University of Chicago Press, 1951–63). References will be in the form of (ST, volume number, page number).
14. Paul Tillich, *The Dynamics of Faith* (New York: Harper & Row, 1957), 97–98.
15. Paul Tillich, "The Significance of the History of Religions for the Systematic Theologian," *The Future of Religion*, ed. Jerald C. Brauer (New York: Harper & Row, 1966), 89.
16. See Paul Tillich, "The Conquest of the Concept of Religion in the Philosophy of Religion," *What is Religion*? ed. James Luther Adams (New York: Harper & Row, 1969), 123.
17. For further development of this idea, see my discussion in "The Significance of Paradox for Theological Verification: Difficulties and Possibilities," *International Journal for Philosophy of Religion* XIV (1983), 171–182.
18. John Hick, "On Grading Religions," *Religious Studies* XVII (1981) 467; idem, "Religious Pluralism," *The World's Religious Traditions*, ed. Frank Whaling (Edinburgh: T. & T. Clark, Ltd., 1984), 158.
19. John Hick, "Religious Pluralism and Absolute Claims," *Religious Pluralism*, ed. Leroy S. Rouner (Notre Dame: University of Notre Dame Press, 1984), 200.
20. See John Hick, "On Grading Religions."
21. John Hick, "Religious Pluralism and Absolute Claims," 193–213.
22. John Hick, *God Has Many Names* (Philadelphia: The Westminster Press, 1980), 75.
23. *Ibid.*, 57.
24. Karl Barth, *Church Dogmatics* II, 2:5.
25. *Ibid.*, IV, 3B: 875; IV, 3/1:354.
26. Ibid., IV, 3/l paragraph 69.
27. For fuller discussion of Barth on this issue, see Robert Jenson, "Religious Pluralism, Christology, and Barth," *Dialog* XX (Winter, 1981), 31–38.
28. Karl Barth, *Church Dogmatics* IV, 3/l:124, 344f.

29. Karl Rahner, "Observations on the Problems of the 'Anonymous Christian,'" *Theological Investigations* XIV (London: Darton, Longman & Todd, 1976), 283.
30. Karl Rahner, "The One Christ and the Universality of Salvation," 218.
31. Paul Tillich, *Christianity and the Encounter of the World Religions* (New York: Columbia University Press, 1963), 81.
32. *Ibid.*, 97.
33. Paul Tillich, *Dynamics of Faith*, 98. See Tom Driver's discussion of Tillich's position in "The Case for Pluralism," *The Myth of Christian Uniqueness*, ed. John Hick and Paul Knitter (Maryknoll, NY: Orbis Books, 1987), 215.
34. *Ibid.*, 97.
35. John Hick, *God Has Many Names*, 36.
36. *Ibid.*, 53.
37. *Ibid.*, 57–58.
38. John Hick, "Religious Pluralism," 154–155. Also see his discussion in "Religious Pluralism and Absolute Claims."
39. *Ibid.*, 155.
40. John Hick, *God Has Many Names*, 105.
41. *Ibid.*, 113.
42. John Hick, "Religious Pluralism," 156–157.
43. *Ibid.*, 163–164.

15

TILLICH, RAHNER AND SCHILLEBEECKX

ON THE UNIQUENESS AND UNIVERSALITY OF CHRISTIANITY IN DIALOGUE WITH THE WORLD'S RELIGIONS

Frederick M. Jelly

APPARENTLY ONE of the most formidable obstacles to the wider ecumenism between Christianity and the other great religions of the world is the Christian conviction and claim that Christianity is the universal religion of the human race based on upon the unique event of Jesus Christ, the Savior of the whole world from the beginning to the very end of history. How can we Christians enter in good faith into an authentic "dialogue" with the members of other religions, since the mutual understanding of such ecumenical or inter-religious conversations is that the conversion of the other is definitely not the intention of the partners in dialogue? On the other hand, if we Christians are not honest and open about our convictions, then the inter-faith dialogue is bound to fail.

I pose this dilemma at the very outset neither because of any sense of hopelessness regarding the "wider ecumenism" between us and the non-Christian religions, nor for the reason that this question has not been confronted before, but precisely because its resolution is so crucial to the possibility itself of inter-religious dialogue. That the claim for the universality of the Christian religion is based on a tradition of long standing hardly requires much explanation to the members of this intra-Christian conference. Although there were sparks of universalism in the Old Testament (cf. Isa. 49:6), still it was not until the definitive revelation of the New Testament that the promised Messiah was clearly portrayed as the One who came to save all (cf. Rom. 10:12–15, Eph. 1:3–23, Luke 2:32 and Acts 13:47 which refers to Isa. 49:6). There is no doubt that the apostles and countless missionaries over the centuries have been impelled by the Spirit to preach the Good News to the ends of the earth. Frequently enough this zeal to evangelize the heathen or "infidel" as the only way of bringing salvation to such people was accompanied by very narrow and negative views of non-Christian religions. More recent theological theories that have attempted to explain how members of these religions, or even those who may have no religious affiliation whatsoever, can be saved—and indeed saved by the sole Savior of all, Jesus Christ, apart from any explicit Christian faith—have been able to remove substantially such narrow negativity without compromising the claim of the Christian religion to universality and also without intending to lessen its missionary zeal.

This paper proposes to summarize three of these theological theories constructed by three 20th-century systematicians: Paul Tillich, the German-born Lutheran who did much of his mature work in America; Karl Rahner, the German Jesuit; and, Edward Schillebeeckx, the Dutch Dominican. Each of these systematic theologians seems to have something significant to contribute towards the resolution of the dilemma confronting us Christians concerning our dialogue with non-Christians. My reason for selecting them is not that their hypothetical constructs answer all of the thorny questions involved in the problem, but because they appear to address the principal issues in the matter. After expounding the opinions of each, I shall offer my reflections about one way in which to combine their main ideas so that we might meet the challenge of the dilemma. All of this will be done without any presumption of arriving at a definitive solution to this basic problem, but with a view towards introducing a dialogue about it with my Christian colleagues at this conference.

Paul Tillich's "Absolutely Concrete" and "Absolutely Universal"

In the introduction to the first volume of his *Systematic Theology*, Tillich addresses the question: Are the claims of Christianity valid for those outside the circle of Christian theology?[1] He maintains that Christian theologians must consider the relationship between the contents of their faith and the religious thinking of non-Christians. They must be prepared to show that trends which are immanent in all religions and cultures are basically questions arising out of the human experience that seek and find their answer in the Christian revelation. The basis of Christian theology's claim to uniqueness and universality is the doctrine of Jesus Christ as the *Logos-Sarx* as the Word made flesh, which was revealed in the Prologue to John's Gospel and was taken up and developed by the early Fathers of the Church such as St. Justin Martyr, St. Irenaeus, St. Clement of Alexandria, etc. Insofar as Jesus Christ is the *Logos*, the divine Word which embraces all the particular *logoi* of the universe, Christian faith has an absolutely universal foundation. And, inasmuch as He truly became *Sarx* (flesh), its foundation is absolutely concrete.

Other theologies lack either concreteness or universality. Priestly and prophetic theologies are concrete but not universal; while, on the other hand, mystical and metaphysical theologies have universality but are deficient in concreteness. Tillich is careful to point out that universality in this context is not to be confused with abstractness which has a limited universality since it is restricted to that whence it has been abstracted. At the same time, the absolutely concrete is not merely a particular whose concreteness is limited by way of excluding other particulars. In applying his formal criteria of ultimate concern to the question, he concludes that the complete concreteness of the personal life of Jesus Christ is the basis of a concern that is genuinely existential, and that his absolute universality as the divine *Logos* called for unconditional, infinite, or ultimate concern.

Tillich is convinced that the *Logos* doctrine of Christianity which identifies the absolutely concrete with the absolutely universal in Jesus Christ is the only possible basis for the Christian claim. In accord with St. Paul's "being in Christ" we can exist in Christ only if He is the absolutely concrete, and, also according to the Pauline subjection of cosmic powers to Christ, only the absolutely universal can overcome cosmic pluralism. In each instance both the absolutely concrete and the absolutely universal must be identified in Christ, since our faith or ultimate concern cannot be committed to Him without both coming together in Him who is the "New Being."

Tillich emphasized the need for a theological history of religion and of culture as the widest source of systematic theology. This would make it possible to take into consideration the religious elements that Christianity has in common with all religions, as well as the demonic distortions found in the religions of the world which are questions, at least implicitly, seeking an answer in the New Being of Jesus as the

Christ. He proposes as the material norm for a contemporary systematic theology the "New Being in Jesus as the Christ as our ultimate concern," and it is the criterion for the use of all the sources of systematic theology, including the widest source, namely, the history of religion and of culture. The concrete biblical portrait of the "New Being" reveals Jesus Christ as the one alone among us in human history who became subject to the conditions of human existence, i.e., our sinful estrangement from our true depth of being in God, without His ever losing unity with that divine depth. That is why the final revelation took place in Christ. He sacrificed Himself entirely (passion and death) and did not lose Himself in so doing (resurrection). He is the perfect medium of divine revelation, completely transparent to the depth of His being, and never permitted the conditioned, the relative, the preliminary in Him to be confused with the unconditioned, the absolute, and the ultimate. This criterion of the "New Being" must always be operative in Christianity itself which would otherwise become another world religion. Even if it were the highest among the religions of the world, this is not sufficient to establish the basis of the Christian claim to universality. What is distinctive of Christianity, therefore, is that this criterion belongs to its very essence and so has received within itself the foundation for its continuous reform. It is precisely this "New Being in Jesus as the Christ as our ultimate concern" that Christianity has to offer the other religions of the world.

Another context of Tillich's reflections upon the uniqueness and universality of Christianity may be found in Volume III, Part IV of his *Systematic Theology*. There he treats of the human quest of unambiguous life through the manifestations of the "Spiritual Presence." This is an application of his Spirit-Christology. It is the Spirit who made Jesus the Christ, i.e., the One in whom and through whom God is definitively and ultimately revealed. Only with the free surrender of his historical existence as Jesus of Nazareth at His crucifixion, does He "become" the Christ, the Spirit who creates the "New Being" in others throughout human history. The creativity of Christ as the "Spiritual Presence" in history gives birth to the "Spiritual Community." Although unambiguous life is manifested in this community, it is fragmentary as indeed was the manifestation of unambiguous life in the Christ, i.e., while life is revealed as overcoming estrangement and ambiguity, it still appears under the conditions of existence and finitude.

This is precisely the paradox of the Christ—to be *in* existence but not *of* it—and so it is also the paradox of Christianity—to be subject to the conditions of finitude but to overcome the estrangement from the ground of being and so to resolve ambiguous relations to the extent that the Christian individual and community share in the "New Being" of the Christ. To be subject to Christ as the central event in history manifesting the "Spiritual Presence" is to belong to the "Spiritual Community" and to be in the "theonomous" situation of reunion with one's divine depth in the midst of the ambiguous relations between religion and culture.

Tillich himself does not identify the "Spiritual Community" with the Christian churches but holds that they represent it "in a manifest religious self-expression." The "Spiritual Community" organized as a church has within itself the principle of self-criticism whereby it can resist the tendencies of absolutizing the finite or of making an idol out of the revelatory medium ("profanization" and "demonization"). This has been shown in the movements of prophetism and the Protestant Reformation according to Tillich. The "New Being" as the norm for a radical self-negation and self-transformation is the reality of the Cross as a symbol of the Christ. Although lacking this criterion of ultimate concern, the members of the "latent Spiritual Community" are teleologically oriented towards its manifest self-expression in their unconscious attraction to the Christ. This explanation of the "latent Spiritual Community," which might clearly include the world religions as such, is not unlike Karl Rahner's theory of "anonymous Christianity" which is also an attempt to provide an intelligible reason for the Christian conviction concerning the universality and uniqueness of God's redeeming love in Christ without restricting it to the Christian churches. Rahner's hypothesis will be discussed in some detail in the next section.

During the fall of 1961, following upon his own direct experience of entering into inter-religious dialogue with representatives from the great religions of the world, Tillich delivered the four Bampton lectures in the Low Memorial Library at Columbia University. They appeared under the title: *Christianity and the Encounter of the World Religions*. The final of these lectures, "Christianity Judging Itself in the Light of Its Encounter with the World Religions," reflects upon the reciprocal relationship and the mutuality of the inter-faith dialogue.

Tillich indicates how much Christianity has historically learned from its encounters with the other religions of the world in reference to its own self-criticism. At the same time Christianity has been a help to the others in their own self-evaluation as religions in their quest for unambiguous life, through the manifestations of the "Spiritual Presence," which is a participation in the "New Being of Jesus as the Christ as their ultimate concern."

Naming the spiritual strength of the "New Being" as Christians do explicitly is not necessary according to Tillich. What matters is that none of the religions allow themselves to remain religions in the narrow and particularistic sense of the term. Only if they are bearers of the "Spiritual Presence" in the world can each one contribute to meeting the common challenge of the secularistic quasi-religions, e.g., world communism.

Christianity and the world religions can and should also learn from their mutual encounter with secularism, which might also be included in the "wider ecumenism" if not the "widest ecumenism." After all, the world religions must express their ultimate concern through the secular as well as the sacred. And when their values are not embodied and expressed in the cultures where they exist (a lack of "theonomy"), then they are regarded by members of that culture as imposed by a particular religious group from outside (a "heteronomy"). This has frequently created the vacuum that has been filled by such ideologies as secular humanism, communism, etc. The religions of the world ought to aim through dialogue at providing the spiritual strength necessary to meet the global issues of justice and peace by bringing the religious influence into the collaborative effort. They shall be able to accomplish this only to the extent that they manifest their religion not as only one particular aspect of life, but as integrating human existence as a whole.

Having considered Paul Tillich's ideas in the matter, let us now turn to the essential elements in the theory of Karl Rahner. Although he appears to be quite compatible with Tillich, as a Roman Catholic systematic theologian he offers a different emphasis, which seems to bring more of the "Catholic substance" of sacramentality into the dialogue with the prophetic critique of the "Protestant principle." And Tillich himself asserted that both the "Catholic substance" and the "Protestant Principle" are needed in order to have a more balanced Christian theology which preserves the realism of the medium without absolutizing it.

Karl Rahner's "Anonymous Christians"

Rahner confronts the dilemma of the Christian conviction in the context of the individual and of the Church.[2] Realistically recognizing the fact that the message of Christ has never been able to gain a foothold in the ancient cultures of Asia even after two thousand years, and that it is just one of many religious explanations of human existence in the West where religion itself is only one of many ways in which we understand ourselves, he still feels obliged to offer some theological rationale for the Christian claim. And he describes this conviction and claim in the following terms: to gain salvation one must believe in God, and not merely in God but in Christ; that this faith is not merely a positive command from which certain circumstances could dispense a person; and that membership in the one true Church of Christ is a necessary means of salvation. But how does one reconcile the necessity of Christian faith with the universal salvific will of God's omnipotent and efficacious love in the face of the fact that so many human beings are not Christians?

Rahner replies that somehow all human beings must be capable of becoming members of the Church. This possibility cannot be only an abstract and logical one, but real and historically concrete. If we Christians truly believe that Christ exercises an influence in the redemption of each individual, then we must be ready to explain how this might be apart from any explicit faith in Him as the Savior of all. Grace, which is the free self-communication of God to His creature, presupposes that human nature is capable of freely and responsibly acknowledging the Creator in his works. The human spirit is by definition entirely open to the creative call of infinite mystery. Summoned by this divine call revealed in creation, the individual awaits a more profound communication or self-disclosure of divinity and even expects it; although such a free revelation of the hidden God is not due to him/her by nature but is a grace or pure gift.

How does this tendency towards God, which is often implicit and inarticulated, include a reference to the incarnate God, Jesus Christ? If we Christians take seriously the mystery of God becoming flesh, then human nature is what God becomes when he freely and lovingly chooses to reveal Himself in the world or that which is outside the divine. From the side of the human, the incarnation of God is the uniquely supreme case of the realization of human nature in general. We come to know ourselves only in the concrete unfolding of our history. And so we are able to recognize in the concrete historical reality of the incarnation, the perfect fulfillment of human potential through the uncreated grace of the hypostatic union or the unity of divinity and humanity in the Person of the Word made flesh. The believer will grasp that the self-communication of grace offered to all and fulfilled in Christ in the supreme mode is the goal of all creation and makes its mark upon an individual's nature even before he/she freely takes a stand about it, since God's word and will are always effective in bringing about what they say and determine.

Rahner calls this determination of human nature in the divine economy of Judeo-Christian salvation and revelation-history the "supernatural existential." This does not mean that one must be a conscious member of this tradition in order to possess it, but the Christian must be able to recognize and name the Christ as the sole Savior of the world. The non-Christian has the "supernatural existential" by reason of being a member of the human race. But even in this condition of being an "anonymous Christian," a person does experience the offer of grace—not necessarily *qua* grace, i.e., he/she may not be conscious of it as a supernatural calling—but does experience the reality of its content. And so if he/she refuses the offer, it does not mean that such a person is left in a state of pure unimpaired nature. It does mean, however, that when the message of Christianity is explicitly received as the definitive divine revelation in and through history, it becomes an expression of the manifestation of grace which one always experiences implicitly in the depths of one's human existence.

If, on the other hand, one does accept this offer of grace, an act of supernatural faith is made even prior to any actual membership in the Church of Christ that may eventually take place. In accepting this grace, regardless of the way in which one may understand and express it in one's own reflective self-understanding, he/she is becoming more than an "anonymous theist," but rather an "anonymous Christian." In the acceptance of oneself as human, with all that implies in terms of living each day in patience and devotion to one's duties towards others, etc., one is in effect accepting Christ as the absolute perfection of his/her own anonymous orientation towards God by grace. The acceptance of this belief is the working of God's grace, which is the grace of Christ, which is the grace of His Church, since she is only the continuation of His mystery in our history.

Of course, this does not mean that every individual, whether or not he/she accepts or rejects the free divine gift of grace in freedom, is automatically an "anonymous Christian." It can refer to those alone who freely say "Yes" to this offer of grace who are moving towards their absolute potential in Christ. In light of this theological theory proposed by Karl Rahner, it would be helpful to quote in its entirety the following paragraph from Vatican II's *Constitution on the Church* (*Lumen Gentium*, n. 16) which he interprets in this context:

> Finally, those who have not yet received the Gospel are related to the People of God in various ways. There is, first, that people to which the covenants and promises were made, and from which Christ was born according to the flesh (cf. Rom. 9:4–5): in view of the divine choice, they are a people most dear for the sake of the fathers, for the gifts of God are without repentance (cf. Rom. 11:39). But the plan of salvation also includes those who acknowledge the Creator, in the first place among whom are the Moslems: these profess to hold the faith of Abraham, and together with us they adore, the one, merciful God, mankind's judge on the last day. Nor is God remote from those who in shadows and images seek the unknown God, since he gives to all men life and breath and all things (cf. Acts 17:25–28) and since the Savior wills all men to be saved (cf. I Tim. 2:4). Those who, through no fault of their own, do not know the Gospel of Christ or his Church, but who nevertheless seek God with a sincere heart, and, moved by grace, try in their actions to do his will as they know it through the dictates of their conscience—those too may achieve eternal salvation. Nor shall divine

> Providence deny the assistance necessary for salvation to those who, without any fault of theirs, have not yet arrived at an explicit knowledge of God, and, who, not without grace, strive to lead a good life. Whatever good or truth is found amongst them is considered by the Church to be a preparation for the Gospel and given by him who enlightens all men that they may at length have life.[3]

Edward Schillebeeckx's "Humanity in Search of the Sacrament of God"

Edward Schillebeeckx, another Roman Catholic systematic theologian, considers Christ as the "primordial sacrament"[4] of our encounter with God. While his theological reflections are mainly concerned with the Christian concept of sacramentality as it applies to the humanity of God in Christ, to the Church and to her seven sacraments, nevertheless he approaches his subject from the viewpoint of "sacrament" in non-Christian religion. There is a solid foundation for his theological hypothesis in St. Augustine who divided the gradual coming into being of the Church into that of the devout pagan as its first phase in history, followed by that of ancient Israel and the Church of the New Israel or Christianity.

Schillebeeckx constructs his theological theory on a similar basis to that of Rahner, namely, that all of humanity receives an inward word of God calling us to a communion of grace with Himself. Although this interior experience of grace causes the recipient to suspect ever so dimly that there is a saving God, he/she does not yet encounter the visible embodiment of that grace, which remains unknown and hidden in the heart. The world of creation, however, does take on a new meaning for such an individual. This world then becomes an actual part of his/her inner yet still "anonymous" (the word is Schillebeeckx's) dialogue with God. However vaguely, life begins to speak a veiled language of salvation in light of this inner experience of grace or anonymous dialogue with the redeeming God.

No matter how limited, this does endow the inward grace with a certain visible manifestation, and all sacramentality is nothing more or less than divinely designated signs or symbols of an invisible grace which is somehow mediated through them. St. Thomas Aquinas spoke of the "sacraments of nature" which have a truly supernatural element (cf. his exposition of Book IV in the *Sentences*, distinction 1, question 2, article 6, solution 3). And they have influenced the outward shape of the sacraments of the Old Covenant and of the Christian Church in the New Covenant. Of course, under the guidance of the explicitly religious and historical revelation to the People of God in the Ancient and New Israel, there was a demythologization of the ambiguous elements in the pagan sacraments of truth that lay hidden in the myths and rituals of pagan sacraments. At the same time, this does not nullify their place in divine Providence in preparation for the Gospel.

Schillebeeckx's theory is not limited to the non-Christians of an ancient past, but very clearly includes them today and till the end of human history. He is convinced that grace never comes to us human beings just interiorly, but must confront us in some visible form as well. No religion, in his opinion, can ever be completely separated from any relationship or orientation to Church and sacrament. And, since every grace comes to us from the one mediator between God and us, Jesus Christ, that Church and sacrament must be essentially Christian. Even though the orientation is implicit and unconscious in individuals, their own religious lives require sufficient sacramentality which derives its meaning and value from the one Savior of the world. To separate religion from Church and sacrament completely is to destroy the life of any religion.

Reflections on These Three Theories and the "Wider Ecumenism"

The points of similarity between the three Christian systematicians should be quite apparent: each one seeks a way of explaining theologically how Christ is truly the Savior of every single human person; each seeks to show that Christ as the one mediator of grace is much more than an "abstract" universal, but a concrete historical reality who truly became one of us in order to accomplish our redemption; and each one wishes more or less to show the role of Christianity as Church in the salvation of non-Christians through history.

It seems that the most significant differences in their theories include the following: Tillich is much clearer about the function of the "Protestant principle" as the prophetic critique according to which the non-Christian religions and Christian churches can ever be reformed; both Rahner and Schillebeeckx are more emphatic concerning the "Catholic substance" or the function and the role of the Church of Christ as a visible and sacramental communion in relationship to the elements of non-Christian religions that appear to be in quest of the Christian message. And Schillebeeckx, while apparently concurring with the essential aspects of Rahner's "anonymous Christians," has concentrated more upon the notion of sacramentality.

For us Christian members of the inter-faith dialogue with our brothers and sisters in the other great religions of the world, I submit that a basic way of helping one another to become better prepared for this encounter is to clarify our own dialogue about the dialectical relationship between the "Protestant principle" and the "Catholic substance." According to Paul Tillich this relationship is very significant for ecumenical conversations. And, just as it is necessary for all the religions of the world to seek a certain religious unity for the sake of our world, so it is most important at this intra-Christian conference on the "wider ecumenism" that we Christians deepen our oneness in Christ and His Church. Generally speaking, what Roman Catholics need is a proper application of the "Protestant principle" to our ecclesiology, particularly in those aspects dealing with our theology of the Church of Christ as a hierarchically structured institution. This is also more or less applicable to the Orthodox and Anglican traditions. On the other hand, what the Protestant traditions seem to be most in need of is an understanding of the Church as the Body of Christ called to mediate the grace of God through the ministries of word and sacrament.

Once we have achieved better balance in our mutual ecclesiologies, then we should be better able to communicate our common Christian conviction and claim to our non-Christian partners in the inter-faith dialogue. The strength of Tillich's theory is that his *Logos-Sarx* and *Spirit Christology* help provide a good basis for the uniqueness and the universality of the Christ event as a prophetically critical principle for the continuous reform of all religions, including the Christian churches, but his weakness is in showing just what role the Church of Christ and her sacraments have in the mediating of salvation. And, while Rahner's and Schillebeeckx's theories clearly show that the Church and her sacraments must be operative in continuing the mystery of Christ in history, they do not seem to be quite convincing about what Christianity has to receive from the other religions of the world. Permit me to conclude my few reflections with a question designed to stimulate our intra-Christian dialogue in this crucial matter: in light of the anonymously Christian elements in the non-Christian religions, might they not be the basis one day of a "Jewish Christianity," a "Moslem Christianity," a "Hindu Christianity," a "Buddhist Christianity," etc.?

Notes

1. Cf. Paul Tillich, *Systematic Theology*, Vol. I (New York & Evanston: Harper & Row, and University of Chicago Press, Three Volumes in One, 1967), 15–18; Vol. III, 111–282 and *Christianity and the Encounter of the World Religions* (New York & London: Columbia University Press, 1969). Cf. also Frederick M. Jelly, *The Notion of Theonomy in Paul Tillich's Systematic Theology: A Thomistic Evaluation for a Theology of Secularity* (Ann Arbor, MI: University Microfilms International, 1981), 19–21, 272–290.
2. Cf. Karl Rahner, S.J., *Theological Investigations*, Vol. VI, *Concerning Vatican Council II* (Baltimore: Helicon Press, 1969), 390–398.
3. English translation is taken from *Vatican Council II*, Vol. 1, Austin Flannery, General Editor (Collegeville, MN: Liturgical Press, 1984), 367–368.
4. Cf. Edward Schillebeeckx, O.P., *Christ the Sacraments of the Encounter With God* (New York: Sheed & Ward, 1963), 7–10.

PART IV

THE WIDER ECUMENISM IN PRACTICE

16

ONE MORE STEP IN A JOURNEY OF MANY MILES

TOWARDS A THEOLOGY OF INTERFAITH DIALOGUE REPORT, RECEPTION AND RESPONSE[1]

Myrtle S. Langley

IN JULY 1984 the General Synod of the Church of England considered a report by its Board of Mission and Unity entitled, "Towards a Theology for Inter-Faith Dialogue."[2] In summing up the two-hour debate, the Right Reverend Barry Rogerson, then Bishop of Wolverhampton, now of Bristol, and Chairman of the Board's Inter-Faith Consultative Group which prepared the report, remarked on a "vigorous debate" and thanked the Synod "for the dialogue that has begun within our own communion at this point."[3] The Synod duly received the report, "commended it for study, reflection and debate in the dioceses and theological colleges," commended the work of the British Council of Churches' Committee on Relations with People of Other Faiths, requesting that Committee to produce an ecumenical study guide on the issues raised in the report, and asked the Standing Committee of Synod and the Central Board of Finance to consider whether the Synod should make an additional contribution to the BCC Committee's work.[4]

Background

The report was itself a response to a previous debate held by the General Synod in November 1981 when considering a Board for Mission and Unity paper on the British Council of Churches' Working Document entitled *Relations with People of Other Faiths: Guidelines on Dialogue in Britain*.[5] *Guidelines for Dialogue in Britain* was in turn a first attempt at a British churches' response to the World Council of Churches' *Guidelines on Dialogue with People of Living Faiths and Ideologies* published in 1979 and commended to member churches "for their consideration and discussion, testing and evaluation, and for their elaboration in each specific situation."[6]

Significantly, however, the British response was also motivated by a newly found awareness of a changed social context, both at local and global levels, in the wake of World War II. No longer, as in 1945, was London the metropolis of a vast empire where nearly all the Hindus and Sikhs in the world, a large proportion of Muslims and an enormous number of Buddhists were subjects of His Majesty; and no longer were the great British missionary societies at work in China and Burma or other closed countries, given unrestricted access to most of the countries of Africa and the Indian sub-continent.

Instead, Britain was the head of a Commonwealth of Nations, many of whose people had been both driven and drawn to live and work in Britain during the booming years of post-war reconstruction, driven in the wake of appalling natural disasters at home, drawn by the strings of "mother country" and the lures of the labor recruiters. These people had changed the face of Britain, racially, culturally, and religiously. The new British society was neither Christian nor secular but religiously plural, or multi-faith.

According to 1985 figures, out of a total population of forty-five million adults (aged 15 years and over) in the United Kingdom, almost seven million, or 15 percent, are practicing members of the Christian churches, while almost a million and a half belong to other religious communities, including approximately 110,000 Jews, 23,000 Buddhists, 170,000 Hindus, 900,000 Muslims (of various kinds) and 180,000 Sikhs. Similarly, out of a total population of 56.6 million, 36.8 million adhere to the Christian churches, and 4.2 million to other religions, including approximately 300,000 Jews, 300,000 Hindus, 1.5 million Muslims,

500,000 Sikhs, and 1.6 million to new and other religious movements. In sum, forty-one million people (or 72 percent of the total population of the United Kingdom) adhere to some form of religion, 65 percent professing Christian faith and over 7 percent professing other faiths.[7] To complete the picture of change, however, it is necessary to note that many of the arrivals from the New Commonwealth are clustered together in certain areas of cities like London, Birmingham, Manchester, Leeds, Bradford, Leicester, and Glasgow so that whole communities take on the character of minority ethnic and religious groups in a predominantly white and culturally Christian society.

On coming for the first time to the proceedings of the November 1981 General Synod debate on the BCC's *Guidelines for Dialogue in Britain* the reader is immediately struck by the 'feel' of a concern arising out of the reality of this multi-faith society. With one notable exception, the tone was generally positive in affirming the four principles of dialogue and commending them to the dioceses "as a guide for action"[8]: (1) dialogue begins when people meet each other; (2) dialogue depends upon mutual understanding and mutual trust; (3) dialogue makes it possible to share in service to the community; and (4) dialogue becomes the medium of authentic witness. One member suggested a fifth principle affirming the significance of dialogue for self-understanding and another moved an amendment asking the Board of Mission and Unity to bring forward a further report on the theological aspects of dialogue in due course. The suggestion for a fifth principle was noted by the Chairman of the Board, the Right Reverend David Brown, Bishop of Guildford, in his summing up and the amendment was moved and carried.[9] It is the requested report on the theological aspects of dialogue to which we now turn.

Report

The report divides into eight sections, numbered by paragraphs from 1–85 and concludes with footnotes and an annotated bibliography.

1. *The Introduction* (1-4) sketches in the background, relating need for guidance to questions of church properties, church schools and hospital chaplaincies in a multi-faith society, affirms the rootedness of theological reflection in the everyday experience of those caught up in inter-faith situations, and undertakes in this matter to act together with other churches on the basis of the Lund Principle.[10]

2. *A Changed Context* (5–13) introduces how early Christianity developed in the context of Greek and Roman cults and philosophies, how Christians have lived at different times side by side with Jews, Muslims

and Hindus, how Britain has become a multi-faith society and how Christians share with those of other faiths an awareness of, and a search for, "the Other, the ground of all being, though they use very different language, symbols and imagery to express it."

3. *Christian Responses to Other Faiths* (14–23) identifies a broad spectrum of views which determine significantly different modes of relating to those other faiths. At one end of this spectrum "the Christian exclusivist theory counts all religions other than Christianity as the product of blindness or even sinful unbelief." Moving along and away from this "the inclusivist theory stresses how Christianity does in fact complete other forms of religion." And at the other end of the spectrum those who hold the pluralist view are concerned with the way other religions are "brought into some kind of larger ecumenical relationship where the truths of each are seen as complementary to each other."[11]

4. *The Bible as Source of Authoritative Guidance* (24) while acknowledging a firm belief in "Scripture as the primary source of authority for the Christian community," it denies that an answer to the question as to the appropriate relationship of Christians to those of other faiths or any other contemporary puzzle is to be discovered "in any single quotation or any one strand of biblical thought."

5. *The Biblical Process* (25–31) affirms that the process of revelation in both Old and New Testaments witnesses to a dialogue between the inherited and the contemporary experience of the individual and the community. A part of that contemporary experience which is brought to bear on the tradition is the experience of other cultures and other religions.

6. *Biblical Pointers* (32–59) under the heads of "the Creating God," "the Covenanting God," "the Electing God," "the Incarnate God," "God as Spirit" and "the Saving and Judging God," explores the unfolding witness to the Triune God as a guide in inter-faith relations. Noteworthy are a discussion of *Logos* theology and its implications for understanding God's activity in the world, a re-examination of Orthodox strictures on the addition of the *Filioque* to the Niceno-Constantinopolitan Creed in relation to the Spirit's origin (proceeding: "from the Father" rather than "from the Father and the Son,")and some detailed exegesis of Acts 4:12 ("And there is salvation in no one else [Jesus Christ], for there is no other name under heaven given among men by which we must be saved") and John 14:6. ("Jesus said to him, 'I am the way, and the truth, and the life; no one comes to the Father but by me.'") These discussions show a non-exclusivist interpretation of these texts and a lengthy exposition of the story of Peter and Cornelius in Acts 10 and 11 as "perhaps the most powerful pointer to the inclusiveness of God's saving activity."

7. *Implications for Inter-Faith Dialogue* (60–80) begins by noting that "the Bible does not offer a comprehensive or definitive solution on the question of the relation of Christians to those of other faiths in the twentieth century." Nevertheless "it does provide sufficient and significant pointers for Christians in their search for a theology of inter-faith dialogue." It proceeds to expound and explore the BCC's four principles for dialogue as (already stated above).

8. *Final Reflections* (81–85) describes inter-faith dialogue as a journey through unfamiliar territory, raising many of the major themes of Christian doctrine, providing opportunity on the way for debates and controversies of past ages to take on a freshness and a new relevance, and forcing another look at personal belief, while listening to one another and the Spirit. In conclusion, the writers of the report make a personal statement: "As more Christians enter into dialogue with those of other faiths we shall be able to discern more clearly what the Spirit is saying to the churches. *For our part we have found a consensus. It can be described as being inclusivist with an exclusivist loyalty to Jesus Christ* (emphasis mine); and words from Bishop David Brown, the Chairman and initiator of the report, who began the journey with them but, sadly, died on the way:

> ...Christ will provide the link by which the different religions will be brought into a deep and mutually enriching relationship with each other....There is much theological work to be done and many generations of dialogue before such a hope can ever come to fruition; but the task is a priority to which the churches must now give their attention![12]

Reception

In opening the debate, Bishop Barry Rogerson claimed that there was no consensus among Christians in their attitudes towards other faiths, but rather a range of starting points, exclusivist, inclusivist and pluralist. The meat of the report, he went on, was to be found in the biblical section, in particular the pointer in the Johannine Prologue to the pre-existent Logos, the even more exciting pointer associated with the work of the Holy Spirit, and the extended exegesis of Acts 4:12 and John 14:6. And dialogue would commence, he concluded, "on the basis of love of our neighbors, a love for their own sake and for God's sake" and would be seen, he hoped, "as part of mission, for it is the means of authentic witness."[13]

Next to speak was Bishop David Young (Ripon) who welcomed the report but wished to affirm that the biblical evidence points to a "Yes" and a "No" which has to be said from the standpoint of Christian faith to world religions. The "Yes" to the religions of the world is said because all men and women in their inner being stand in relation to God in their essence....the "No" to the religions of the world is said because they are the constructs of fallen men and women...![14]

Canon Gareth Bennett (Oxford University) began by stating that for many Christians the whole subject of inter-faith dialogue is deeply unwelcome, the reason being "that they fear the kind of liberalizing theology which makes Christ just one religious teacher among many and compromises the claim that in him God has acted fully and decisively." But the various faiths have come out of their geographical isolation and are now face to face and "if we do not listen to each other, do not seek to understand, do not seek to share whatever it is that we can, we are in danger of creating communities of mutual incomprehension which will make our inner cities, our schools and our social services areas of conflict, and we may well miss occasions of deepening our own understanding of faith as we engage in dialogue....So this dialogue needs a sound theology, and the question is: can we find a way of appreciating whatever is good and true in other religions while at the same time strongly reaffirming our belief that in Jesus Christ we have the same disclosures of God to man, his decisive act? I think we can."[15]

Bishop John Taylor (Winchester), while welcoming the report as one more step in a journey of many miles towards "opening ourselves to the ideas of totally different world views from our own" and comprehending that "our Lord Jesus is to be found sovereign of those worlds as well as our own, but not in our ways," nevertheless drew attention to "certain aspects of inaccurate thinking," particularly in the paragraphs which deal respectively with "the eternal Logos and unique incarnation" and "the *Filioque* Clause." His penetrating critique is worth quoting at length.

> I am a little worried by certain aspects of inaccurate thinking in this report. It is not because I reject it, but because I hope we shall continue to do this sort of thing, but we must be very, very accurate in the use of our words and of our own theologies. For example, on page 18, which deals with the eternal Logos and unique incarnation, it quotes a very happy quotation from William Temple. Temple starts: "The Light that lightens every man," and he says "without ceasing His creative and sustaining work, added this to it, that He became flesh...." This is interpreted in the following paragraph as "the unique expression of God as being in Jesus Christ," which is not quite the fullness of "The Light that lightens every man" nor the incarnation; and then it goes on to speak about "other manifestations of the Logos in other places and at other times." Even the use of that phrase ought to have reminded them of the first two verses of the Epistle to the Hebrews, but did not apparently. We read on the next page of "other manifestations" of the Logos, "other revelations" and then of the "fullest revelation of God in Jesus Christ." In other words, there is the suggestion all along that we are dealing with something that is of the same kind but of a little

higher voltage in Jesus Christ. That is not what Temple's quotation is talking about, and it would have been truer and more accurate to say "The continuous illumination of people everywhere by the Logos and the one manifestation of that Logos in a human life." That is the kind of accuracy we must cling to unless we are in fact to become fuzzy.

Then on page 20 the report does not do justice to the Filioque Clause, and if this had appeared in a serious debate on the Filioque Clause it would have made nonsense. It reads: "....the advent of the Spirit in the world was dependent upon the Son." The introduction of the phrase "into the world" suggests that by the Son we mean the incarnate Son, which is not at all what is meant in the Filioque Clause. The Filioque Clause is talking about the very nature of the Trinity in which we do not identify the Son with the incarnate Son exclusively, and it reflects the fact that the Spirit is proceeding from the Father and the Son—in other words, it speaks of the existence of the Spirit in the eternal exchange between Father and Son. The Spirit is the flow of love, the flow of inter-relationship and exchange, between Father and Son in all eternity. That is not making the Spirit dependent on the Son, but dependent upon and within the very being of God. We must be accurate.

On page 24 the report says, "There is no suggestion in the context that Jesus is claiming to be the 'whole of God.'" I do not want to enter into what Jesus actually claimed; we are dealing with the Fourth Gospel anyway; but Robinson, only two lines above, says, "The Father is perfectly reflected in him." In that word it means completely reflected in him. We would never believe that there is a partial revelation of the Father in the Son. That is another bit of inaccuracy and it is the kind of dangerous inaccuracy which can lead us one step forward into the kind of syncretism that is obviously scaring the Synod. "He is the truth." All through the Fourth Gospel the article is used of "the truth." It means the total reality. It is not just part of the truth. We must be accurate.

If we really do hold that somehow in the incarnate Son we are able to see the truth that is truth for every man, then we can begin to look for that truth outside the Church. We have to start with that conviction and then we are perfectly free to expose ourselves to all the shocks of discovering that truth outside the Church; for we must realize—and herein lies our humility; not in the kind of way partly suggested in this report, but the true humility in relation to other religions—that all religions lie under the judgment of Christ and his Church and Christianity most of all. We do not reflect the Christ perfectly. We can look for that truth of Christ in the insights of other world views, and if only we will start by listening and learning and discovering the strange lunar landscape of other religious attitudes to life, then it suddenly dawns upon us with a shock of recognition that indeed Jesus Christ has a sovereign relevance to every man's world.[16]

Many other, differing and conflicting, views were expressed: the report cited biblical evidence of the openness of Israel to surrounding cultures and religions but failed to deal adequately with Israel's stubborn resistance to other traditions; the "sweet reasonableness" of the report acted as a narcotic; the report was in danger of dividing people into different categories as they opted for one or other of the three stances and indeed, at times, appeared to "prescribe" the inclusivist stance. One speaker (formerly Hindu), having welcomed the original debate, even confessed to being confused and begged the Synod not to send the report down to the dioceses or deaneries; it would "drive them barmy... you may find a cosmic Christ in other religions, but the crucified Christ, the risen Christ, in no other faith."[17]

But despite these reservations and criticisms it was probably such sentiments as those expressed by the Very Reverend Alan Warren, Provost of Leicester, which won the day:

> I speak as The Provost of a city in which I have worked off and on now for nearly 20 years, and even the off-section was six very happy years as a Canon at Coventry Cathedral, a city which also knows something about immigration. Leicester is now very much a multi-faith and multi-race city. I hope to make a contribution to this debate in perhaps a slightly more practical and pragmatic way.
>
> I certainly support the general terms of this report, although I do go along with other speakers in saying that I am most uncomfortable about the idea of dividing people into positions of exclusivist, inclusivist or relativist, and so on. I know that these are only meant as guidelines, but I do think they can push people into compartments where they do not really belong.
>
> ...I want to bring the Synod's attention...to those paragraphs which suggest that dialogue with those of other faiths is a medium for authentic witness...and I am speaking as one who is unashamed to call himself an Evangelical....
>
> Of course, I long and I pray for all men, women and children to come to know the love of God in Christ Jesus, and I believe there is full salvation in no other name, but to suggest that my neighbors, some of whom are my personal friends, have no insights into truth, nothing to offer and cannot even offer anything in terms of worship to God—and I stress that a key part in this dialogue is our approach to them in their worship—seems to me to smack not of religious conviction but of bigotry....
>
> ...I would like to quote from paragraph 78 in the report, which says: "In dialogue authentic witness is not only given in the words we speak but in the manner and bearing of the life we live. Human frailty and sin mean that Christians have always to struggle towards consistency between the message they proclaim and the image they present in life." I certainly go along with that very much, and I believe that in simple terms of courtesy and caring Christian love towards my fellow human beings there is witness....
>
> I would like to stress that this sort of loving in practice, not in theory, the loving which means sharing and welcoming and sometimes I believe even encouraging those of other faiths, is usually costly and is certainly always open to misunderstanding, although we are all going along the same road approach. But I honestly believe that it is worthwhile. Living in a city like Leicester, an abrasive materialistic society, where the name of Jesus Christ for most people is no more

than a mild or popular swear word, it seems to me to be totally realistic as well as Christian to welcome and encourage other people who come in with that firm belief in God, a strong moral code and a strong sense of family values.

...Pablo Casals once said, "Never be afraid to be human." I believe that the main direction and thrust of this report is no more than a Christ-like human response to our fellow human beings, and personally I wish it an effective and constructive journey through the dioceses and the theological colleges.[18]

Response

My purpose in this paper is not to provide any critique of the report; that, as we shall see, has been done by others. It is rather to identify, present and evaluate some of the responses.

First, the implementations of Synod's three decisions. The report is on its way in the dioceses and deaneries, "still selling" as the Secretary of BMU put it; the Inter-Faith Consultative Group produced in 1987 its own in-house discussion of responses entitled "Yes and No"; and at least one diocese has produced a document as a result of setting up its own working party.[19] The study guide met with some difficulties but is under way and ought to appear soon. The necessary financial support for the work of the BCC Committee on Relations with People of Other Faiths was secured and a future for its executive officer assured.

Second, the response of the Conservative Evangelical wing of the Anglican Communion. *Anvil*, which describes itself as "an Anglican Evangelical Journal for Theology and Mission," in its third issue for 1984, included a critical essay entitled "Inter Faith Dialogue" by Christopher Wright, Lecturer in Old Testament at Union Biblical Seminary, Pune, India together with a brief counter-response by Christopher Lamb, Coordinator of the BCMS/CMS Other Faiths Theological Project in Birmingham and member of the group which produced the report. The general tone of Wright's article is negative towards the report and defensive of an exclusivist position. While he makes valuable hermeneutical points, particularly when expounding Old Testament material, he misrepresents the report's understanding of dialogue and inclusivist stance.[20] In November 1984 the Church of England Evangelical Council discussed the report and commissioned a small steering group to make a contribution to the ongoing discussion. This was published in 1985 in the form of a booklet by Christopher Sugden entitled *Christ's Exclusive Claims and Inter-Faith Dialogue*.[21] It reads somewhat like a string of related but diverse comments, taking issue with the inadequacies of "the three-category spectrum," challenging religious experience as an adequate starting point or valid criterion, criticizing the selectivity of the choice and handling of the biblical texts, attacking the "ahistorical" nature of the report's Christology, and claiming compatibility for the four principles of dialogue "with a commitment to the exclusive claims of Christ."

Third, the Anglican Consultative Council, and the Lambeth Conference 1988. At its discussions in Nigeria in 1984, the Anglican Consultative Council had considered Christian-Muslim relations, a discussion which led into the wider area of inter-faith contacts prompted in part by the Church of England Report. "We thought," says one of the discussions's interpreters, "the book needed a greater emphasis on the doctrine of redemption, and we question some of its biblical exegesis, as well as the selectivity of biblical texts. People from non-Western societies especially found the approach too academic and cerebral, and thus it was classified as largely irrelevant to them." Commitment to inter-faith relationships was, however, to be maintained with an emphasis on living in cooperation in the world with differing faith communities and by Christians witnessing to their faith through the service of those in need.[22] A mark of this commitment is the placing of the report on the Lambeth Conference Agenda for 1988, with the addition of a postscript in the form of an essay from Pakistan by Bishop Michael Nazir-Ali. Nazir-Ali's critique falls into two parts: the first pointing to the fact that the original Consultative Group which produced the report lacked representation from Asian, African, and Latin American communities resident in Britain, being thus deprived of vital historical and contemporary experience of inter-faith encounter; the second focusing on a variety of biblical and theological deficiencies in the report.[23]

Fourth, further afield the report has been noted by the World Council of Churches and the Vatican. By and large, however, it has not been the subject of theological comment in broad church circles in Britain.

Future

As a result of the foregoing perusal and examination of the field, it is my considered opinion that the future lies with urgent, open, and maximum dialogue between peoples of different faiths, with theological reflection arising out of this contact. Thinking in the field of inter-faith relationships, which is based on text without context and on personal experience which fails to seek to enter into the experience of others, can lead only to a new sterility based on old concepts.

Notes

1. The title is taken from the comments made by the Right Reverend John V. Taylor (then Bishop of Winchester, now retired and sometime missionary in Uganda and General Secretary of the Church Missionary Society) during the Synod debate on July 11, 1984 at York: "I welcome this report, particularly the first word of its title 'Towards a Theology for Inter-Faith Dialogue.' I believe it is, in a journey of many miles, for we have hardly begun, not to whittle away the faith, but to have enough faith to expose ourselves to the ideas of totally different world views from our own" (General Synod July Group of Sessions 1984 Report of Proceedings, Volume 15, No. 2, London, CIO Publishing, 1984, 798).
2. "Towards a Theology for Inter-Faith Dialogue," A Report of the Board for Mission and Unity of the General Synod of the Church of England (London, CIO, 1984), hereinafter referred to as the report. It was initiated by Bishop David Brown, Chairman of the Board for Mission and Unity and also of the British Council of Churches' Committee on Relations With People of Other Faiths.
3. Report of Proceedings, Volume 15, No. 2, 803.
4. *Ibid.*, 805.
5. *Relations with People of Other Faiths: Guidelines on Dialogue in Britain*, Working Document published on the authority of the Committee for Relations with People of Other Faiths (London, BCC, 1981). Re-issued in a Revised Edition entitled *Relations With People of Other Faiths: Guidelines for Dialogue in Britain* (London, BCC, 1983); hereinafter referred to as the BCC's *Guidelines for Dialogue in Britain*.
6. Geneva, WCC, 1979; hereafter referred to as the *WCC's Guidelines*.
7. Peter Brierley *UK Christian Handbook 1987/88 Edition*, Bromley, Kent etc., Marc Europe *et al.,* 1986, 129–53.
8. The Reverend D.R.J. Holloway (Newcastle): "It is for this reason that I am worried about the model that we get in this BCC report, the model of fellow pilgrims. This is the model of the WCC originally. I submit that it is neither catholic nor apostolic, nor is it Anglican, because I am not a fellow pilgrim; I do not believe I am or want to be with, for example, the Moonies, with Jim Jones' Temple, with the New Church of Satan. Ah, it may be said, but we are talking about the higher religions. How do you separate off the higher religions?... I prefer that old model of D.T. Niles of the two beggars, one of whom is pointing the other beggar to where food can be found. I do not believe there is arrogance in that, but rather I believe that the failure to do that is being selfish." (General Synod November Group of Sessions 1981 Report of Proceedings, Volume 12, No. 3, London, CIO, 1981, 1022).
9. *Ibid.*, 1017–1048.
10. What came to be known as "the Lund Principle" was enunciated at the third Faith and Order Conference of the World Council of Churches held at Lund, Sweden, in 1952. It was a representative of the Church of England, Oliver Tomkins (then Secretary of the Faith and Order Department in Geneva and later Bishop of Bristol), who first propounded it, by posing the question: "Should not our Churches ask themselves...whether they should not act together in all matters, except those in which deep difference of conviction compel them to act separately?"
11. "Exclusivism," "Inclusivism" and "Pluralism" as categories were first set out in detail in Alan Race, *Christian and Religious Pluralism* (London: SCM Press, 1983). Alan

Race was a member of the group which prepared the report.

12. David Brown, *All Their Splendour*, (London: Collins Fount, 1982), 223.
13. *Report of Proceedings*, Volume 15, No. 2, 781–784.
14. *Ibid.*, 784–786.
15. *Ibid.*, 786–788.
16. *Ibid.*, 798–800.
17. Vijay Menon, *ibid.*, 797–798.
18. *Ibid.*, 790–792.
19. *Inter-Faith Dialogue in the Diocese of London* (London, Diocesan Church House, 1986).
20. *Anvil*, Vol. 1, No. 3, (1984), 231–260.
21. Christopher Sugden, *Christ's Exclusive Claims and Inter-Faith Dialogue*, Grove Pastoral Series No. 22 (Bramcote, Notts: Grove Books, 1985).
22. *Towards a Theology for Inter-Faith Dialogue*, Lambeth Conference 1988 Edition, published worldwide for the ACC in 1986 (UK Edition, London, CIO, 1986).
23. Michael J. Nazir-Ali, "That Which Is Not to Be Found but Which Finds Us," *Towards a Theology for Inter-Faith Dialogue* (Lambeth Conference 1988 Edition), 41–51. At Lambeth the bishops rejected a paper on Christian-Jewish relations, accepting instead an entirely re-written version entitled "Jews, Christians and Muslims: The Way of Dialogue." The new draft was much influenced by the Palestinian-born Christian Arab, the Right Reverend Samir Kafity, President-Bishop of the Episcopal Church of Jerusalem and the Middle East. It recognizes the desirability of dialogue with all faiths but gives a special place to the relationship between Christianity, Judaism, and Islam—the Abrahamic faiths. "Dialogue," it maintains, "is the work of patient love and an expression of reconciliation. It involves understanding, affirmation and sharing—three 'ways' developed at length."

17

INTERRELIGIOUS DIALOGUE

NEXT STEP FOR CONSERVATIVE PROTESTANT INTELLECTUALS IN AMERICA?

Richard Quebedeaux

IN THE YEARS following the Civil War, which ended in 1865, profound changes occurred in the intellectual climate of American society that challenged the prevailing Protestant theology and seemed to many to threaten their understanding of the Christian faith. Psychological studies tended to reduce religion to phenomena of sociology and anthropology. New comparative work in religion challenged the uniqueness of Christianity. Darwinism, geology, and the new methods of biblical study, especially the "higher criticism" of the German universities, called the authority of the Bible into question.

In the Church, a major new emphasis on the responsibility of the Church for society developed in the latter part of the nineteenth century, later called the "Social Gospel." Drawing upon the new biblical criticism, it concentrated on the ethical teachings of the Scriptures, rather than the traditional teachings of God's revelation. Many Christian intellectuals were positively influenced by the Social Gospel and other new trends in American thought and adapted their theological understanding and ecclesiastical practice to them. In time these thinkers were described as "modernists" or "liberals," and they gradually became the dominant authority in the hierarchies of the major Protestant denominations during the course of the twentieth century.

As all this was taking place, however, there were also those in the churches who saw the new theology as a threat to the Christian faith, and who rallied their forces to take a stand against further inroads. The core of this grouping were the "fundamentalists," those who identified themselves with a movement which emerged at the turn of the century and took on recognizable form after World War I. The name of this still-thriving school of thought is derived from a series of twelve short booklets entitled *The Fundamentals* (1910–15),[1] written by a number of prominent theological conservatives (including intellectuals) and distributed widely throughout the English-speaking world. These doctrinal tracts set forth the "fundamentals of the faith" in defense of traditional orthodoxy against modernism. Five fundamentals came to be regarded as the absolute essentials of the Christian revelation—the "inerrancy" of the Bible, the virgin birth of Jesus, his "substitutionary atonement," his bodily resurrection, and his imminent visible and personal return.

Fundamentalism became an *opposition* movement against the liberals who had departed from orthodox Christian belief, and it has been in such opposition that fundamentalists found their identity. But by the late 1920s, it became clear that the fundamentalists had failed to capture the major American denominations, a fact which resulted in the formation of a number of (mainly Baptist and Presbyterian) splinter denominations by those who left the larger liberal groupings. Others organized independently of the denominations and worked through separated fundamentalist colleges and seminaries, missionary and evangelic associations, publishing houses and periodicals.

Throughout the 1920s and 1930s, fundamentalism took on a literalist mode of biblical interpretation and a sectarian, and scattered, ecclesiastical organization. It moved into a cultural time warp, rejecting almost all of the values not only of religious liberalism but also of the wider society as a whole, and equating any form of liberalism with out-and-out secularism. Thus, the movement was marginalized with respect to the mainstream of American Protestantism, a process which was aided by its *exclusivist* stance. This stance insisted that only Christians can inherit "heaven" after death, and that fundamentalists alone are "true Christians." All other religious traditions are false, and their adherents are doomed to eternal torment in hell.

By the 1940s, a small group of younger theologians, who had grown up in fundamentalism, sparked a new movement they termed "neo-evangelicalism," identifying it with the more "mainstream," nonsectarian character of the eighteenth and early nineteenth century evangelical revivalism of the Great Awakening in America. This moderating trend took on structure in 1942, when some 150 delegates representing 40 Protest ant denominations met in St. Louis, Missouri and launched the National Association of Evangelicals (NAE). The NAE was founded by small, "formerly" fundamentalist denominations, together with individuals still in the more liberal denominations, who were eager for an instrument of co-operation in between what they regarded as the liberal Federal Council of Churches (later, the National Council of Churches) and the strict fundamentalist American Council of Christian Churches, established earlier.

The new organization was supposed to serve as an instrument for a united evangelical witness in evangelism itself, church and state issues, broadcasting, public relations, Christian education, and mission work at home and abroad. Although the intellectual leadership of the NAE was largely Baptist and Presbyterian of a strong doctrinally oriented Reformed bent, the organization also attracted major pentecostal and holiness denominations which had previously emphasized testimony, experience, and sanctification (sometimes expressed as social reform) more than doctrine. But during the 1940s, 1950s, 1960s, and 1970s, these denominations moved toward the larger evangelical consensus in doctrinal matters.

In this discussion, conservative Protestants are those who refer to themselves as fundamentalists, evangelicals (the term "neoevangelical" fell into disuse by the late 1960s), or Pentecostals, and who would generally identify with the NAE's basic concerns, even if they are not formally related to that organization. To the outside observer, conservative Protestants are still entirely exclusivist in their religious orientation, incapable of "dialogue" even with other Christians and certainly not with members of other religions. But the prominent intellectuals within this grouping have changed, sometimes dramatically, especially since the 1960s, and may well be ready for "the wider ecumenism." Our purpose here is to trace and examine the reasons for such a change among them.

Just as in the hierarchies of the major Protestant denominations, intellectuals—theologians, journalists, and others—have had the key role in shaping the subtle ideological and relational changes of direction within conservative Protestantism as a whole. They, ultimately, manipulate the symbols of understanding by which the people at large conceptualize reality.

Fuller Theological Seminary

To accommodate the interests of the growing number of scholars within evangelical ranks during the late 1940s and 1950s, Fuller Theological Seminary, Pasadena, California, was established in 1947 as an interdenominational graduate school of theology, in large degree through the efforts of Harold John Ockenga, then pastor of Park Street Church, Boston. Carl F.H. Henry and Harold Lindsell were among its first faculty. Both were later to become editors of *Christianity Today*, since 1956 the chief intellectual barometer of the conservative Protestant movement. After his first media-attracting revival in Los Angeles in 1949, the young fundamentalist evangelist, Billy Graham, aligned himself with the "new evangelicals"; and their intelligentsia, including Ockenga, joined Fuller Seminary's board of directors and later provided funds to found and maintain *Christianity Today*.

It was at Fuller that the first intellectual changes occurred within modern conservative Protestantism. In 1972, after years of debate, the seminary removed the "inerrancy clause" from its statement of faith, signed by all faculty members, most of whom were well-educated in higher biblical criticism (several at Harvard). The notion of biblical inerrancy, that the Bible is "free from error in the whole and in the part," had been the principal roadblock in the way of evangelical theologians' legitimacy in the larger theological academy. The removal of this doctrinal requirement for Fuller faculty—a "liberal" act—enhanced the development of critical theological studies there, and the creation of a full-fledged school of psychology, and a school of world mission which emphasizes the social-scientific study of religion.

By the 1980s, Fuller Seminary had, in some ways, become nearly as modernist in its general orientation as "mainline" Protestant schools like Princeton Theological Seminary. Furthermore, by then, most of the other faculties of evangelical colleges and seminaries had already followed the spirit of Fuller's example. The gradual acceptance of the historical-critical method of biblical interpretation, and of the social and behavioral sciences, applied even to religion, greatly weakened evangelical doctrinal exclusivity. But there were numerous other contributing factors as well to the breakdown of conservative Protestant sectarianism.

Charismatic Renewal

In terms of ecclesiology, the doctrine of the pure, completely orthodox, evangelical church or denomination waned considerably, especially after the "charismatic renewal" or "neopentecostal" movement emerged in

1960. In this movement, mainline denominational Christians (e.g., Anglicans, Lutherans, Presbyterians, and, by 1967, Catholics) received the pentecostal "gifts of the spirit" outlined in I Cor. 12–14—including "speaking in tongues," divine healing, and prophecy—practiced them in their own churches, and accommodated them to the nonsectarian religious style of mainline liberal Protestantism and Catholicism. When white fundamentalist Pentecostals, most notably those of the Assemblies of God (an NAE charter member), began praying and worshipping with mainline Christian ministers and laity during the last three decades, they could no longer easily condemn them for their denial of inerrancy, their sacramental liturgies, their espousal of baptismal regeneration, and the like—beliefs and practices once publicly repudiated by evangelical theologians. Not a few within the charismatic renewal leadership were intellectuals—theologians and writers—who, in the course of time, led many of their nonpentecostal evangelical counterparts in a more broadly ecumenical direction, focusing on "spiritual" rather than doctrinal commonalities.

The Jesus People Movement

The secular "counterculture" of the mid-to-late 1960s was a well-known movement of idealistic youth whose "radical" and permissive values and mores ran counter to those of the established society of that time. Conservative Protestantism had its own version of the counterculture in the Jesus People movement, which followed on the heels of charismatic renewal in the late 1960s (many of the Jesus People were charismatic), and challenged the conservative and traditional lifestyles of the evangelical elders. The secular counterculture influenced the Jesus People movement politically, because it legitimated protest in the evangelical ranks. In addition, the social, cultural, and moral permissiveness of the secular counterculture gradually seeped into that movement—with long-term effects on the whole of conservative Protestantism.

In the Jesus People movement, communal and "alternative" lifestyles flourished, replacing the conservative Protestant stress on the priority of the nuclear family. An emphasis on "simple living," for a time, repudiated the material upward mobility of traditional evangelicals. The fundamentalist Christian taboos against social dancing, alcohol, and tobacco were rejected, and some were even experimenting with drugs. More importantly, the Jesus People legitimated "Satanic rock n' roll" (as the fundamentalists saw it) by creating a new genre of "Christian" rock music. At first, the eroticism in secular rock n' roll was subdued in this brand of sacred music, but as secular rock moved from "suggestive" to "explicit" in the 1970s and 1980s, Christian rock and *its* performers became suggestive (as in the case of Christian vocalist Amy Grant).

The Jesus People had disappeared by the mid-1970s, but the exclusivism of the wider evangelical community had been permanently shaken at the level of culture and society. The social experimentation of the Jesus People remained acceptable, and a measure of moral relativism took hold within evangelical ranks. Many of conservative Protestantism's intellectuals supported these trends in their teaching and writing.

Jimmy Carter and the Movement Left

Though they didn't realize it at first, evangelical theologians were gradually becoming much like their liberal Christian counterparts. Changes in conservative Protestant thinking suggested a subtle shift from transcendence to immanence, from a stress on the hope of a literal heaven and avoidance of a literal hell to a focus on building a just society on earth. During the period from about 1966 to 1976, a number of evangelical intellectuals moved to the political left, away from the once-solid alignment of conservative Protestantism with the right wing of the Republican party. Gravitating around U.S. Senator Mark Hatfield of Oregon, a new breed of evangelical social activist rose up in the mid-1970s, claiming to be "radical Christians," and championing left-oriented causes from pacifism and nonviolent resistance to liberation theology. *Sojourners*, the now well-known, even chic, radical evangelical monthly, was founded in 1971, and in many ways charted the new course of leftward movements; while other evangelical publications, including *Christianity Today*, became increasingly "sophisticated," and attracted the attention of more mainline Protestants and Catholics.

In many ways, the political liberalization of the evangelical intelligentsia in the 1970s was epitomized by the election in 1976 ("the year of the evangelical") of Jimmy Carter, the "born-again" Southern Baptist, to the U.S. Presidency, as a moderately liberal Democrat. With that event, moreover, conservative Protestantism, after half a century on the margins, symbolically entered the mainstream of American society. Evangelical exclusivism had at once been dealt a mortal blow.

Relational Theology and Popular Psychology

"Relational theology" in evangelicalism emerged in the late 1960s and matured in the 1970s, as a reaction against the rational and scholastic doctrinal emphases of many conservative Protestant churches. Most prominent among relational theologians at that time were Keith Miller, best-selling Anglican author; Lloyd Ogilvie, senior minister of Hollywood's

First Presbyterian Church; and Bruce Larson, author and senior minister of University Presbyterian Church in Seattle.

In *The Relational Revolution* (1976),[2] Larson insisted that "the kingdom of God is in truth the kingdom of right relationships"—to God, to one's self, to "significant others" (family, friends, and colleagues), and to the world (the rest of humanity "whom one can choose to love or ignore"). Relational theology was profoundly influenced by the secular human potential movement and its psychological, relational, and small-group techniques and theories, as well as its therapies, which were regularly taught at Fuller Seminary. Larson stressed his conviction that "the quality and scope of relationships and the ability and willingness to relate are marks of orthodoxy rather than doctrine, ethical performance or spiritual heroism." Thus, by making theology relational instead of conceptual, these theologians further softened the doctrinal (and relational) exclusivism of conservative Protestantism.

Popular psychology from the secular world affected the evangelical intelligentsia in relational theology, while the "positive thinking" struck a chord among the conservative Protestant masses. Rooted in the nineteenth century "New Thought" (or "mind-over-matter") movement, this popular mode of thinking was a reaction against the Calvinistic pessimism about the possibility of *eradicating* human sinfulness and sinful propensity. It was also a reaction, at a time of increasing evangelical upward mobility, against the delayed material gratification (i.e., "pie-in-the-sky-by-and-by") once inherent in conservative Protestantism. All of this led to the gradual development of a full-fledged "doctrine of prosperity"—based on positive mental attitudes—which became an integral part of modern evangelical and fundamentalist popular theology, and was most visible among the prominent television evangelists, Schuller among them. Psychology, once a "tool of Satan" in conservative Protestantism, was now its salvation, weakening its social exclusivism even further.

Academic Respectability

Fuller Seminary, with its critical, well-published faculty, became the center of evangelical scholarship. But other seminaries, also operating on an interdenominational model, rose or were revitalized to meet Fuller's academic challenge. Most important among these were Gordon-Conwell Theological Seminary, South Hamilton, Massachusetts; Trinity Evangelical Divinity School, Deerfield, Illinois; and Talbot Theological Seminary, La Mirada, California. Evangelical colleges like Wheaton in Wheaton, Illinois, and Westmont in Santa Barbara, California, gained stature, while three conservative Protestant television evangelists started their own modern universities. Oral Roberts University was founded in the 1960s, and achieved full regional accreditation in almost record time. It was followed, in the 1970s, by Pat Robertson's CBN University in Virginia Beach, Virginia, and Jerry Falwell's Liberty University, Lynchburg, Virginia.

Numerous evangelical scholars produced noteworthy theological, historical, and sociological studies in the 1970s and 1980s; and the lists of forthcoming books by evangelical publishers like Eerdmans and InterVarsity Press suggested far more liberal political, social, and theological themes and stances than were published by them previously. Although *Christianity Today* maintained its basically conservative stance (far more so than Fuller Seminary), other evangelical magazines like *Sojourners*, *The Reformed Journal*, and *Daughters of Sarah* (a feminist journal) moved solidly to the "left" politically and socially, while they retained some of the evangelical symbolism.

More evangelical scholars became active in their professional societies during the 1970s and 1980s. The Society for Pentecostal Studies was formed, and a well-attended evangelical studies theme group was established by the American Academy of Religion (AAR), and held its sessions at the professional society's annual meetings. Liberal Protestant theological journals began to take evangelical scholarship seriously and published articles by evangelical authors and reviews of their books; while feminists, gays, and lesbians, and political activists on the left within conservative Protestantism formed their own organizations such as Evangelicals for Social Action, Evangelical Women's Caucus, and Evangelicals Concerned (about homosexuality). When these elites became known within liberal Protestant (and Roman Catholic) circles, academic and otherwise, new relationships occurred, bridges were built, and conservative Protestant exclusivism in higher education, theological and secular, no longer served a useful purpose.

Evangelicals in Dialogue

"Dialogue with evangelicals" became a new catchphrase among believers, especially liberal Protestants, Catholics, and Jews, by the mid-1970s. The prestigious American Theological Society elected Carl F.H. Henry to a term as president, succeeding Gordon Kaufman of Harvard. Union Theological Seminary in New York, that great bastion of liberalism, hired two Pentecostal professors, and Harvard Divinity School announced that it was seeking endowment for a professorship of evangelical Christianity. Established ecumenical conferences, which had repudiated the born-again in a previous era, now welcomed conservative Protestant scholars, pastors, and activists as featured speakers.

With all this respect coming from its old archenemy, liberalism, the evangelical movement—its intellectuals anyway—no longer saw the antichrist behind such modernist organizations as the National Council of Churches and the World Council of Churches, which had an especially positive contingent of evangelical leaders present at its 1983 General Assembly in Vancouver. And thanks to charismatic renewal, the wall between Catholics and evangelicals broke down as well. No longer were Protestant liberals and Roman Catholics consigned to hell, as in the not-too-distant past.

As to dialogue with other religions, that also emerged within some elite evangelical circles in the mid-1970s. There had long been a positive feeling toward Judaism in fundamentalism, because its "dispensational" theology, popularized by the Scofield Reference Bible, gave a special role to the Jews in the approaching millennium. Celebrities like singer Pat Boone and bestselling author Hal Lindsey regularly wore a star of David around their necks during the heyday of the Jesus People movement. By 1975, a major academic dialogue between evangelical Christians and Jews took place, at which one wondered whether there had *ever* been any conflict between the two groups. (See Marc H. Tanenbaum, Marvin R. Wilson, and A. James Rudin, eds., *Evangelicals and Jews in Conversation*.[3]) And in 1978, a similar dialogue occurred between a number of prominent evangelicals and members of the Unification Church, which most conservative Protestants would term a new religion, not a branch of Christianity. (See Richard Quebedeaux and Rodney Sawatsky, eds., *Evangelical-Unification Dialogue*.[4])

The Universalist Impulse

A "saved and lost" school of Christian thought, conservative Protestantism always repudiated the "universalist" notion that, ultimately, all people, including nonbelievers, would inherit eternal life in heaven. Part of the evangelical critique of Karl Barth in the 1950s and 1960s had to do with the universalism in his theology and in neorthodoxy more generally. (Barth later became very popular among evangelical intellectuals.)

As the 1960s turned into the 1970s, however, heaven, hell, and the afterlife were discussed less in intellectually oriented books and articles by evangelicals. Interest centered more on the here and now, politics, culture, and society. Mass evangelism declined in popularity, and, by the 1980s, Billy Graham had become something of an anachronism among evangelical intellectuals. But even *he* questioned the old assumptions that everyone, including the Jews, would be lost, in a highly controversial interview in the January 1978 issue of *McCall's*. (The touchy parts of that piece were later repudiated by Graham, but the interviewer, a highly respected New York journalist, writing under a pseudonym, still has the tapes.) Then, Charles Kraft, an anthropologist at Fuller Seminary's school of world mission, published his *Christianity in Culture*,[5] which, like much earlier liberal Protestant works, argued for the "contextualization" of the Christian message. The book explicitly and implicitly questioned certain traditional theological and ethical norms, culturally rooted, which had been taught as *mandatory* for Christians in every culture. Kraft insisted that all religion originates in a specific culture, and if it wants to be "relevant" in another culture, its teaching must be properly contextualized. Many evangelical leaders feared that this kind of thinking would ultimately impede evangelism, since it seemed to relativize Christian doctrine.

Although most evangelical media still affirm the external "lostness" of all persons outside of belief in Jesus Christ, an increasing number are simply silent in the matter, while numerous evangelical scholars move ever closer to an essentially universalist position. The March 20, 1987, issue of *Christianity Today* included a symposium on universalism. Here evangelical theologian Clark Pinnock now argues for the mere extinction of those outside Christ, rather than their eternal punishment in hell; while Neal Punt, a pastor in the highly Calvinistic Christian Reformed Church, declares that all will be saved except those who "finally persist in refusing to have God in their knowledge." He terms this "biblical universalism," and insists that it "breaks down barriers between people. It promotes a feeling of genuine concern and mutual trust. It helps overcome prejudices that arise out of fear because we view others apathetically—or worse still, with suspicion. On this basis we are to view all persons as heirs of the kingdom of heaven."

The New Christian Right

To be sure, the liberalization and resulting breakdown of exclusivism among evangelical intellectuals have not gone unchallenged. In the mid-1970s, Harold Lindsell published his *Battle for the Bible*,[6] "exposing" the liberal trends, especially at Fuller Seminary and in the theological schools of the conservative Southern Baptist Convention (Billy Graham's denomination). The rise of the so-called "New Christian Right" later that decade, led by Jerry Falwell and other television evangelists, was, in part, a reaction to the new liberalism close to home, not just to the "secular humanism" on the outside.

In 1985, Tony Campolo, a Baptist sociologist and popular evangelical speaker at youth conventions, was accused of espousing universalism (that Jesus is mystically present in every person) in his book *A Reasonable Faith*.[7] The president of Campus Crusade for Christ's theological seminary wrote a 35-page critique of the work, insisting that Campolo is not an evangelical, because he espouses "Marxism, humanism, existentialism, and pantheism," and should no longer be invited to speak at the large evangelical youth rallies sponsored by leading conservative Protestant organizations such as Campus Crusade. The popular author denied the charges. A formal trial was held with trusted evangelicals, including former assistant to Richard Nixon, Charles Colson, as judges. Campolo was acquitted in this case, but some of the "leading liberals" among modern evangelical theologians did lose their credibility and jobs within the evangelical community during the last decade, largely over their rejection of the fundamental doctrine of biblical inerrancy. Nevertheless, these measures have had little *real* impact within the colleges and seminaries of the world of conservative Protestantism. Academic liberalism is hard to eradicate.

Furthermore, at the same time the New Christian Right was exposing theologically liberal and politically leftward trends in evangelicalism, some of its own mentors were also being influenced by modernity. Jerry Falwell's "Moral Majority," established in the late 1970s, was actually a "liberal" phenomenon within fundamentalism because, for the first time fundamentalists were encouraged to associate—and work—with *any* political conservatives, including Mormons and atheists, for the common cause.

Falwell later took the bold step of defending the Reverend Sun Myung Moon who had been convicted on charges of income tax evasion and spent thirteen months in prison. When the television evangelist associated himself with the Unification Church's religious liberty activities on behalf of its founder—and others similarly charged—he also accepted invitations to speak at Unification-sponsored anti-communist conferences where Unification theology was presented and discussed. While this may sound odd—a fundamentalist leader cohorting with a "false messiah" (as many fundamentalists and evangelicals saw Moon)—it seemed a natural outgrowth of Falwell's book, *The Fundamentalist Phenomenon*,[8] which was actually written by two of his professors. Like the writings of the neoevangelicals of the 1940s, it repudiated much of fundamentalism's sectarianism and exclusivism and called for at least a moderate openness to the wider society and its concerns.

Conservative Protestants and Interreligious Dialogues

Since Christian ecumenism and, even more so, interreligious dialogue have largely been the prerogative of highly educated, urbane elites, many of whom have had a wide range of intercultural experience, it is no wonder that marginalized conservative Protestants in America have been excluded and have excluded themselves. In 1978, George Gallup found that the typical conservative Protestant is a white female Southerner, aged 50 or over, with a high school education, and a very modest income. Of the evangelical-fundamentalist movement as a whole (28 percent of all Americans), 63 percent are women, 50 percent live in the south, 27 percent live in the Midwest. A mere 15 percent are college graduates and professional or business people, with 25 percent having completed only grade school, and 60 percent high school alone. Sixty percent of all conservative Protestants live in small towns or rural areas, with only 9 percent in large cities. Forty-five percent are manual workers, 42 percent Baptist, and 22 percent members of small conservative denominations. In 1978, 51 percent earned under $10,000 annually, with only 28 percent making more than $15,000.[9] Although Gallup's definition of "evangelical" (i.e., born-again, Bible-believing in all matters, and concerned about evangelism) included non-whites (23 percent of the sample), our discussion of intellectual currents in conservative Protestantism excludes all of the black church (except those who were schooled and socialized in white fundamentalist or evangelical institutions), since blacks were not included in the white fundamentalist-modernist controversy, and are not guilty parties in the present debate.

The above social statistics have probably changed somewhat since 1978 with upward social mobility, but conservative Protestantism as a whole remains marginal in the wider society. What this means is that the liberalized group of evangelical intellectuals is indeed a small one, yet a growing one which has successfully manipulated the evangelical symbols in a way that allows the "evangelical" designation to be interpreted much more broadly than in the past.

As yet, there has been very little formal interreligious dialogue undertaken by conservative Protestants, probably because very few of their intellectuals have been invited. (But see, for instance, Virginia Ramey Mollenkott's *Women of Faith in Dialogue*,[10] which is a dialogical collection of essays on the specific concerns of women, not only by Christian and Jews, but Muslims as well, and includes a sample interreligious service of worship. Mollenkott is a prominent evangelical Christian feminist theologian.) This is not to say that conservative Protestants, any more than most of their liberal counterparts in "mainline Christendom," will be eager to start the process. (They, too, will have to be dragged along at first). The point to be made, however, is that the once-pervasive blanket of evangelical exclusivism is worn and has many holes in it. So let the dialogue begin.

Notes

1. Chicago: Testimony Publishing Company, 1910–1915.
2. Waco, Texas: Word Books, 1976.
3. Grand Rapids, Michigan: Baker Book House, 1978.
4. New York: Rose of Sharon Press, 1979.
5. Maryknoll, New York: Orbis Books, 1979.
6. Grand Rapids, Michigan: Zondervan, 1976.
7. Waco, Texas: Word Books, 1985.
8. Garden City, New York: Doubleday, 1981.
9. Albert J. Menendez, "Who Are the Evangelicals?," in *Christianity Today* (January 27, 1978), 42.
10. New York: Crossroad, 1987.

For a full account of the gradual liberalization of the conservative Protestant intelligentsia, see the following works:

James Davison Hunter, *Evangelicalism: The Coming Generation* (Chicago: University of Chicago Press, 1987).

Richard Quebedeaux, *The Young Evangelicals* (New York: Harper & Row, 1974).

___*The World Evangelicals* (San Francisco: Harper & Row, 1978).

___*By What Authority: The Rise of Personality Cults in American Christianity* (San Francisco: Harper & Row, 1982).

___*The New Charismatics II*. (San Francisco: Harper & Row, 1983).

___"We're on Our Way, Lord: The Rise of Evangelical Feminism in Modern American Christianity," in Ursula King, ed. *Women in the World's Religions: Past and Present* (New York: Paragon House, 1987), 129–144.

___"Conservative and Charismatic Developments of the Later Twentieth Century," in Charles H. Lippy and Peter W. Williams, eds. *Encyclopedia of the American Religious Experience* (New York: Scribners, 1988), 963–976.

18

EXPERIENTIAL MOMENTS OF INTERRELIGIOUS ENCOUNTER

FROM A PASTOR'S DIARY

Romesh Philip Modayil

I COULD HAVE entitled this paper differently and called it "The Gospel of Dialogue According to a Pastor!" In fact, that is what inter-faith dialogue is all about—"good news"! And I have good news indeed as far as my experiences in inter-religious encounter are concerned. In this paper I would like to share two significant inter-faith encounters I have had as a Christian minister, two religious encounters specifically related to religious ritual. The first, an encounter with Hinduism concerning the ritual of marriage; the second, an encounter with Islam concerning the ritual of a worship service. In sharing these experiences with you I hope to highlight the amazing possibilities of inter-religious encounter in a pluralistic society like that of India.

As Indians, we gradually began to realize our unity in diversity during the early years of our struggle for independence from British colonialism. Regardless of caste or creed, we had one common objective—to live as one people in a free land! What actually transpired was however something quite different—we were now a people divided according to the religion we professed: Muslims in Pakistan and Hindus in India. Nevertheless, the people who remained in India resolved to continue the common task of now building a free, democratic, and secular republic in which everyone could preach or practice his own religion without fear or hindrance. Unfortunately, however, that generation of Indians is beginning to pass away, and the trend today is somewhat in the opposite direction. The generations of post-independent India are becoming increasingly captive to thoughts and ideas about "unity in similarity"— similarity in language, in religion, in tribe, or in caste. My experiences tell me that this trend can be reversed and joyfully, too!

During my three years as the pastor of a large Protestant congregation in New Delhi, the capital of India, I have had many an opportunity to participate in religious dialogue with sisters and brothers of other faiths. My position as a Christian minister particularly enabled me to meet and befriend other religious leaders, and this made our encounters all the more exciting and challenging. One of my most challenging yet happiest encounters was with a priest and leader of the Arya Samaj, a reactionary and forceful Hindu organization.

The Arya Samaj, founded by Swami Dayananda Saraswati and established in 1875 at Bombay, is a dynamic organization extremely active in Hindu society today. Dayananda stood for the creation of an Indian nation which would have a common religion and culture. One of his basic aims was to rally the people of India against the growing influence of Christianity and against any further inroads that Islam could make in Indian society. India had been ruled by Muslim overlords in the past and many of them (e.g., Aurangzeb) had undoubtedly encouraged the propagation of Islam. It was now the turn of the Christians as represented by Great Britain to rule the country and, in Dayananda's view, to proselytize as well. He was however convinced that "Aryan was the chosen people, Vedas the chosen gospel, and India the chosen land."[1] Just as Martin Luther's Reformation cry was 'Back to the Bible,' Dayananda's clarion call was 'Back to the Vedas.'[2]

Hence foreign religions like Christianity and Islam had no place in India and adherents of these religions were to be converted or re-converted to Hinduism through the 'Shuddhi' (or 'purification') movement which he initiated. Dayananda also objected to the educational system introduced by the British in India, particularly to the spread of the English language. He saw the system as being geared towards promoting the cause of Christianity and Western culture in India. "The Mission Schools also taught that the superiority of the Europeans over the Indian was the gift of the Son of God."[3] Besides, the missionary, while criticizing the evils inherent in Hindu society, would proudly declare the Christian community to be free from such curses, and at the same time maintain the absolute superiority of the Christian Scriptures.[4] Small wonder that Dayananda was provoked into becoming a firebrand, militant nationalist with all its communal undertones.

The modern Arya Samaj has, to a large extent, inherited the militant posture of its founder and continues to strive to establish a dynamic and cohesive Hindu society throughout the country. Christians are still considered as foreigners (the Muslims too, for that matter) whose political, cultural and religious loyalties lie beyond the borders of India. The members of this and other Hindu cultural or political organizations seem to be oblivious of the fact that Christians have been living in India at least since the beginning of the fourth century C.E., if not earlier, and that even later, many people embraced Islam or Christianity only to escape the rigid and oppressive Hindu caste system. But this has to be said of the Arya Samaj: that they too are vehemently opposed to the caste system as well as to idol-worship.

I think I have said enough to serve as an introduction to what I am now going to narrate. Two years ago I received an unusual request from the parents of a Christian girl asking me to help concelebrate her marriage to a man who belonged to the Samaj. The marriage was to take place according to the rites of the Arya Samaj. I confess that I was astounded at first and then learned that they had earlier approached other Christian priests known to them and who had declined their offer either on the grounds of 'religious conscience,' or out of fear of their congregations. On subsequent inquiry I realized that all I needed to do was to read a passage from the Christian Scriptures and pronounce a benediction. I decided to take up the challenge.

The reception I received when I arrived for the late-night function in my cassock was anything but warm. The ushers at the entrance looked away as I walked in; and the moment I seated myself among the other guests, those on my left and right got up and left their seats. The boys who were serving the light refreshments would quite deliberately pass me by and serve the guests nearby. I began to understand the concept of untouchability. Most of the guests were members of the Arya Samaj; and, although there were a few Christians too representing the bride's party, I was the most conspicuous one with my cassock. The girl's parents were profusely apologetic and suggested that I ought not to have come dressed in my clerical gown. But they themselves were guests of the bridegroom's family and therefore not in a position to appreciably reduce my discomfort. When the dinner was served (this normally takes place before the wedding ceremony itself) I was told rather curtly by one of the ushers that I could eat with the servants after the guests had eaten.

The arrival of the Arya Samaj priest was quite another story. Received personally by the bridegroom's parents and elders of the family, he was escorted to the podium at the center where the marriage ceremony was to take place. There was a flurry of activities around him while members of the family remained in attendance. The dinner was brought to him by the bridegroom's father himself. The welcome was quite appropriate, for a Christian minister in India would have the same kind of reception in a similar setting if the parties involved were Christians.

Just before the ceremony began, the bride's family was told that the Christian benediction should take place only after the priest and the guests had left. I learned that the Hindu priest had earlier vehemently objected to my presence at the ceremony and only agreed to my being there for the sake of the bride's parents and on the condition that I should have no part in the program as long as he and other members of the Samaj were there. This was acceptable to me. The bride herself had already become an Arya Samaji through the Shuddhi ceremony, a necessary precondition for the marriage.

The ceremony proceeded according to plan while I remained a curious looker-on in the background. I was fascinated by some of the rites used in this ritual, particularly as the priest made every effort to explain in simple Hindi to the bridal pair and to the gathering the ancient Sanskrit terminology used in the 'mantras' he was chanting. I found many similar points of contact with our own Christian marriage service.

Soon after the ceremony was over the guests got up to congratulate the young couple and then leave. It was at this point that the father of the bride requested me to proceed with my part of the program immediately. Much to the chagrin of the priest and the bridegroom's parents, I invited the couple to an adjacent podium and sat down cross-legged with them on the platform. That raised a few eyebrows as it was expected that I would have them kneel before me. I noticed that just a few members of the bride's family were standing around us while most of the others were making their exit.

I began by reading, or rather chanting, St. Paul's letter on love (1 Cor. 13) in Sanskrit, using a copy of the New Testament in Sanskrit I had taken along with me. People were flabbergasted and stopped in their tracks to listen. They were expecting the usual rendering of some passage from the Bible in English. (English is quite often assumed to be the mother-tongue of Christians in India, although less that 20 percent actually use it.) I then proceeded to explain what I had chanted, just as the Hindu priest had also done. Since I too was now using the *lingua franca*, it drew the attention of not only the bridegroom's family and guests, but also of the Arya Samaj priest. They seemed to have evinced a keen interest in what I had to say. Making use of the opportunity I proceeded to explain the concept of Christian marriage and its responsibilities and suddenly it did not sound so alien after all! I wound up the service with the Aaronic benediction in Hebrew, pointing out that this was the original language of the Old Testament.

Another false notion that Christianity's Scriptures have always been in English was demolished. It was now the turn of the Arya Samaj priest to be fascinated by what I did and had to say. In an ensuing discussion I was able to tell him about some of the indigenous rites of some Christian marriages in India and went on to give him a bird's eye view of the long history of Christianity in India. The priest was excited and demanded that I address some of his colleagues who were leaders of the Arya Samaj. I gratefully accepted his invitation.

There was now a perceivable change in the attitude of the bridegroom's family toward me. I was treated with the same respect and cordiality accorded the Hindu priest. I had quite certainly made an impression.

At the follow-up meeting with the priest and his colleagues at his headquarters two weeks later, I was able to deal at length with the false notions many Hindus have about Christianity and Christians. The meeting was indeed an eye-opener for most of them. Inherited prejudices were swiftly swept aside and a beginning was made wherein the Arya Samaj leaders were now in a position to appreciate some of the 'Indianness' of Christianity in India. Of course strong objections were voiced to factors like proselytization, but they did not stand in the way of good and wholesome dialogue. Today the priest and I are good friends and continue to build on the foundations we laid two years ago.

I ask myself what was that "magic word" or sudden revelation that completely changed the situation for me on that wedding night? The answer is simple: It was the lifting of the veil of ignorance. In this case it was the realization that Christianity was not identical and equivalent to Western civilization and culture, which in turn meant that all Christians in India were not necessarily beef-eaters, blind imitators of Western customs and behavior, and loyalists of Britain or the USA. But it took a real flesh and blood encounter to dispel these notions. Undoubtedly the priest, his colleagues, and the wedding guests must have talked about their new-found knowledge with their friends and acquaintances, and the circle of awareness will only grow larger. Yet there are those who will say that my case was an exception and will continue to hold fast to their cherished prejudices. It is my contention, however, that this "risk factor" is minimal, and it is only in the constant exposition of the truth of ourselves that any meaningful step can be taken towards the removal of the barriers of ignorance. I shall say a little more on this in a general comment at the end of the description of my second significant inter-religious encounter.

While I was studying for my M.A. in Islam at the Jamia Millia Islamia, a Muslim university in New Delhi, I had the privilege of interacting with religiously oriented Muslim teachers, students, and leaders. A Christian priest studying Islam in a Muslim university aroused the curiosity and, at times, the hostility of some of my Muslim brethren. I often found myself in the midst of argumentative discussion, having to clarify my basic position as that of being a seeker of truth and a promoter of peace and understanding between religious communities, and not a confidence trickster aiming to seek converts to Christianity from the Muslim faith. It took a great deal of time, patience, and persuasion before I could invite some of them to witness a Christian worship service. I am not speaking here of liberal-minded Muslims, many of whom had already attended Christian worship services both in Protestant as well as Catholic churches, who were quite open to the truth of Christianity as I was to the truth of Islam. I am speaking rather of those rather conservative and zealous Muslims (and I am not using the term in a negative sense) who are not only devoted to the cause of Islam, but also who command a great deal of respect and authority in the Muslim community. Of course, it was necessary for me to make a few preliminary explanations to my guests: e.g., in the church, unlike in the mosque, men, women, and children sit together for worship; in urban churches people would normally go into the church without first removing their footwear; and that singing and music were an integral part of Christian worship. Having said all this, I was now ready to welcome them into the church in which I was ministering.

One of the first items that impressed my visitors was the relative simplicity of the church's interior—a sanctuary devoid of artistry and imagery, a conspicuously bare altar, and monotonous rows of simple benches. What they had heard or seen in print of churches was quite the opposite. "It reminds us so much of a mosque," they remarked. The singing of the hymn to the accompaniment of Indian instruments as the service was being conducted in the Hindustani language, a language that is almost identical to Urdu, the *lingua franca* of the Muslim community in India, was a source of delight to my friends. They were now able to follow the entire service. The participation of the laity in the reading of the Scriptures, in the collecting and the presenting of the offerings, and in the rendering of special hymns was appreciated. They were particularly happy to note the respect we show by standing up when the Scriptures are read. They paid keen attention to what was being said in the sermon and were ecstatic at the exchange of the greetings of peace, something very similar to the Islamic custom. By the end of the service they were a transformed people, transformed in their thinking about Christianity and Christians. This, of course, did not mean that their other notions of Christianity had disappeared, but they had allowed themselves to alter one or two of their preconceived notions about Christianity. This was a big step indeed.

The matter did not end there. The big Muslim feast of *Bakrid* was coming up soon. I suggested that we could have a common token celebration of the feast in the church. The idea struck a responsive chord in their minds and we began to plan for it.

Bakrid is a commemoration of Abraham's sacrifice of his son. The difference in the Qur'anic story is that Abraham (Ibranim in Arabic) took his first-born son Ishmael with him to sacrifice him to God, and not Isaac according to the Old Testament. There are also small differences in detail as regards the story, but by and large the story is the same. The main point anyway in both narrations is that Abraham's love for God was so genuine that he did not even withhold his own son from God. We therefore decided to praise God together in a celebration of worship for Abraham's faithfulness and, above all, for God's enduring love for Abraham and all his descendants, including us.

The worshippers included a number of my Muslim friends, both liberal as well as conservative, some of their colleagues and friends, a few members of my congregation and other interested people. We began the celebration with a '*Qawwali*'—a popular form of singing with the Muslim community in which two groups of singers or participants express their thoughts on a particular theme in a stylized form of singing. The theme in this case was the praise of God in the words of the 24th Psalm. Towards the end of the '*Qawwali*' most of the gathering was joining in with the singers. This was followed by a recitation of the passage in the Qur'an in which the Abrahmic story of the sacrifice is narrated. A brief '*Qutba*' (sermon or address) based on the passage was then given by one of the Muslim leaders. There was a brief time for meditation during which some of the Muslim worshippers performed their prayers according to their ritual, while the others remained in silent prayer or thought. Then followed the reading of the biblical account of the sacrifice, from the book of Genesis and a homily based on it. The language used throughout the service was naturally Urdu/Hindustani. I led the worshippers in a prayer thanking and praising the one God of all for the opportunity of worshipping together and for His great love for us, His children and creatures, the descendants of Abraham. We concluded the service with an exchange of greetings of peace in the Islamic way. We then went on to celebrate the event in a feast of the sacrifice in which we broke bread together and shared the meat that was specially prepared by the members of the Muslim community for the occasion. It was indeed possible for the '*Ahl-i-Kitab*' (the People of the Book = the Christians) and the '*ummah*' (the Muslim community) to worship and celebrate together.

Once again, what was it that really broke the ice that enabled such a common celebration of worship? The answer is the same: the lifting of the veil of ignorance. In this case it was the realization that there was indeed a lot that was similar and not just dissimilar in Muslim and Christian tradition. And when there is so much similarity, factors of dissimilarity seem to pale into relative insignificance. Of course, it is always possible to read about these things and to talk about these things, but the fact remains that once again it took a real physical participation to dispel preconceived notions. My Muslim friends, particularly those who hold the status of leaders in their community, would have undoubtedly shared their new thoughts and ideas about Christianity with other colleagues, friends, and family and, I am sure, will continue to do so in the future too; but this communication would probably be far more authentic and acceptable than that of a Christian trying to say the same thing. Those with a vested interest in keeping our communities apart will continue to ridicule such ideas but that should and must never deter us in our endeavors to expose the truth of ourselves in the best ways possible.

Ignorance is in my experience the greatest deterrent to inter-religious understanding and co-operation. It is not religion or faith or belief itself that is the problem, but ignorance as regards the customs, habits, tradition, and culture associated with a religion or system of beliefs. When I consider the issue of inter-religious dialogue in the Indian context, I no longer think in terms of a theological dialogue (though it is an important and necessary part of dialogue between scholars and even religious leaders belonging to different religious persuasions), but in terms of cultural dialogue which includes the whole gamut of customs and habits, language and tradition. It involves setting the record straight as regards prejudices by a conscious and physical participation in each other's affairs. It involves an act of body, mind and will acting in conjunction. Above all, when I think of inter-religious dialogue, I think of it in terms of an act of love and an act of humility.

One of the scribes asked Jesus: "Which commandment is the first of all?" Jesus answered: "The first is, 'Hear, O Israel: The Lord our God, the Lord is one; and you shall love the Lord your God with all your heart, and with all your soul, and with all your mind, and with all your strength.' The second is this, 'You shall love your neighbor as yourself.' There is no other commandment greater than these." (Mark 12:28–31) Jesus was of course quoting the Law of Moses, but he picked out the two commandments that involved a person's capacity to love in the entirety of his or her humanness. This kind of love or loving involves every conceivable dimension of the human being—the emotional, the spiritual, the mental, and the physical. To love with all your heart and soul and mind and strength is the maximum capacity utilization of one's emotional, spiritual, mental, and physical faculties. One is expected to love God in this way and in like manner, one's neighbor. To love your neighbor as yourself is precisely this—to love one's neighbor to the complete extent that one's heart, soul, mind, and strength will go. It is this act of love that one requires in inter-religious encounter, especially in the context of widespread ignorance about one's neighbors. At times the process can be painfully slow and frustrating, but then we must ask ourselves what is this love that is required of us so completely. As St. Paul describes it: It is patient and kind; neither jealous nor boastful, not arrogant or rude. It does not insist on its own way; it is not irritable or resentful; it does not rejoice at wrong, but rejoices in the right. Love bears all things, believes all things, hopes all things, endures all things (1 Cor. 13:4 –7). Only when we learn not to think of such love as an utopian ideal, but use it in a very deliberate sense in inter-religious encounter, can there be a radical transformation of the ignorance in society, paving the way for harmonious interdependence and co-operation.

When one considers the sheer magnitude of the problem in India, with almost 800 million people belonging to different religions, castes, tribes, language-groups and cultures, the task of fighting the ignorance that divides us would seem insurmountable. But that may not really be the case, for more often than not, most people want to play "Follow the Leader." Whenever there is communal strife or discord, there is invariably just a handful of people who are responsible for the flare-ups and misunderstandings. Granted that a few of them may have vested interests, but others are often misled or misinformed about certain things. It is here that we can play our conciliatory roles using dialogue as the key.

It is said that when the Christian missionaries of yesteryear were involved in mass conversions in India, they would often take a hose-pipe and spray the assembled crowds with water as a mark of their baptism. They only needed to convince the village headman or the tribal chieftain, and the entire village or tribe would come forward to be baptized without asking questions. The same principle would have worked with the Arya Samaj priest and the Muslim leaders with whom I had had those remarkable encounters. It is like throwing a pebble into a pond and watching the ripples. Each ripple forms a concentric circle which grows bigger and bigger till it encompasses the entire pond. One important point in the above example is "watching the ripples." It may be necessary from time to time to do some follow-up work and see how things are progressing. One has to watch out for distortions and misinterpretations along the way. This requires a cooperative venture involving both parties in the dialogue and their followers.

This brings me to the role I play in my own community and the responsibility I have towards it. As a pastor of a large urban congregation, first and foremost I would have to be able to carry my flock with me in such a venture—by no means an easy task. It implies a gradual but steady process of conscientizing the people and then enabling them to participate fruitfully in such dialogue, preferably to other religious communities. They would also need to be "watching the ripples" and doing their part of the follow-up work. While this process is going on in my community, it is my hope that it is simultaneously going on in, for example, the community of the Arya Samaj priest—a synchronous activity that would eventually lead to a wide dissemination of better knowledge. At the same time it would be my duty to bring my fellow-ministers into this venture too and encourage them to do the same thing with their congregations. Sometimes the greatest challenges and the worst disappointments come from within one's own community, which can put at nought one's painstaking efforts with other communities. It could mean starting all over again, but in the long run it would be well worth the effort.

A beginning has been made. The few interested 'dialogists' are going about their business with a sense of urgency and a feeling of genuine concern. But they have "miles to go before they sleep" and need to encourage many, many more to join them in their enterprise. India has a great future indeed—a future that can be blessed with the dynamic interdependence and fellowship of her people. Let us not wait till it is too late!

Notes

1. Quoted in Pander, Dhanpati, *The Arya Samaj and Indian Nationalism (1875–1920)* (New Delhi: S. Chand & Co., 1972), 15.
2. Quoted *ibid.*
3. *Ibid.*, 28.
4. *Ibid.*

Contributors

Marcus Braybrooke, an Anglican, is Vicar of Christ Church, Bath, United Kingdom. He edits *Common Ground*, the journal of the Council of Christians and Jews and *World Faiths Insight*, the journal of the World Congress of Faiths. He is the author of *Together to the Truth, The Undiscovered Christ of Hinduism, Inter-Faith Organizations 1893–1979*, and edited the report *Inter-Faith Worship*.

M. Darrol Bryant is Chairman of the Department of Religious Studies and Associate Professor of Religions and Culture at Renison College, University of Waterloo, Waterloo, Ontario, Canada. He is the author/editor of more than a dozen books including *God: The Contemporary Discussion* (1982), *The Many Faces of Religion and Society* (1985) and *Interreligious Dialogue* (1989).

Francis Xavier D'Sa is Professor of Indian Religions and Philosophy; Coordinator, Postgraduate Studies in Philosophy, Jnana Deepa Vidyapeeth; Director, Department of Sanscrit and Symbolism, Snehasadan Institute for the Study of Religion, Pune, India. He is the author of *Gott, der Dreieine und der All-ganze. Vorwort zur Begegnung zwischen Christentum und Hinduismus* (1987).

Donald W. Dayton is Professor of Theology and Ethics, Northern Baptist Theological Seminary. He is President of the Society for Pentecostal Studies and of the Wesleyan Theological Society, Lombard, Illinois. He is the editor, with M. Darrol Bryant, of *The Coming Kingdom*.

Joseph H. Fichter is Emeritus Professor of Sociology at Loyola University, New Orleans. Holder of a Ph.D. in Sociology from Harvard University and three honorary doctorates, Dr. Fichter has taught at several universities in the USA, Europe, and South America. He has written more than thirty books and numerous articles.

Martin Forward is secretary to the British Methodist Church's Committee for Relations with People of Other Faiths. He worked at the Henry Martyn Institute of Islamic Studies, Hyderabad, India, from 1975 to 1977. From 1977 to 1982, he was Methodist chaplain to London University, and from 1982 to 1988 was a pastor in a multi-faith area of Leicester. He is the editor of *God of all faiths*.

Durwood Foster is Professor of Christian Theology, Pacific School of Religion and Professor of Systematic Theology, Graduate Theological Union, Berkeley. He is also a Methodist minister, California-Nevada Conference, United Methodist Church, California.

Monika K. Hellwig is Professor of Theology at Georgetown University, Washington, D.C. She was past President of Catholic Theological Society of America. She has written numerous books including *The Eucharist and The Hunger of the World*, *Understanding Catholicism*, *Sign of Reconciliation and Conversion: The Sacrament of Penance for Our Time*, and *Jesus: The Compassion of God.*

John Hick is Danforth Professor of the Philosophy of Religion at the Claremont Graduate School, California. He is the author of twelve books and editor of eleven and has previously taught at Cornell University, Princeton Theological Seminary, Cambridge University, and the University of Birmingham, England.

Frederick M. Jelly, a Dominican, is Dean of Studies and Professor of Theology, Mt. St. Mary's Seminary, Emmitsburg, Maryland. He is the author of *Madonna: Mary in the Catholic Tradition* (1986).

Myrtle S. Langley is presently a Diocesan Missionary, Diocese of Liverpool, United Kingdom. She was extensively involved in missionary and educational work in Kenya and in interreligious dialogue. She holds a Ph.D. in anthropology from the University of Bristol and has authored several articles and books including *The Nandi of Kenya: Life Crisis Rituals in a Period of Change*, *Ethical Dialogue with Other Religions*, and *Equal Women: A Christian Feminist Perspective*.

Romesh Philip Modayil is a Methodist minister, Delhi Regional Conference, Methodist Church in India. He is also a member of Board of Directors, Theological Research and Communication Institute, New Delhi, India.

Joseph Osei-Bonsu is Lecturer, Department of the Study of Religions, and Catholic chaplain at the University of Ghana, Leon, Ghana. He was editor of *Ghana Clergy Review* and *Ghana Bulletin of Theology*.

Geoffrey Parrinder is Emeritus Professor of the Comparative Study of Religions, London University, and Fellow of King's College, London. He is also an ordained minister of the Methodist Church of Great Britain. A prolific writer, he is the author of thirty books on world religions, with translations in ten languages, including *Jesus in the Qur'an* (1965), *Avatar and Incarnation* (1970), *A Dictionary of Non-Christian Religions* (1971), *Worship in the World's Religions* (1961), and *Mysticism in the World's Religions* (1976).

Peter C. Phan, a native of Vietnam, graduated summa cum laude from London University. He holds a doctorate of theology degree from the Salesian Pontifical University, Rome, and a doctorate of philosophy from London University. Besides contributing numerous articles to learned and popular journals, he has written several books including Social Thought, Culture and Eschatology, Eternity in Time, and Grace and the Human Condition. He is the general editor of an eight-volume series in systematic theology. Formerly a professor of theology at the University of Dallas, Texas, he currently teaches systematic theology at the Catholic University of America, Washington, D.C.

Richard Quebedeaux, holder of a Ph.D. from Oxford University, is a senior consultant for New ERA and author of several books on evangelical Christians including *The Young Evangelicals, The Worldly Evangelicals, By What Authority: The Rise of Personality Cults in American Christianity*, and *The New Charismatics II*.

Robert P. Scharlemann is Commonwealth Professor of Religious Studies, Department of Religious Studies, University of Virginia, Charlottesville, Virginia. He is the author of several books including *Thomas Aquinas and John Gerhard*, *Reflection and Doubt in the Thought of Paul Tillich*, and *The Being of God.*

Mary Ann Stenger is visiting Assistant Professor in Religious Studies at the University of Louisville, Kentucky. She is the author of several papers and articles on inter-religious issues, including "The Problem of Cross-cultural Criteria of Religious Truths," *Modern Theology* 3:4 (July 1987).

Index

F

G

H

I

T